Guide to the Recommended

COUNTRY INNS

of the Rocky Mountain Region

"In addition to covering the basic information, Mrs. Kennedy also conveys a sense of the unique flavor of the individual inns she describes, and very often their innkeepers as well. Especially helpful are the detailed instructions on how to get to each inn and the indexes at the back, which group the inns by categories."
—Barbara Bannon, *Utah Holiday* magazine

"The book has a unique charm that extends a most personal invitation to stop, stay, and share warm hospitality in unusual surroundings. If you plan a trip, this book will give you all the information you need, in depth, with a most friendly touch. Read it, plan with it, take it along.
—Harrison Lane, *Montana* magazine

D1041702

The "Guide to the Recommended Country Inns" Series

"The guidebooks in this new series of recommended country inns are sure winners. Personal visits have ensured accurate and scene-setting descriptions. These beckon the discriminating traveler to a variety of interesting lodgings."
—*Norman Strasma, publisher of* Inn Review *newsletter*

The "Guide to the Recommended Country Inns" series is designed for the discriminating traveler who seeks the best in unique accommodations away from home.

From hundreds of inns personally visited and evaluated by the author, only the finest are described here. The inclusion of an inn is purely a personal decision on the part of the author; no one can pay or be paid to be in a Globe Pequot inn guide.

Organized for easy reference, these guides point you to just the kind of accommodations you are looking for: Comprehensive indexes by category provide listings of inns for romantic getaways, inns for the sports-minded, inns that serve gourmet meals . . . and more. State maps help you pinpoint the location of each inn, and detailed driving directions tell you how to get there.

Use these guidebooks with confidence. Allow each author to share his or her selections with you and then discover for yourself the country inn experience.

Editions available:

Guide to the Recommended Country Inns of
New England • Mid-Atlantic States and Chesapeake Region
South • Midwest • Arizona, New Mexico, and Texas
Rocky Mountain Region • West Coast

Guide to the Recommended
COUNTRY INNS
of the Rocky Mountain Region

Colorado • Idaho • Montana
Nevada • Utah • Wyoming

by Doris Kennedy
illustrated by Duane Perreault

A Voyager Book

The Globe Pequot Press

Chester, Connecticut 06412

Library of Congress Cataloging-in-Publication Data

Kennedy, Doris.
    Guide to the recommended country inns of the Rocky Mountain region.

    ("Guide to the recommended country inns" series)
    "A Voyager book."
    Includes index.
    1. Hotels, taverns, etc.—Rocky Mountains Regions—Guide-books. 2. Resorts—Rocky Mountains Region—Guide-books. I. Title. II. Series.
TX907.K426   1987   647'.947801   87-8691
ISBN 0-87106-816-8 (pbk.)

Manufactured in the United States of America
First Edition/First Printing

Contents

How This Guide Is Arranged vii
Inn-sights. ix

Colorado: The Eastern Slope 1
Colorado: The Western Slope. 69
Idaho 147
Montana. 173
Nevada. 203
Utah. 225
Wyoming 265

Indexes

Alphabetical Index to
   Inns 289
Inns with Restaurants or
   That Serve Dinner by
   Special Arrangement . . 291
City Inns 292
Guest Ranches and
   Farms. 292
Romantic Inns 293
Rustic Inns. 294
Inns near Downhill
   Skiing. 294
Inns near Cross-country
   Skiing. 295
Inns with Swimming
   Pools. 296

Inns with Hot Tubs. 297
Inns with Working
   Fireplaces or Wood-
   burning Stoves in Some
   Guest Rooms 298
Inns with Wheelchair
   Access. 298
Inns with Special
   Features for Children . . 299
Inns with Age and
   Behavior Preferences
   Pertaining to Children . 299
Inns That Permit Pets . . . 300

*T*his book is dedicated to my husband and fellow "inn peeper," Gary Kennedy, who not only photographed every inn I chose to include so the publisher's artist could sketch from his photos but also proofread all 70,000 words, chauffeured me, humored me, encouraged and consoled me. This book is the result of our combined efforts. Thanks, Gar.

How This Guide Is Arranged

The country inns, historic hotels, mountain lodges, and guest ranches in this book are arranged alphabetically: by state, by town within each state, and by inn name within each town. My guideline for dividing Colorado between "The Eastern Slope" and "The Western Slope" was the Continental Divide.

You will find a map preceding each chapter with numbers corresponding to the facing index. This is for your ease in finding the geographical location of each inn. The special-category indexes in the back of the book are to help you find those inns providing features that are important to you. There is also an alphabetical index to all the inns in the book.

The 🐾 🐾 are not intended as a rating system. Their purpose is to point out some of the things about an inn that I thought were particularly interesting, pleasing, or unusual.

The "D" found at the end of an inn selection stands for Doris and means I couldn't let you go without telling you one more thing that especially fascinated me.

I have personally visited every inn included in this book, have attempted to discern what makes each special, and am happily sharing my discoveries with you. Establishments paid absolutely nothing for inclusion in this book, nor, under any circumstances, was compensation accepted for such inclusion.

If you have a favorite inn you think I should know about, I'd love to hear from you in care of my publisher so that I can consider it for this book's next edition.

Caveats

Rates: The rates quoted are those in effect at the time of my visit. Although they may change slightly, this information will give you a general idea as to cost. It is always a good idea to call ahead. The following abbreviations are used consistently throughout to let you know exactly what, if any, meals are included in the room price.

EP:　European Plan. No meals are included in the price of the room.

EPB: European Plan plus breakfast. A *full* breakfast is included in the price of the room.

MAP: Modified American Plan. A full breakfast and dinner are included in the price of the room.

AP: American Plan. A full breakfast, lunch, and dinner are included in the price of the room.

Where a *continental* breakfast is included, I have stated this fact.

Air conditioning: In some of the write-ups, I have stated that there is no air conditioning, but do keep in mind that many of these locations are at very high altitudes, so nights are likely to be quite cool. Unless I have said otherwise, you can expect to find air conditioning.

TV: If there is no mention of TV in the preliminaries of a particular story, your room should contain a TV set. This sort of amenity can change, however, so if it's important to you, inquire when making your reservation.

Smoking: Unless otherwise specified, smoking is permitted.

Children: I have stated age and behavior preferences indicated by individual innkeepers. There is also an index in the back of the book listing inns with restrictions. If I've made no mention of children, the little darlings are welcome. You know your children best. The description of each inn will help you decide if it is the sort of place where they would be happy and you would be comfortable having them there.

Pets: Well-behaved pets are permitted at some inns. I have noted the ones where this is the case and also have included an index listing the inns where Felix and Bowser will be welcome. Without exception, though, innkeepers want to be advised ahead of time that you are bringing your furry friend because some inns have a limited number of rooms suitable for pet occupancy.

Wheelchair access: I have specified which inns are wheelchair accessible. There is also an index in the back listing the establishments with this type of accommodation. Some inns have additional features for the exceptionally challenged. Best to inquire. If I have made no mention of wheelchair accessibility, regrettably there is none.

Inn-sights

Writing this book has brought me many unforgettable moments. None of these special experiences need be exclusively mine, however. They, and more, are out there waiting for anyone who cares to search them out.

I remember walking to dinner in Unionville, Nevada, under stars so bright they seemed to touch the ground; in Kellogg, Idaho, I was met with an innkeeper's smile as wide as his chef's hat was high; I viewed the pleasant town of Manti, Utah, from my hosts' carriage pulled by a faithful mare named Tillie; I walked the old Oregon Trail, just outside of Glenrock, Wyoming, and found wagon ruts and a gravestone dated 1860. In Telluride, Colorado, during film-festival week, I stood in awe as movie great Jimmy Stewart sauntered through the sitting room of an inn I was visiting. And then there were the shaggy mountain goats zigzagging down the hillside near Essex, Montana, and the yearling bear cub lumbering along just up the road. At dinner table after dinner table, I silently pledged to try to duplicate the wondrous morsels set before me by generous innkeepers. (And, at the same time, I promised myself to eat only food with zero calories for the next year!)

There are so many adventures waiting, so many intriguing inns to discover, so many fascinating people to meet. As you take the road "less traveled by," I wish you many "happy innings."

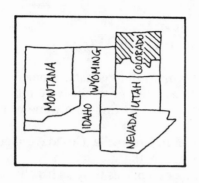

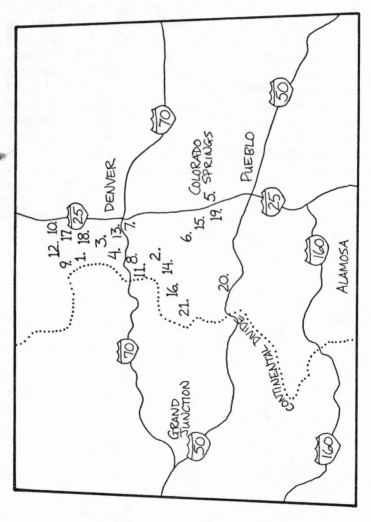

Colorado: The Eastern Slope

Numbers on map refer to towns numbered below.
Dotted line on map indicates Continental Divide.

1. Allenspark,
   Allenspark Lodge..2
   Wild Basin Lodge...4
2. Bailey, Glen-Isle on the Platte...................................6
3. Boulder,
   The Briar Rose...8
   The Gold Hill Inn and Bluebird Lodge.....................10
   Hotel Boulderado..12
   Pearl Street Inn...14
4. Central City, The Golden Rose Hotel...........................16
5. Colorado Springs, The Hearthstone Inn........................18
6. Cripple Creek, The Imperial Hotel.............................20
7. Denver,
   Cambridge Club..22
   The Oxford...24
   Victoria Oaks Inn..26
8. Empire, The Peck House......................................28
9. Estes Park,
   The Aspen Lodge at Estes Park............................30
   Black Canyon Inn..32
   River Song Inn...34
   The Stanley Hotel..36
   Wanek's Lodge at Estes....................................38
10. Fort Collins, Helmshire Inn...................................40
11. Georgetown, The Hardy House...............................42
12. Glen Haven, The Inn of Glen Haven..........................44
13. Golden, The Dove Inn..46
14. Grant, Tumbling River Ranch.................................48
15. Green Mountain Falls, Outlook Lodge........................50
16. Leadville, Historic Delaware Hotel............................52
17. Loveland, Sylvan Dale Ranch..................................54
18. Lyons, Peaceful Valley Lodge and Guest Ranch.................56
19. Manitou Springs, Gray's Avenue Hotel.........................58
20. Salida,
    Ponderosa Lodge..60
    The Poor Farm Country Inn................................62
    Sweet Adeline's..64
21. Twin Lakes, Inn of the Black Wolf............................66

Allenspark Lodge
Allenspark, Colorado
80510

Innkeepers: Larry Christine and Dorothy Mueller-Christine
Address/Telephone: 184 Main Street (mailing address: P.O. Box 326);
  (303) 747–2552
Rooms: 15, including 1 suite; 4 rooms and suite have private bath; all
  have sink.
Rates: $18.95 to $37.95, single; $24.95 to $39.95, double; EP. No pets.
  TV in lobby only. No air conditioning (not needed; elevation 8,500
  feet). MasterCard and Visa accepted.
Open: All year.
Facilities and Activities: No meals served. Restaurants within walking
  distance. BYOB. Hot tub, game room, gift shop, dance area. Nearby:
  antique shops, Rocky Mountain National Park; hiking, fishing,
  horseback riding, mountain climbing, downhill and cross-country
  skiing.

Larry and Dorothy met in this tiny town of only 300 residents when she was both owner of and cook at the Meadow Mountain Cafe and he raised pigs on a nearby farm. Larry arranged to collect the restaurant scraps for feeding his pigs and, in the process, fell in love with the cook. They have since married and combined their energies and talents into restoring the town's old landmark lodge into a fine country inn.

Made of ponderosa pine inside and out, the lodge has been added on to several times over the years, and every guest room is different in size and shape. ☞ There's even a triangle-shaped room, which was probably built that way simply because it happened to fit the outside dimensions of the building.

The Honeymoon Hideaway Suite has windows on three sides, and ☞ one can sit in its claw-footed tub and look out on a meadow sometimes sprinkled with wildflowers, other times covered with a blanket of snow. This room has an unusual ceiling. It has seven pointy angles where seven roofs come together.

☞ The trailhead to 7,000-foot Longs Peak is only five miles from the inn. There are two routes up the mountain, and both the walk-upright kind of climber and the hang-on-for-dear-life type often stay at the inn, rising at 3:30 A.M. for the seven-mile trek. Both Larry and Dorothy have made the climb, so they are a good source of information on the venture.

Dorothy doesn't serve meals at the inn, but you can always find a cup of coffee and sometimes hot cider and a roll. Guests get a discount on meals at the Meadow Mountain Cafe, and I'd recommend that you take advantage of this offer. This is where the locals gather, and you just might time it right to get in on an impromptu guitar session while enjoying your homemade soup and fresh hot bread.

There is a five-star restaurant called The Fawn Brook Inn just around the corner from the lodge. Its menu is extensive, and the dining is excellent.

How to get there: Allenspark is north of Denver and Boulder, on Highway 7 between Lyons and Estes Park. Inn is in center of community.

Wild Basin Lodge
Allenspark, Colorado
80510

Innkeepers: Randy and Sandy Good
Address/Telephone: Highway 7 (SR 1320); (303) 747–2545
Rooms: 4, including 2 suites; all with private bath; 2 dormitory rooms
with bunk beds, shared bath.
Rates: $48 to $55, single and double; EPB. Phone for dorm rates. No
pets. No air conditioning (not needed; elevation 8,300 feet). No
smoking in dining room. MasterCard, Visa, American Express accepted.
Open: All year.
Facilities and Activities: Breakfast, lunch, dinner, and Sunday smorgasbord available during summer; Saturday dinner and Sunday
smorgasbord only during winter. BYOB. Horse stables. All rooms
overlook river. Nearby: Rocky Mountain National Park; horseback
riding, hiking, fishing, downhill and cross-country skiing.

Although this inn is nestled in the mountains at an elevation
of 8,300 feet, from Denver it is not necessary to cross any passes
in order to reach it.

Folks come here for a variety of reasons. In summer,
there's 🖝 excellent fishing in mountain lakes, streams, and the
North St. Vrain River; and the numerous trails in adjacent Rocky

Mountain National Park are perfect for hiking or riding horse-back. In winter, one can ☛ cross-country ski right out the back door. Others come to read that "put-aside" book they've been trying to get to or just rest on the deck overlooking the river.

Fall is a special time because that's when the aspen trees turn to shimmering gold, highlighted by the evergreen of surrounding pine trees.

And Randy's good home cooking is getting quite a reputation, too. He uses an old family recipe for his fried chicken, and it is special indeed. The salad bar has all the usual items, plus some uncommon ones such as sauerkraut salad. Randy's Western omelet, made with ham, green pepper, onion, and mushrooms, is outstanding, as is his cheddar-cheese soup. The ☛ Sunday smorgasbord, offered during the summer and early fall, has become an area tradition.

The guest rooms are upstairs, and ☛ each has a balcony overlooking the river. The suites have both a front and a river view. All rooms are furnished in contemporary décor and open onto a large sitting room. There is also a good-sized dormitory on the lower level, perfect for large groups.

While I was visiting, several members of a Sweet Adeline Barbershop Quartet organization were staying at the inn, and there was a lot of spontaneous harmonizing going on. They were having a great time, and so were those of us who were fortunate enough to be there at that particular time.

How to get there: Inn is on Highway 7, northwest of Denver, 14 miles south of Estes Park and 22 miles north of Lyons.

Glen-Isle on the Platte
Bailey, Colorado
80421

Innkeepers: Gordon and Barbara Tripp
Address/Telephone: P.O. Box 128; (303) 838–5461
Rooms: 14 share 7 baths; 23 cabins, all with private bath.
Rates: $35, single or double, inn; $40, single or double, cabins; EP. $35
per day per person, AP. Pets allowed, $2 per night. No TV. No air
conditioning (not needed; elevation 7,830 feet). Well-behaved chil-
dren only, please. Credit cards not accepted.
Open: Inn and dining room, June 6 to September 8; cabins, all year.
Facilities and Activities: Full-service dining room during summer.
BYOB. Alcohol allowed in guest rooms only. Gift shop. Children's
playground, 1-mile private stream stocked with trout every 2 weeks,
stocked pond. Cookouts, all-day picnics, square dancing, billiards.
Nearby: hiking, fishing, horseback riding, sledding, ice skating,
cross-country skiing.

The old Colorado and Southern Railway no longer brings
long-skirted ladies and properly attired gentlemen to Glen-Isle for
a reprieve from the city. No, these days they arrive via automo-
biles, dressed in jeans and shorts or ski clothes. But that is about
all that has changed at this Adirondack-style hideaway, fifty miles
southwest of Denver.

☛ An antique-lover's paradise, the fourteen-room inn is packed with beautiful period pieces. Every room, hallway, nook, and cranny reveals wonderful one-of-a-kind treasures.

Barbara's roots go deep here. Her grandparents bought the inn in 1923, and, from early childhood, she spent her summers playing innkeeper. Today, she does most of the cooking and lends a warm, down-home feeling to the place.

If you are into ☛ doll collections and Indian artifacts, you'll have a great time here. Barbara has been collecting all types of dolls since she was eight years old and has one of the most complete collections of Indian dolls in the United States. And Gordon has an ☛ outstanding selection of Indian cradle boards from many, many tribes, including the Lakota Sioux, Iroquois, and Cherokee. Barbara also assembles doll houses and furnishes them with thousands of detailed miniatures. And these items are on display in the common rooms for guests to enjoy.

Folks come from miles around to dine on ☛ hearty, home-style meals served either in the dining room, from an outdoor chuck wagon, or from the porch buffet. Sundays boast of roast turkey, fried chicken, and lemon or banana-cream pie, all fresh from Barbara's kitchen.

The guest rooms are upstairs, and the three in the round section of the building are particularly charming; but I think my favorite is "H," with its oak bedstead, lowboy dresser, washstand, and rocker. Add to this a 4' x 5' silver-dust mirror, hand-crocheted bedspread, pillow shams, and dresser scarf, and you can imagine why I chose this room.

All the rooms have ruffled curtains, antique pitchers, bowls, and chamber pots and look out on giant pine trees planted as seedlings by Barbara's grandfather. Quite a place!

How to get there: On Highway 285, 50 miles southwest of Denver, 1 mile southwest of Bailey. Inn is on south side of highway.

The Briar Rose
Boulder, Colorado
80302

Innkeeper: Emily Hunter
Address/Telephone: 2151 Arapahoe Avenue; (303) 442–3007
Rooms: 11; 6 with private bath.
Rates: $49 to $75, single; $65 to $95, double; EP. Continental breakfast
   included. Pets allowed. Wheelchair accessible. Portable air condi-
   tioning. No cigars or pipes, please. Well-behaved children only,
   please. All major credit cards accepted.
Open: All year.
Facilities and Activities: Dinner available if requested ahead. BYOB.
   Complimentary fruit, afternoon tea, and sherry. Nearby: University
   of Colorado, Pearl Street Mall; fishing, hiking, biking.

   The moment you meet innkeeper Emily Hunter, you know
you've made a new friend. This former English teacher, world
traveler, and patron of the arts has a special knack for making
guests feel immediately welcome and comfortable at The Briar
Rose. Join her for complimentary afternoon tea or sherry, and
inquire about the year she spent sailing around the world with
her husband and two young sons.
   The Briar Rose, built in 1904 and used as a family residence
until 1982, is a red-brick, English-style cottage filled with an-

tiques and surrounded by a large, shaded yard. All beds are covered with down comforters, some exactly like the puffy feather beds of Europe. The Rose Room, upstairs, is tucked under a sloped ceiling and has a private balcony and a small sitting area, shared with only one other room.

Emily and her staff will serve breakfast of croissants, cranberry muffins, homemade jams and jellies, European-style yogurt, fresh-squeezed orange juice, and coffee or tea either in your room, in the formal dining room, or, best of all, on the sun porch. Here, quart Mason jars filled with jam line one shelf, while carnations, roses, wildflowers, and blossoms of every description hang drying from the ceiling, eventually to become the potpourri that Emily has sitting in small china dishes throughout the house.

Emily also serves dinner upon request. She has a chef on call, and, provided you order early enough, he will accommodate with a choice of entrée. A specialty is turkey pie with puff-pastry topping, vegetable salad, a light dessert, and complimentary wine.

If you are there on the last Sunday of the month, be sure to join other guests and Boulderites as well for Emily's High Tea. Live chamber music is provided, and, during intermission, a delicate feast of cucumber-and-roast-beef sandwiches, strawberries and imported Devon cream, scones, crumpets, tea, and coffee is served.

How to get there: From I–25, take Highway 36 to Boulder. Turn left at Arapahoe Avenue and go six blocks. The Briar Rose is at the intersection of Arapahoe and Twenty-second streets.

D: *The kitchen cookie jar, always filled with shortbread delights, is there for your pleasure. Don't miss it!*

The Gold Hill Inn
and Bluebird Lodge
Boulder, Colorado
80302

Innkeepers: Frank and Barbara Finn
Address/Telephone: Salina Star Route; (303) 443–6461
Rooms: 9 share 4 baths.
Rates: $36.50, single or double; EPB. No pets. No TV. No air condition-
ing (not needed; elevation 8,200 feet). Credit cards not accepted.
Open: Lodge and restaurant, May 1 through October.
Facilities and Activities: Restaurant open weekends the month of No-
vember. Breakfast served to lodge guests only. No lunch. Restau-
rant serves dinner only. Lounge. Hot tub. Nearby: hiking, fishing,
old mines and cemeteries to explore.

The Bluebird Lodge was built in 1872, and, seventeen years
later, poet and 📰 newspaperman Eugene Field wrote his famous *Casey's Table d'Hote* while a guest in the inn. The poem is
said to have been written about this place, and it is interesting to
note that many lines still apply, such as "This Casey was an
Irishman—you'd know it by his name. And by the facial features
appertainin' to the same . . ." Today's owner is Frank Finn, and,
believe me, he's as Irish as they come!

Clarence Darrow is said to have stood on the hotel's stairway and recited Field's entire poem to a gathering of Bluebirds (a group of working women who frequented the lodge in the '20s and for whom it is named).

Built of rough-hewn logs, the rustic lodge and inn hug the unpaved main street of this once-thriving gold-rush town, which is now home to 150 residents at best. The Bluebird, with its antique furnishings, is nicely complemented by the Finns' Gold Hill Inn restaurant next door.

Barbara and Frank's son, Chris, is chef, and ☞ his six-course dinners are major productions. The appetizers during my visit were ham with herb cheese, apples and shrimp, and blue-fish mousse. The cold soup was boysenberry; the hot was oriental vegetable. There is always a choice of four or five entrées, such as smoked, stuffed trout and steak-and-kidney pie. Then come three fresh vegetables (you don't have to choose—you get all three), salad, and hot bread. The dessert cart featured sour-cream–apple pie, caramel pears, and frozen strawberry mousse. This was followed by a cheese-and-fruit tray.

Deborah Finn Millennor and husband Gary, hosts at the Bluebird Lodge, serve a dandy complimentary breakfast of shoofly pie, apple-raisin-bread pudding, or thick slices of French toast in the formal dining room each morning.

During my stay, a group showed up for a "mystery weekend," and they had a terrific time. They came in costume, each dressed for his or her particular part, and it was exciting just to watch. This is a fun place.

How to get there: The most direct route to Gold Hill is via the city of Boulder. Take Canyon Blvd. west, turn right onto Ninth St., then left onto Mapleton Ave. Follow the winding road to Gold Hill. Inn is on left.

DP Perreault

Hotel Boulderado
Boulder, Colorado
80302

Innkeeper: Sid Anderson
Address/Telephone: 2115 13th Street; (303) 442–4344
Rooms: 103; all with private bath.
Rates: $59 to $99, single; $69 to $109, double; EP. No pets. Wheelchair accessible; some rooms designed for handicapped. All major credit cards accepted.
Open: All year.
Facilities and Activities: Three restaurants, 3 bars. Whirlpool bath in some rooms, complimentary passes to health club; fresh flowers in all rooms. Nearby: University of Colorado; Award-winning, entertaining, great for people watching, Pearl Street Mall; fishing, hiking, biking.

At the turn of the century, desiring to attract tourists and notables to their community, the residents of Boulder banded together and raised the necessary funds to build a luxury hotel. Although of one mind when it came to building, there was a sometimes angry, sometimes comical split in opinion over the choosing of a proper name for the hotel. In an attempt to be original and to avoid being imitated, a combination of *Boulder* and *Colorado* was suggested; and, after much disagreement and quarreling, the name Boulderado was finally accepted.

And the visitors did come, many of whom were celebrities the likes of Ethel Barrymore, Clarence Darrow, Robert Frost, Helen Keller, Bat Masterson, and Louis Armstrong.

Today's Boulderites are as proud as ever of their Boulderado, and it is definitely 🖝 *the* place to meet friends and be seen.

In the lobby, 🖝 a domed canopy of stained glass provides a mellow glow over the entire area, including the Mezzanine Lounge. 🖝 A cantilevered, cherry-wood staircase holds court at one end of the lobby, and elegant pieces of period furniture are strategically placed to encourage good conversation or restful solitude.

Each guest room is individually decorated with authentic antiques and tasteful color schemes. Feel like splurging? Do as I did and reserve a suite on the fifth floor, accessible via 🖝 a tiny 1908 Otis elevator. My sitting room was fitted with dormer windows; a sea green, circle-backed settee with matching chairs; black cherry carpet; and lamp with silk fringe shade. The bedroom sported a wicker peacock chair, king-size bed, and gorgeous grandfather clock.

The Boulderado provides dining for just about all tastes. The Steak Porch features prime beef, and Winston's offers a fine selection of fresh fish specialties. I must admit, though, that my choice was pasta on this particular night, and I wasn't disappointed in Franco's Pastaria. This 🖝 basement bistro presents a red-checkered-tablecloth atmosphere combined with laughter, gaiety, and a pasta bar with six delicious sauces. There are also meatballs and bread and . . . that settles it. I must go back!

How to get there: From I–25, take Highway 36 to Boulder. Turn left onto Arapahoe Avenue and proceed to 13th. Turn right on 13th to Spruce. Hotel is on the corner.

D: *Hotel historian Silvia Pettem has written a most entertaining book about the Boulderado's coming of age. Entitled* Legend of a Landmark, *it is available from Westview Press.*

Pearl Street Inn
Boulder, Colorado
80302

Innkeepers: Yossi Shem-Avi and Cathy Surratt
Address/Telephone: 1820 Pearl Street; (303) 444-5584
Rooms: 7; all with private bath.
Rates: $58 to $85, single; $68 to $95, double. Includes continental-plus
  breakfast. Pets allowed. All major credit cards accepted.
Open: All year.
Facilities and Activities: Breakfast served in guest rooms or dining room.
  Complimentary sherry, wine, or champagne every day at 5:00 P.M.
  Bar. Room service. Concierge services. Nearby: award-winning
  Pearl Street Mall, shopping, 25 restaurants within 5-block radius;
  University of Colorado; fishing, hiking, biking.

   Yossi and Cathy have modified this attractive red-brick Victorian into an elegant, contemporary, and, at the same time, old-
fashioned inn. The old and new are blended in such a skillful
way, the two distinct styles merge to produce a meld of perfection.
   Enter the front door and find ☞ the sort of place where you
catch your breath in awe. The first time I came here, I think I
must have turned in two complete circles before I settled down to
look in just one direction. From the sitting room, you can see into

the gallery, where fresh-flower-laden, white-linen-covered tables are encircled by black laquered chairs, and quality art enhances the creamy walls.

French doors lead to a☞ beautiful, brick-walled inner courtyard. Arranged around a fifty-year-old apple tree and garnished with white wicker and tubs of bright flowers, it is the focus of this truly intimate inn. All the rooms open out onto this area, with those upstairs having a balcony–walkway as well.

Each guest room has a fireplace (the bridal suite has *two*), complete bath, down comforter with German duvet, fine pieces of period furniture, wooden or brass-and-white-iron bed, and lovely Indian dhurries, elegant pastel throw rugs from Bombay.

Dinner is served for groups of ten or more if arranged in advance. You would do well to ask if there is one of these group affairs scheduled during your stay—if there is and if there is room, Cathy will prepare a private dinner just for you. A sample menu might be fresh basil-and-goat-cheese canapés, chicken Paillard, orange-flavored braised red cabbage, oven-roasted potatoes, French bread, lemon mousse, and apple brandy. Cathy trained at the Cordon Bleu in Paris. Need I say more?

Israeli-born and formally educated in hotel management, Yossi is a most cordial host and provides guests with ☞ every amenity a hotel concierge would offer and more: complimentary wine, dining recommendations, and turn-down service with a carafe of ice water and an English mint.

How to get there: From I–25, take Boulder exit north to Boulder. Highway becomes 28th Street. Turn left on Pearl Street. Inn is on the left.

෴

D: *One last word. This inn is immaculate. It absolutely sparkles.*

The Golden Rose Hotel
Central City, Colorado
80427

Innkeeper: Suzanne Travis
Address/Telephone: 102 Main Street (P.O. Box 8); (303) 582–5060
Rooms: 26; 15 with private bath, 11 share 5 baths.
Rates: $48 to $96, single or double, from June through October; $38 to
  $76, single or double, from November through May; EP. No pets.
  No TV. No air conditioning (not needed; elevation 8,456 feet). Well-
  behaved children only, please. All major credit cards accepted.
Open: All year.
Facilities and Activities: Four hotel restaurants. Continental breakfast
  at small charge. Bar. Hot tub, sauna, turn-down service with pillow
  mint, and wake-up call if requested. Nearby: Central City Opera,
  jazz festival, dinner theater, restaurants, cabarets, shopping, museums; hiking, fishing, horseback riding, jeep tours, downhill and
  cross-country skiing.

This fine old (1874) Italianate hotel is at its height of
grandeur. ☛ Fine antiques grace every room; the walls are
sheathed in silk-screened wallpaper imported from Italy; and the
bathrooms boast marble floors and shiny brass fixtures.

In the lobby, oak-parquet floors, teardrop-crystal chandeliers,
and a sweeping white-maple staircase set the stage for this most

elegant structure. Pause to admire the magnificent 1849 square baby grand piano, brought in sections across the plains long ago by someone who could not bear to leave it behind.

Upstairs, skylights give an open feeling to short hallways leading off in all directions. Small sitting areas beg you to rest awhile, and the tiny library has a unique collection of microfilms from the local newspaper dating back to 1863, when Central City's gold-mining boom earned it the title of "the richest square mile on earth."

Room 5, my favorite, has a wine-colored carpet; huge armoire; heavily embossed, pale pink wall covering; and a two-foot-wide ceiling border in an original Victorian pattern, copied and silk-screened in England.

The carved mahogany sleigh bed in Room 1 was brought by oxcart over the "Oh My God Road," which clings precariously to the side of the mountain. I have traversed this hair-raising route, and it's a wonder ox or cart made it, let alone this fine piece of furniture!

Suzanne serves early-morning coffee and tea in the lobby; across the street and two doors up, The Teller House presents breakfast, lunch, and dinner in four charming dining rooms. I lunched in the Atrium, a four-storied glass-enclosed patio with green latticework walls and balconies, white tables, and white wicker chairs. Dinner in the Little Kingdom Room proved to be another pleasurable experience with, among other delights, a fine wiener schnitzel sautéed in white wine, lemon, and fresh parsley and served with red cabbage.

How to get there: At junction of I–70 and Highway 119, turn north, then left onto 119 to town of Black Hawk. Turn left along main street of Black Hawk and proceed to Central City. Hotel is on left.

✱

D: *Notice the famous "Face on the Barroom Floor," inspired by Hugh Antoine d'Arcy's poem "Madeline" and painted as a lark in 1936 by Herdon Davis on the floor of the Teller Bar. It has become part of Central City's folklore.*

The Hearthstone Inn
Colorado Springs, Colorado
80903

Innkeepers: Dot Williams and Ruth Williams
Address/Telephone: 506 North Cascade Avenue; (303) 473–4413
Rooms: 25; 23 with private bath, 2 share 1 bath.
Rates: $50 to $85, single; $58 to $95, double; EPB. No pets. No TV. Air
conditioning on third floor only (not often needed on other floors;
elevation 6,012 feet). No smoking in dining room. MasterCard, Visa,
American Express accepted.
Open: All year.
Facilities and Activities: Picnic lunches available. BYOB. Coffee, tea,
iced tea always available. Lots of personal service. Nearby: Pikes
Peak, cog railroad, Air Force Academy, Will Rogers Shrine of the
Sun, Cave of the Winds, Royal Gorge; shopping, restaurants; hik-
ing, fishing, cross-country skiing, ice skating.

A tremendous amount of time, thought, toil, and tenderness
went into making these two circa-1885 mansions, ☞ connected
by a carriage-house walkway, into a magnificent country inn.
Ruth and Dot, same last name but not related, met in graduate
school. With the help of friends, they completely remodeled the
interior, refinished all the furniture, and hung 792 rolls of wall-

paper. Ruth works as a psychotherapist, and Dot, who has a master's degree in social work, is the full-time innkeeper.

From the elegantly appointed parlor to the third-level former servant's quarters, every room has its own personality. I liked the fact that 🖝 all unoccupied guest rooms have their doors wide open, making choosing a place to spend the night a journey of discovery. Up a few steps, down a couple more, around the corner, 🖝 the hallways go every which way, lending a secluded feeling to the rooms.

It would be fun to stay a week, each night in a different chamber. I particularly like the Solarium with its white-iron-and-brass bed and lattice-covered balcony, where you can have a private breakfast, if you choose. The purple grapes on the dresser scarf match those on the antique basin and pitcher. 🖝 There's a lot of attention given to detail here.

Other rooms include The Study, with window seat, oak-manteled fireplace, and gleaming brass bed; The Fireside Room, with fireplace, king-size iron-and-brass bed, private porch, and round, beveled-glass window; and Mountainside, small and cozy with a magnificent view of 14,000-foot Pikes Peak.

Mornings bring dining-room tables laden with 🖝 gourmet goodies such as Hearthstone Inn French toast, made with *breaded* French bread and topped with spiced butter and gingered whipped cream. Unique! Or how about puffy popovers called Dutch babies, gingerbread muffins, honey-crunch baked apples, or strawberries Romanoff? Recipes for these and other delectable delicacies are available in a book put out by the inn.

There are plenty of places for dinner close by. I suggest you try La Petite Maison for fantastic French cuisine.

How to get there: From I–25, take Exit 143 east (away from mountains) to third stop light. Turn right onto Cascade Avenue and proceed 7 blocks. Inn is on the right, on the corner of Cascade and St. Vrain.

The Imperial Hotel
Cripple Creek, Colorado
80813

Innkeepers: Wayne and Dorothy Mackin, Steven and Bonnie Mackin
Address/Telephone: 123 North Third Street (mailing address: P.O. Box
   957); (303) 689–2922 or (303) 471–8878
Rooms: 26; 12 with private bath, 14 share baths; all have sinks.
Rates: $28 to $33, single; $35 to $40, double; EP. No pets. TV in TV
   room only. No air conditioning (not needed; elevation 9,500 feet).
   All major credit cards accepted.
Open: Mid-May through mid-October.
Facilities and Activities: Full-service dining rooms. Lounge. Melodrama
   theater. Nearby: shopping, restaurants, museums, ghost towns,
   mine tours, narrow-gauge railroad; hiking, fishing, jeeping.

   The Imperial was built immediately following Cripple Creek's
disastrous 1896 fire and, except for two years during World War
II, has operated as a turn-of-the-century-style hotel ever since.
   The staunch, Victorian-strict exterior leads one to underes-
timate the splendor found inside. Completely ☞ furnished with
elegant antiques, this hotel is "Gay Nineties" at its best. It hosts
three formal dining rooms and several smaller, more intimate
dining areas; The Thirst Parlour sports a beautiful antique back

bar and cherry-wood pool table; and many a miner bellied up to the century-old bar that embellishes the Red Rooster Room.

All the guest chambers are delightfully furnished. There isn't a one I wouldn't want to stay in, but my favorite is Number 50, on the second floor. It has a ☛ unique bed—an astoundingly ornate and intricately designed French repoussé made of hammered copper. This room also has a bird's-eye maple dresser with oval mirror and a claw-footed bath tub. Room 51, across the hall, has a magnificent cherry and black walnut bedstead, fashioned for a bishop in 1850.

The Imperial's ☛ Melodrama Theatre has been applauded by such noteworthy publications as *Life* magazine, the *New York Times,* and the *Denver Post.* In its fortieth year, it uses legitimate scripts written from 1800 to 1920 and has played to more than a million theatergoers, including many celebrities.

Breakfast is à la carte, and lunch and dinner are both à la carte and buffet. I had the Sunday buffet, and it was fantastic: corn chowder, curried turkey, glazed duck, roast pork, prime rib, rice pilaf, potato puffs, and chocolate mousse are only a few of the many, many selections. Dinner/melodrama packages are available and are a bargain, considering the enjoyment gained.

Cripple Creek is rimmed by the Sangre de Cristo Mountain Range and surrounded by headframes and ore dumps, marking the sites where, long ago, fortunes were made in gold and silver mining. The town is not a "has been," however. Business is brisk in the small shops and restaurants, and many of the mining properties are being given a second look, as the area is once again being seriously considered for gold production.

How to get there: From I–25 at Colorado Springs, take Highway 24 west to town of Divide. Turn south onto Highway 67 and proceed to Cripple Creek. From Bennett Ave. (Cripple Creek's main street), turn right onto N. Third. Hotel is on the left.

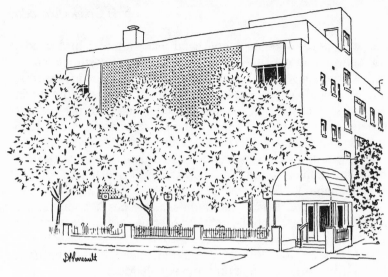

Cambridge Club
Denver, Colorado
80203

Innkeeper: Jeff Paap
Address/Telephone: 1560 Sherman Street; (303) 831–1252
Rooms: 27 suites; all with private bath.
Rates: $110 to $155, single; $130 to $175, double. Includes continental breakfast. Corporate rates available. Well-mannered pets permitted. All major credit cards accepted.
Open: All year.
Facilities and Activities: Dining room. Bar. Numerous special amenities; please see text. Nearby: state capitol, U.S. Mint, business district, shopping, restaurants, museums, parks, professional sporting events; hiking, fishing, biking. Downhill and cross-country skiing approximately 50 miles away.

I have found an inn, sequestered away on one of Denver's tree-shaded, downtown streets, that has ☛ one of the most extensive personal-attention programs I have ever experienced. If you like being pampered, if you have someone you want to impress, or if your ego could use a boost, follow me to the Cambridge Club.

Built in the 1940s, just steps from Colorado's gold-domed capitol and only a few blocks from Denver's business district, the inn has a plain exterior that belies the grandeur found inside. The entryway, carpeted in plush, rich green, is startlingly beautiful, with tiny lights reflected from polished brass, shiny mirrors, beveled glass, and warm oak paneling. Upstairs, ☛ the guest rooms are ultra-elegant and enriched with French Provincial antiques; canopied, cherry-wood four-posters; crystal chandeliers; wet bars; and butler pantries.

My goal is to spend a night or two in the Huntsman's Suite. It has a white couch, red-leather highback chairs, one-of-a-kind art work on forest green walls, and a massive desk guaranteed to make anyone feel like a corporate executive. The bedroom, an explosion of rich reds, boasts an exquisite bed and a brass valet stand.

And now to the ☛ special amenities: packing and unpacking service; vouchers for shoeshines and garment pressing; turndown service with cognac and truffles or milk and cookies; terry robes and baskets of imported toiletries; stocked butler pantries; fresh flowers and fruit baskets; continental breakfast delivered to your room along with the *Wall Street Journal;* and a chauffeur-driven Lincoln limousine to take you wherever you want to go within a twenty-mile radius—all complimentary.

Jeff keeps a file on all guests so that when they return, their pantry contains *their* preference in soft drinks and the valet knows *their* favorite wine label and preferred breakfast hour. Add to this the twenty-four-hour room service that brings you anything from a full breakfast to a midnight dinner of chicken cordon bleu or filet mignon, the latter served with care, one course at a time, by a most conscientious waiter. Or if you choose, the American bistro-style dining room downstairs offers excellent regional cuisine.

How to get there: From I–25, take 6th Avenue exit east to Lincoln Street. Turn left onto Lincoln and drive to 16th Street, turn right onto 16th, then right onto Sherman, and proceed the ½ block to the inn.

◌֍◌

D: *A recent visitor from London was heard to say, "When I walk in, they remember my name, what I drink, my favorite newspaper, and that I take tea with lemon, no sugar. What a marvelous little hotel!"*

The Oxford
Denver, Colorado
80202

Innkeeper: James Shofstall

Address/Telephone: 1600 Seventeenth Street; (303) 628–5400, (303) 628–5411, or (800) 228–5838 (outside Colorado only)

Rooms: 81; all with private bath.

Rates: $105 to $300, single; $135 to $300, double. Includes continental breakfast. Special weekend packages available. No pets. Wheelchair accessible. Well-behaved children only. All major credit cards accepted.

Open: All year.

Facilities and Activities: Full-service dining room. The Corner Room Lounge and Cruise Bar. Complimentary fruit basket, sherry, and biscuits. Turn-down service with chocolates, daily newspaper, shoeshine, concierge and room service, valet parking. Nearby: shopping, Center For The Performing Arts, state capitol, U.S. Mint, museums, professional sporting events; hiking, fishing, biking. Downhill and cross-country skiing approximately 50 miles away.

Located one-half block from Denver's historic Union Railroad Station and billed as "Denver's Grand Small Hotel," the four-star-rated Oxford is indeed ☛ grand and yet small enough to provide an abundance of personal services. When it first opened its doors in 1891, it was touted as having the ultimate in amenities and boasted several dining rooms, a barber shop, Western Union office, stables, saloon, electric and gas lighting, and bathrooms and separate water closets on each floor. Rooms went for $1 to $2 per night.

During World War II, the troop trains arriving at Union Station filled every nook and cranny of the hotel with military personnel, and Denver residents served hot sandwiches, coffee, and doughnuts in the lobby twenty-four hours a day.

A ☛ major restoration, from 1979 to 1983, involved an investment of more than $12 million. Previous remodeling atrocities were removed; paint was lifted from sterling-silver chandeliers; custom carpeting was loomed to match the original; and the rooms were filled with rare English and French antiques. ☛ A mint-condition grand piano once owned by Baby Doe Tabor, the society-snubbed second wife of millionaire mineowner Horace Tabor, enhances one end of the lobby.

The Corner Room presents live jazz six nights a week, and the Cruise Bar, with velvet-covered booths and indirect red- and blue-neon lighting, is pure, unadulterated Art Deco.

Upstairs, ☛ spacious hallways embrace small alcoves where sherry and biscuits are served every afternoon at five.

My choice of room was Number 208, where ☛ I found a fruit-and-cheese bowl waiting on the bedside table, a plush robe in the closet, and Godiva chocolates on the down pillows. The white-marble fireplace with beveled mirror and oak mantel is set off beautifully by a midnight blue carpet. This room also has a gigantic armoire and charmingly petite bathtub. In the morning, a complimentary continental breakfast appeared along with the daily newspaper.

Chef Charles Heaton presides over breakfast, lunch, and dinner in a European-café atmosphere, with entrées ranging from fresh seafood to Cantonese roast duck with plum sauce and fresh mint. Suggestion: Try the duck, golden glazed, succulent, and outstanding. For dessert—a chocolate-and-coffee éclair or perhaps the fruit mousse.

How to get there: From downtown Denver, take 18th Street north to Union Station. Turn left and drive 1 block to 17th Street. Turn left again. Hotel is on the right.

Victoria Oaks Inn
Denver, Colorado
80218

Innkeeper: Gary Stephens
Address/Telephone: 1575 Race Street; (303) 355–1818
Rooms: 10; 2 with private bath, 8 share 2 baths.
Rates: $49 to $125, single; $69 to $125, double. Includes continental-plus breakfast. No pets. TV in sitting room only. Well-behaved children over 3 years old only. All major credit cards accepted.
Open: All year.
Facilities and Activities: Full breakfast, lunch, and dinner can be catered in; menus available. BYOB. Hot tub, robes; complimentary wine, sherry and snacks; laundry facilities; free airport pickup and return. Nearby: three major parks, natural-history and other museums, botanic gardens, zoo, state capitol, U.S. Mint, theater, professional sporting events, restaurants, extensive shopping facilities; recreation centers, hiking, fishing, biking. Downhill and cross-country skiing approximately 50 miles away.

Proud and stately, this grand 1879 Victorian is garnished with a wide, curving veranda, elaborate balustrade, and oak front doors framed by white pillars. Located in Denver's historic Capitol Hill district, within walking distance to restaurants, parks, museums, and downtown, it is also only one block from major bus lines.

26

This inn has 🖙 all the amenities of a first-class hotel, including extra thick and comfy monogrammed robes, special soaps (also monogrammed with the inn's "V"), fresh flowers, and telephones. 🖙 Complimentary wine and cheese are served in the afternoons, and there is evening sherry. Gary also provides a 🖙 no-charge pickup and return to Stapleton International Airport, an extensive security system, outdoor hot tub, laundry facilities, and room service. He also has bicycles and motor scooters to rent.

If the continental breakfast of hot croissants and Danish, fruit plate, coffee, and freshly squeezed orange juice isn't sufficient, Gary will order in a full breakfast for you at a nominal charge. You may eat in the large, beautifully appointed dining room or have your breakfast brought to your room. Lunch and dinner, too, can be catered from menus he has for your perusal.

For eating out, I recommend Acappella's for moderately priced seafood and a good selection of ethnic sandwiches. For more elegant dining, I suggest the quaint and romantic Café Alta for American and continental cuisine. Both are within a few blocks of the inn.

The bright and cheery parlor at Victoria Oaks has tiled and mirrored fireplace, elegant antique pieces, window seat, and lots of plants. Although the first- and second-floor guest rooms are more spacious, and two have private bath and fireplace, I think 🖙 I like the cozy, sloped-ceiling third-level rooms the best. Each is painted in a ripe shade of blueberry, raspberry, or grape ("raspberry" has a great view of the city), has lovely furnishings, and is reached by climbing the sweeping, majestically carved oak staircase with its overhead chandelier and window-seated landings.

How to get there: From downtown Denver, go east on East Colfax to Race Street. Turn left onto Race and proceed 1 block. Inn is on the corner of Race and 16th Avenue.

The Peck House
Empire, Colorado
80438

Innkeepers: Gary and Sally St. Clair
Address/Telephone: 83 Sunny Avenue (mailing address: P.O. Box 428);
   (303) 569–9870
Rooms: 11; 9 with private bath.
Rates: $35 to $60, single or double; EP. No pets. Wheelchair accessible.
   No TV. No air conditioning (not needed; elevation 8,600 feet). All
   major credit cards accepted.
Open: All year.
Facilities and Activities: Breakfast for guests only at nominal charge.
   Lunch on Saturdays all year, every day during summer. Dinner and
   champagne brunch all year. Picnic lunches for hikers. Bar. Hot tub.
   Fresh flowers in guest rooms. Nearby: Victorian village of
   Georgetown; hiking, fishing, downhill and cross-country skiing.

Nestled against a wildflower-strewn hillside in the small
mountain community of Empire, The Peck House is ☞ the oldest inn still operating in Colorado. Flanked by a full-length veranda facing Empire Valley and the snow-covered peaks beyond,
it was built as a private residence in 1860 for miner James Peck
and his family. Hospitable folks, they welcomed as house guests
friends and strangers alike. When finances became a little tight,

28

the Pecks took to charging a nominal fee for overnighters. The establishment became a regular stagecoach stop, and many a mining executive returned East with glowing tales of the comforting oasis he had found in the middle of the Rocky Mountain wilderness.

Today, innkeepers Gary and Sally St. Clair carry on that same tradition by extending a warm welcome to all who wander in. Gary reigns over the kitchen and is town mayor as well. Sally has a degree in horticulture, and the flowers throughout the premises reflect her skill.

All the rooms are furnished with antiques, including some Peck originals brought west by wagon train. The old-fashioned parlor is strictly Victorian and is carefully watched over by an oval-framed portrait of a stern but beautiful Mary Parsons Peck.

The grandest room, The Governor's Quarters, is located on the ground floor and features private bath, deep rose walls, and elegant, dark walnut furniture. Across the hall, The Bridal Suite is dressed in blue and trimmed in gold touches. And next door, The Garden Room is perhaps the nicest "nest" of all. Light and airy, with gold and green Victorian wallpaper and bird's-eye maple furniture, it opens onto the front porch and offers a peaceful view of the valley.

While a warm fire crackled in the dining-room fireplace, I enjoyed trout stuffed with cornbread dressing, baby shrimp and mushrooms, potatoes au gratin, and a chocolaty, nutty, ice creamy dessert that was a meal in itself.

How to get there: From I–70, west of Denver, exit north onto Highway 40. Empire is only 2 miles up the road. Inn is on the right.

❋

D: *If you happen by on the first Sunday following the Fourth of July, don't miss the ☛ Annual Empire Frog Race. Begun by Gary for the local children, it attracts as many adults as youngsters.*

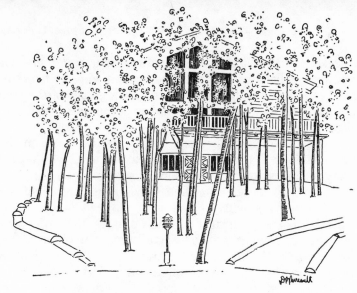

The Aspen Lodge
at Estes Park
Estes Park, Colorado
80517

Innkeeper: Buddy Surles
Address/Telephone: Highway 7, Long's Peak Route; (303) 586–8133
Rooms: 36 in lodge, 21 luxury cottages; all with private bath.
Rates: $75 to $105 per person, AP. Children 3 to 10 years old, 50 percent discount; 2 and younger, free. Phone for EPB and EP rates. No pets. Wheelchair accessible; 2 rooms fully equipped for handicapped. No air conditioning (not needed; elevation 9,100 feet). TV in public alcoves only. All major credit cards accepted.
Open: All year.
Facilities and Activities: Dining room, lounge. Sunday brunch. Conference facilities. Heated outdoor pool, exercise equipment, hot tub, racquetball, tennis; hayrides, sleigh rides to working cattle ranch; horseback riding, hiking, cross-country skiing, snowmobiling, ice skating, jeep tours, children's programs, baby-sitting. Nearby: white-water rafting, golf, downhill skiing.

What began as a fur trapper's cabin in 1910 has been skillfully developed into a luxury dude ranch with ☞ the warmth of a small inn. Quite an achievement! And innkeeper Buddy Surles deserves much of the credit. With down-home friendliness and genuine Western hospitality, he encourages guests to "prop up your feet in front of the fireplace. We want you to feel at home here." The entire staff calls you by name, and they behave as though they are there only for you.

Made of pine, the lodge is the largest log structure in Colorado. Original Western Art is featured throughout the building; and a twenty-four-foot moss rock fireplace graces the main room, where cushioned, handmade aspen-wood couches almost insist that you sit a while. If a log building can be called exquisite, this one qualifies!

The guest rooms are color coordinated beautifully; the beds have quilted coverlets and ruffled skirts; and each room has one wall made of logs, their crossed ends protruding from the corners. Brass lamps on writing desks, fan ceiling lights, and panoramic views of craggy mountain peaks all add to this fine mix of rustic elegance.

A special moment for me happened as I walked from the lodge to the dining room along a stone pathway and through a glen of whispering aspen trees: I saw snowcapped 14,000-foot Long's Peak awash with moonlight. Breathtaking!

The food here is excellent. The barbecued ribs are delightfully flavored, and the meat virtually falls from the bones. I hope you get a chance to try the house dessert, a layered masterpiece of crushed walnuts, cream cheese, silky chocolate pudding, whipped cream, and more walnuts. Isn't that something! And if you catch a trout in the stocked private lake, Chef Roger Rowles will cook it to perfection for you.

How to get there: From I-25, take Highway 34 west to the town of Estes Park. Turn left at first stop light onto St. Vrain Ave. Go 8 blocks, turn onto Highway 7. Continue for 7 miles. The lodge is on the left.

D: See Charlie Eagle Plume's authentic Indian-made works of art, only 4 miles down the road. A Blackfeet Indian, Charlie has operated his Trading Post since 1917.

Black Canyon Inn
Estes Park, Colorado
80517

Innkeepers: Gary Lodmell and Sondra Joyce
Address/Telephone: 800 MacGregor Avenue (P.O. Box 4654); (303)
586–8113
Rooms: 33; all with private bath.
Rates: $35 to $80, May 20 through October 31; $25 to $60, November
1 through May 19; EPB. Pets allowed. Wheelchair accessible. No
air conditioning (not needed; elevation 7,522 feet). Nonsmoking
rooms available. MasterCard, Visa, American Express, Diner's Club
accepted.
Open: All year.
Facilities and Activities: Gourmet restaurant, Tulip Lounge, Fireside
Lounge. Outdoor heated pool, hot tub, sauna, some rooms with
fireplaces. Nearby: Historic MacGregor Ranch, town of Estes Park,
Rocky Mountain National Park, Lake Estes; hiking, horseback
riding, downhill and cross-country skiing, golf.

Executive Chef Carlo Castiglione likens his role at the Black
Canyon Inn to that of an orchestra conductor—and oh, what a
symphony of epicurean delights he creates! Having worked
as ☞ chef in several Arizona four-star restaurants, he now be-
stows his talents on this high-mountain inn.

My dinner began with crispy circles of *lavosh*, an Armenian bread served with herb butter. Next came a bowl of creamy potato soup; homemade whole wheat rolls; and a tender, tasty steak au poivre sautéed with mushrooms and green peppercorns, flamed with cognac, and finished in a cream sauce. All this on candlelit pink linen, surrounded by lilting piano music. When it was time for dessert, my waiter suggested that I have my ☞ Grand Marnier fudge cake in front of the fire in the loft lounge. I did. It was truly memorable.

The accommodations are in both a main-lodge chalet and scallop-edged cottages trimmed in colors that match their wildflower names: Forget Me Not, Thimble Berry, Wild Iris, Butter Cup, and Columbine. Cedar paneling, thick carpeting, ruffled table cloths, pillows and bedspreads, fireplaces, and small sitting areas make these pretty little cottages mighty inviting, indeed. My choice was Columbine, named for Colorado's state flower and situated on a knoll ☞ overlooking a meadow where a large herd of elk often comes to graze.

Breakfast, buffet style, included granola with fresh fruit, scrambled eggs, croissants, bacon, sausage, juice, and coffee. This was served in the dining room, but a continental breakfast is also available for those who would like to have it brought to their rooms.

This inn is ideally located only one mile from the town of Estes Park, close to Rocky Mountain National Park, and within walking distance of Historic MacGregor Ranch, now a museum.

How to get there: From I–25, take Highway 34 west to the town of Estes Park. Turn right at first stop light onto Highway 34 bypass. Turn right again onto MacGregor Avenue. Inn is on the right.

River Song Inn
Estes Park, Colorado
80517

Innkeepers: Gary and Sue Mansfield
Address/Telephone: P.O. Box 1910; (303) 586–4666
Rooms: 6; 2 with private bath, 4 share 2 baths; plus carriage-house suite
with bath, 1 cottage with bath.
Rates: $30 to $75, single; $40 to $85, double; EPB. No pets. No TV. No
air conditioning (not needed; elevation 7,522 feet). No smoking
inside inn. Children 12 years and older welcome by prior arrangement in carriage house only at $10 per child per night. Credit cards
not accepted.
Open: All year.
Facilities and Activities: Dinner and box lunches by reservation. BYOB.
Located on 27 acres of land with easy hiking trails. Nearby: Rocky
Mountain National Park; restaurants, shopping; hiking, fishing,
sailing, mountain climbing, golf, tennis, wildlife seminars, downhill
and cross-country skiing, snowshoeing.

I don't think I've ever seen a more meticulously designed,
decorated, and furnished country inn.

The most luxurious accommodation is called Chiming Bells,
and it is nearly impossible not to gasp as you get your first glimpse.
A shiny brass bed gleams above the emerald green carpet; a moss

rock fireplace fills one corner; and ☛ skylights open the pine-planked cathedral ceiling to the sun and stars. In the small parlor, one finds a crimson Victorian settee and walnut platform rocker; in the bathing area, a sapphire blue oversized, recessed soaking tub and ☛ redwood-paneled double shower with skylight.

The carriage-house suite has a white-pine four-poster covered with red plaid bedspread and pillow shams to match; a raised-hearth, freestanding wood stove; private bath; sun deck; and large sleeping loft.

Forget-Me-Not features Sue's grandmother's high-backed bed and dresser set; Shooting Star has a Jenny Lind spool bed; and others have beds of iron and brass or wood.

I sat for a long time in the many-windowed dining room, enjoying the ☛ aroma of apples baking in nutmeg and cinnamon sauce. Sue is an excellent cook and makes many delectables such as apple pandowdy, blueberry cobbler served with vanilla yogurt, and corn fritters topped with genuine Vermont maple syrup. Dinners are country style; they are the perfect culmination to a day out-of-doors and include fresh-baked breads with perhaps corn chowder, vegetable-beef or split-pea soup, and a simple dessert. The soup pot sits on the corner wood stove, and guests help themselves, ladling to their hearts' content.

Plush off-white couches and an ice blue carpet add elegance to the living room, where one entire side is a ☛ window with a magnificent view of tall pines and mountains. Books line two walls, a warm fire crackles in the fireplace, and the grandfather clock periodically chimes the hour. All's well at River Song.

How to get there: Going west on Elkhorn Avenue, Estes Park's main street, turn left onto Moraine Avenue and proceed 4 blocks. At first stop sign, turn right onto Highway 36. At stop light (1.2 miles) turn left onto Mary's Lake Road. Watch for River Song Inn mailbox just across bridge. Turn right to inn.

The Stanley Hotel
Estes Park, Colorado
80517

Innkeeper: Harry Graham
Address/Telephone: 333 Wonderview Avenue (mailing address: P.O. Box
   1767); (303) 586–3371, (800) 762–5437 within Colorado
Rooms: 91; all with private bath.
Rates: $55 to $105, single; $60 to $110, double; $150, suite; EP. No
   pets. Wheelchair accessible. No air conditioning (not needed; ele-
   vation 7,600 feet). MasterCard, Visa, American Express accepted.
Open: All year.
Facilities and Activities: Full-service restaurant. Lounge. Gift shop.
   Outdoor pool, sauna, tennis; award-winning theater productions,
   weekly fine-arts series, weekend entertainment in the lounge.
   Nearby: Rocky Mountain National Park; shopping; hiking, fishing,
   horseback riding, wildlife photography, downhill and cross-country
   skiing.

   Perhaps the best way to describe The Stanley Hotel is to say
that it is tastefully grandiose. Built in 1909 by Freeland O. Stanley,
designer of the photographic dry-plate process and inventor of
the Stanley Steamer automobile, The Stanley is a fine example of
extravagant Georgian architecture, both inside and out.
   As I strolled the expansive lobby, paused to admire

the 🖙 rare, 1906 mint-condition Stanley Steamer on display, entered the music room with its white-columned fireplace and circa-1909 Steinway, and wandered through the walnut-paneled billiard room and into the small gallery of antiquities and ancient art, it was easy to imagine how it must have felt to be part of the Gatsby era.

These public areas are large enough so that, even on Sundays, when The Stanley serves an eight-entrée champagne brunch followed by a free classical concert, the feeling of spaciousness remains.

A grand staircase in the center of the lobby leads to the second and third floors, where lovely wallpapered rooms are furnished with an assortment of white iron, brass, four-poster, and canopied beds; claw-footed bathtubs; and elegant writing desks, some original to the inn. A gleaming, solid-brass 1909 Otis elevator, run by a hand lever and affectionately known to innkeeper Harry Graham as "Otis the First," transports guests to their quarters.

The MacGregor Room features continental cuisine and is renowned for its New York steak au poivre, which Chef Frank Abeyta prepares table-side. What a marvelous way to feel special! I advise, just once, though, ordering lightly and then fully indulging in the dessert menu. How about 🖙 bananas Flambé, cherries jubilee, or, not nearly so spectacular but absolutely delicious, raisin bread pudding? The MacGregor Room looks out onto an unbeatable vista of massive mountains, alpine meadows, and Lake Estes.

Owners Frank and Judith Normali are deeply dedicated to the preservation of The Stanley, and innkeeper Harry Graham is always close at hand to see to the needs of every guest.

How to get there: From I–25, take Highway 34 west to the town of Estes Park. Turn right at first stop light and immediately right again onto Wonderview Avenue. The Stanley is on the right.

Wanek's Lodge at Estes
Estes Park, Colorado
80517

Innkeepers: Jim and Pat Wanek

Address/Telephone: 560 Ponderosa Drive (mailing address: P.O. Box 898); (303) 586–5851

Rooms: 4 share 2 baths.

Rates: $31, single; $38, double. Includes continental breakfast. No pets. TV in sitting room only. No air conditioning (not needed; elevation 7,600 feet). No smoking inside inn. Well-behaved children considered. Credit cards not accepted.

Open: All year.

Facilities and Activities: Dinner and picnic lunches available on weekends if requested ahead. BYOB. Outdoor deck with barbecue. Nearby: Rocky Mountain National Park, Lake Estes; shopping; hiking, fishing, horseback riding, wildlife photography, golf, downhill and cross-country skiing.

This inn sits on an acre of natural grass and giant ponderosa pines, ☞ not far from Trail Ridge Road, the loftiest continuous highway in America, and Rocky Mountain National Park, home to bighorn sheep, black bear, bobcat, mountain lion and more than 200 species of birds and 500 species of wildflowers.

If you can't stay a week, plan to come on a weekend because

that's when Jim, on request, cooks up meals to please the fussiest of gourmands. ☞ The first guest to make reservations for dinner gets to choose the entrée—and this chef is so gifted, the choice can be just about anything. French, German, Italian, Greek, or Chinese, Jim won't disappoint you. I hope you get a chance to try his Czechoslovakian potato soup. Flavored with caraway and dill, it's thick and delicious. All items are made from scratch with only natural ingredients, no salt is used, and the seasoning is done exclusively with herbs. Pat and Jim also pack tasty sack lunches for hikers and skiers.

Breakfast is continental: homemade sweet rolls, applesauce-nut bread or oatmeal muffins, three kinds of juice, and coffee or tea.

The guest rooms feature fresh flowers and ☞ line-dried linens scented by pine trees and clean mountain air. Rooms upstairs open onto a common sitting room with television and large windows. The broad outdoor deck has a barbecue grill for guest use, and this would be a great place to cook a steak or a hot dog or two. Supplies are only a few blocks away. Or after a day of hiking or skiing, come back to Wanek's for a shower or a soak and then it's off to the picturesque town of Estes Park for dinner at your choice of many restaurants. Molly B's in Gaslight Square, where I had a tasty lunch, serves breakfast, lunch, and dinner, with an emphasis on seafood.

How to get there: From downtown Estes Park, go east on Highway 36 to Stanley Avenue. Turn right onto Stanley and right onto Ponderosa Drive. You will wind around for about ¼ mile. Inn is on the left.

Helmshire Inn
Fort Collins, Colorado
80524

Innkeeper: Jim McIver
Address/Telephone: 1204 South College Avenue; (303) 493–4683
Rooms: 27; all with private bath.
Rates: $51, single; $56, double; EPB. No pets. Wheelchair accessible;
  some rooms fully equipped for handicapped; elevator Braille
  equipped. All major credit cards accepted.
Open: All year.
Facilities and Activities: Complimentary coffee, tea, cocoa at all times;
  complimentary wine after 5:00 P.M. BYOB. In-room refrigerators
  and microwaves. Nearby: shopping; Colorado State University
  across the street, Roosevelt National Forest, Kodak plant tours; river
  and lake fishing, swimming, boating, downhill and cross-country
  skiing.

Old English on the outside and a skillful blend of elegance,
country charm, and avant-garde convenience on the inside—this
may sound like an odd mix, but it really works. The ☛ lobby is
absolutely plush, with thick, blackberry–ice cream carpet; lavender walls; soft, plump sofas; fine wood pieces; and cut-glass
lamps. The guest rooms are beautifully appointed with contemporary furnishings. And lilac linens cover the round oak tables in

the dining room, where only in-house guests are served. The pace is thus pleasant and leisurely.

Chef Erik Stukenberg produces remarkable breakfasts from his small kitchen. Sometimes it's a puffy soufflé; other days it could be blintzes. The morning I breakfasted here, Erik outdid himself with a feather-light quiche and an assortment of his breads, including both apple and cherry kuchen, blueberry-swirl bread, cinnamon bread, and raisin muffins. Add to this the cantaloupe, fresh strawberries and pineapple, fresh-squeezed orange juice, and Columbian coffee, and you have a veritable feast.

Erik will also arrange dinners upon request. For eating out, I highly recommend The Café François. If you can muster the courage to walk past the delectable French pastries long enough to order from the menu, you will be in for a wonderful meal.

The housekeeping at the Helmshire is on a level with the most meticulous I've ever seen. Every one of the many rooms I looked into was spotlessly clean: not a speck of dust, not a single wrinkle in the bed covers, nary a footprint on the carpet.

☛ Directly across the street from Colorado State University, the Helmshire is a favorite with visiting professors from all over the world. The campus is a great place to muse an hour or two in the library, take in a lecture, or enjoy a walk. Is it the profusion of energy? I'm not sure, but there is something about a college campus that always feels good.

How to get there: From I–25, take Exit 265 west toward Colorado State University. Turn right onto College Avenue. Inn is on the right.

D: *A large bar of hard-milled soap, imported from France, waits on the bathtub. A real touch of class!*

The Hardy House
Georgetown, Colorado
80444

Innkeeper: Sarah Schmidt
Address/Telephone: 605 Brownell Street (mailing address: P.O. Box 0156); (303) 569–3388
Rooms: 3; 1 with private bath.
Rates: $35 to $55, single; $45 to $55, double; EPB. No pets. TV in parlor only. No air conditioning (not needed; elevation 8,500 feet). Smoking permitted in 1 guest room only and in common rooms with other guests' permission. Well-behaved children over 10 years of age only. Credit cards not accepted.
Open: All year.
Facilities and Activities: Dinner available if arranged for in advance. BYOB. Picnic lunches. Special-occasion packages. Storage for ski equipment. Nearby: museums, many antique and specialty shops, Victorian-house tours, mine tour, narrow-gauge passenger train; hiking, fishing, cycling, downhill and cross-country skiing.

Painted candy apple–red with snow-white picket fence, shutters, balustrade, and gingerbread trim, the eye-catching exterior of this 1877 🖝 Victorian doll house is only the beginning.

Inside, the cozy parlor centers around a large, potbellied stove that heats the room and warms the cider in winter. The downstairs suite has 🖝 its own potbellied stove, a claw-footed tub, and a private sitting room, where one can have an intimate breakfast and sometimes watch bighorn sheep grazing on the hillside.

Upstairs, you can snuggle beneath a goose-down comforter amid papered walls, sloped ceilings, and the sweet scent of a wooded forest emanating from the cedar-lined closet. Open the window to the swishing of a 100-year-old blue spruce and the rush of nearby Cleark Creek and be guaranteed a good night's sleep.

Sarah is an accomplished chef, and her love of cooking will be your gain. (If you stay here often, you may gain in more ways than you intended!) Mornings bring fruit, granola, egg dishes, lemon bread, rum-raisin muffins, or maybe a "touch of sherry" coffee cake with penuche icing.

🖝 If you caught a fish from the creek the day before, Sarah will cook it for your breakfast. You're not a fisherman? Not to worry. She has a friend who fishes for her; so just let her know when you make your reservation that you would dearly like to start your day with fresh, pan-fried trout, and you're apt to get just that.

Dinner is available if requested in advance. Served on china, with crystal and silver, it may consist of soup or chowder, salad, bread made from scratch, an entrée such as Sarah's grandmother's recipe for chicken and noodles, and, *la pièce de résistance,* apple Devonshire, with sour cream, cinnamon, and nuts.

How to get there: From I–70, take Exit 228 into Georgetown. Turn right onto Brownell Street. Inn is on the right.

∽

D: *I found tasty little surprises all over the house: a dish of chocolates by the front door, shortbread cookies in the parlor, and, best of all, a whole basketful of melt-in-your-mouth meringue mushrooms in each bedroom. These perfectly shaped sweets, with their undersides carefully dipped in chocolate, are a Sarah specialty.*

The Inn of Glen Haven
Glen Haven, Colorado
80532

Innkeeper: Mark Maher

Address/Telephone: 7468 County Road 43 (mailing address: P.O. Box 19); (303) 586–3897

Rooms: 8; all with private bath.

Rates: $40 to $75, single or double. Includes continental breakfast. No pets. No air conditioning (not needed; elevation 7,000 feet). No TV. Well-behaved children only, please. MasterCard, Visa, American Express accepted.

Open: All year.

Facilities and Activities: Full-service restaurant. Bar and wine-tasting room. Nearby: Rocky Mountain National Park; hiking, fishing, horseback riding, nature trails, downhill and cross-country skiing.

Innkeeper Mark Maher is a soft-spoken, gentle man who is rightfully proud of his Old English, hunting lodge–style inn. With its rich red carpeting, dark wood-paneled walls, and glowing fire in the stone fireplace, the main room is perfect for making friends and holding quiet conversations. Upstairs, the bedrooms reveal ☛ half-canopied beds and top-quality antiques. The strong medieval-England influence throughout makes the inn truly romantic.

And guess what. There is a secret room! The tiny library, cozy and warm, has a sliding bookshelf wall that, when pushed to one side, reveals a hidden old-world wine-tasting cellar. Here one can sit on little benches amid racks of wine bottles while savoring wonderful tastes and aromas by the glass.

The dining room could get by on appearance alone. The whole room is bathed in a lovely rosy glow emanating from predominantly red stained-glass windows and reflecting off scarlet tablecloths set with genuine silver and crystal.

Mark is chief chef, and what a magnificent job he does! Every evening brings another of his specialties, all equally good. My favorite? I think he really outdoes himself with his steak escoffier. This is a remarkably flavored fillet mignon in a Cabernet-Sauvignon butter sauce, served with either wild rice or cream-of-almond soup, house salad, and homemade breads. It is a meal not easily forgotten.

From December 25 to January 5, The Inn of Glen Haven presents a traditional "Twelve Days of Christmas" celebration. A different theme is followed each evening, featuring, among others, a pheasant night, a venison night, and a wild-pig night. Because it has become so tremendously popular, there are actually two wild-pig nights. On these occasions, a twenty-member choir parades the roasted pig through the dining room while singing the Boar's Head Song and, later, leads the guests in caroling. Early reservations are a must if you plan to join in the revelry.

How to get there: From I–25, take Highway 34 west to the town of Estes Park. Turn right at first stop light onto Highway 34 bypass. Turn right again onto MacGregor Avenue. At MacGregor Ranch, the road turns right and becomes Devils Gulch Road. Continue on Devils Gulch Road for about five miles to Glen Haven. The inn is on the right.

✳

D: *Ask Mark to show you the many false walls where, during the inn's "speakeasy" days, guests found refuge from law-enforcement raids.*

The Dove Inn
Golden, Colorado
80401

Innkeepers: Ken and Jean Sims
Address/Telephone: 711 14th Street; (303) 278–2209
Rooms: 4; 2 with private bath.
Rates: $29 to $44, single; $34 to $49, double; EPB. Children under age
6 free. No unmarried couples, please. Pets and smoking permitted
in East Room (downstairs room) only. MasterCard, Visa, American
Express accepted.
Open: All year.
Facilities and Activities: BYOB. Crib and rollaways available. Bikes,
including a tandem, for rent. In-room phones available. Shuttle
service from Denver's Stapleton Airport. Nearby: Buffalo Bill's grave
and museum, Coors Brewery Tours, Colorado School of Mines, National Earthquake Center, Heritage Square (artisan and entertainment village), museums; restaurants, shopping; hiking, fishing,
downhill and cross-country skiing.

Hidden behind a giant blue spruce and covered with an
abundance of climbing ivy, this enchanting Victorian cottage has
been standing on a quiet side street in Golden (only twelve miles
west of Denver) since 1889.
Doves enhance the mailbox, the guest-room doors, the stair-

way, and the breakfast napkin rings. There are others, too. See how many you can spot.

The guest rooms are country gingham in décor. Room Five is done in blues, with the print in the bedspread and curtains matching that in the wallpaper. It has two white iron beds with tiny hand-painted flowers on the headboards. The room directly across the hall has a writing desk in a bay-window alcove, brass bed, and navy blue ruffled curtains and bedspread made by Jean. A container of candy and a unique basket made from pine needles by Ken's grandfather sit on the dresser. Still another attractive room is on this floor, plus a shared bath with ☞ the longest bathtub I've ever seen.

The fourth guest room is downstairs and has its own entrance, private patio, and a queen-size antique brass bed that Ken ingeniously made by putting together two twin beds.

Jean has been associated with interior decorating for many years, and her expertise is evident throughout the inn. Ken is a freelance corporate pilot, and when he's not flying, his inn duties include being a plumber, a maintenance man, and an assistant to the chef (Jean).

Breakfast is buffet style and includes a hot dish such as scrambled-egg casserole with lots of cheese, a fruit compote, bacon or sausage, and ☞ Grandma Holmberg's cinnamon rolls, homemade by Jean's mother. When she comes to visit, Grandma fills the freezer with them, and you and I are the lucky recipients of her culinary skills.

For dinner, you have only to walk across the street to the ☞ 14th Street Ristorante for reasonably priced authentic Italian cuisine. I suggest the broccoli, cheddar-, and mozzarella-cheese calzone and the vermicelli-chicken salad. Jan and Salvatore Russo operate this small and intimate restaurant in the restored 1904 former home of Mildred Delaney, known throughout the Golden area for her contributions to the advancement of music and culture.

How to get there: Go south on Washington Street (Golden's main street) to 14th. Turn left onto 14th and proceed ½ block. Inn is on the right.

Tumbling River Ranch
Grant, Colorado
80448

Innkeepers: Jim and Mary Dale Gordon
Address/Telephone: P.O. Box 30; (303) 838–5981
Rooms: 12 in 2 lodges, plus 13 cabins; all with private bath.
Rates: Adults, $750 per week; children aged 6 to 11, $550 per week;
   children aged 2 to 5, $450 per week; AP. No pets. No TV. No air
   conditioning (not needed; elevation 9,200 feet). Credit cards not
   accepted.
Open: May 1 to October 1.
Facilities and Activities: BYOB. Fireplace in each unit, daily maid service; heated outdoor pool, sauna; game room, square dancing,
   horseback riding, rodeo activities, 4WD trips. Complete program for
   children age 3 and older (optional). Nearby: Pike National Forest,
   wildlife, mining towns; hiking, fishing, white-water rafting.

If you like the jeans, sweatshirts, barns, and animals part of
dude ranching, but you also appreciate fancy guest rooms and
extraordinary dining, you're going to like it here.

Tumbling River Ranch has several cottages and two lodges,
the most unusual being The Pueblo, built for the daughter of
Adolph Coors of Colorado beer fame and used for many years as
her mountain home. It is classically Spanish-Indian in design;

Indians from Taos, New Mexico, participated in the building's construction and the decorative carving of the wooden beams. 🐾 Indian rugs, adobe walls, beehive fireplaces, small alcoves for books and artifacts, and strings of hanging, dried red peppers add to the authenticity of this inn's Southwestern ambiance. A large sitting room with massive fireplace, a game room, a lounge, an attractive dining area, and seven lovely guest rooms, each with its own fireplace and bath, make this, without a doubt, my choice of lodging.

The second lodge, built in the '20s for a former Denver mayor, also exhibits an abundance of warmth and charm. It has five guest rooms, each with fireplace and bath, and a dining room and lounge from which one can sometimes 🐾 spot bighorn sheep grazing on the hillside.

Mary Dale is in charge of the kitchen, and food preparation is taken seriously. All is made from scratch, and Jim proudly says that the mashed potatoes even have a few lumps, attesting to the fact that they are the real thing, not box variety. (They are also made with *real* butter and *real* cream!) There are lots of cookouts, and a favorite seems to be Jim's Brunch, celebrated each Tuesday. Imagine for a moment an open fire, 🐾 Jim's *3½-foot* frying pan with 150 eggs scrambling all at once, potatoes browning, bacon crisping, cowboy coffee perfuming the air . . . Incidentally, do you know the recipe for cowboy coffee? The author is anonymous, probably to keep from being shot!

Cowboy Coffee

Dump two pounds coffee in pot.
Add jist 'nough water to wet it down good.
Boil fer two hours.
Next, throw in a hoss shoe.
If the shoe sinks,
     the coffee ain't done.

How to get there: From Denver, take Highway 285 southwest to Grant. Turn north onto Guanella Pass Road. Ranch is on the left.

Outlook Lodge
Green Mountain Falls, Colorado
80819

Innkeepers: Impy Ahern and family

Address/Telephone: 6975 Howard Avenue (mailing address: P.O. Box 5); (303) 684–2303

Rooms: 12; 4 with private bath, 8 share several baths.

Rates: $30 to $35, single; $35 to $40, double. Generous continental breakfast included. Well-mannered pets allowed. TV in parlor only. No air conditioning (not needed; elevation 7,800 feet). MasterCard and Visa accepted.

Open: Memorial Day through Labor Day.

Facilities and Activities: BYOB. Yard, patio, use of barbecue and kitchen. Nearby: swimming pool, bingo, trout-stocked lake; Pikes Peak, cog railway, U.S. Air Force Academy, North Pole (amusement center for young children); hiking, fishing, tennis, horseback riding.

Perched high on a hillside, almost in the shadow of 14,000-foot Pikes Peak, the Outlook Lodge was ☛ built in 1889 as a parsonage for visiting ministers and their families. In the 1920s, it was sold and reopened as an inn.

A hand-carved, golden oak staircase, creaking from the tread of many footsteps, leads from the Victorian parlor to the upstairs guest rooms. ☛ Many of the original furnishings remain, and the antique-filled rooms appear much as you'd expect they did at the turn of the century, except for the addition of new wall and floor coverings.

The lemon yellow claw-footed tub in one of the shared bathrooms was the first such luxury item in Green Mountain Falls; ☛ during the '20s, the enterprising owner of the inn rented it out to the townspeople for twenty-five cents a bath, including hot water, soap, and towel. An old-time resident still remembers seeing folks patiently waiting in line with their towels draped over their arms.

The front veranda looks out through tall pines and blue spruce to the town below. Down the hill to the right, next door to the inn, is "The Little Brown Church in the Vale," said to be the inspiration for the hymn of the same name.

Breakfast is "all you can eat" and includes homemade scones, cinnamon rolls, and Impy's special Hawaiian bread (made with pineapple, macadamia nuts, and bananas) or another specialty, Rocky-Mountain-High muffins, a bran muffin that bakes with an exceptionally high peaked top that Impy ices with white frosting to represent snow. You have a choice of juices and the coffee pot is always on.

Guests have full use of the parlor, dining room, and kitchen. ☛ You are welcome to fry up your catch of trout, pack a lunch, or cook your evening meal on the patio barbecue. There's even an extra fridge for guests' supplies.

Several restaurants are within walking distance. I recommend the Li'l Pantry for homemade soups, breads, and pies and the Pub & Grub, built of logs with stone fireplaces, for complete dinners.

How to get there: Take Highway 24 west from Colorado Springs to Green Mountain Falls turnoff. Inn is on the left.

❧

D: *Be sure to ask Impy about the origin of the upright piano in the dining room. And to think it ended up in a former parsonage!*

Historic Delaware Hotel
Leadville, Colorado
80461

Innkeeper: Jill Murwin
Address/Telephone: 700 Harrison Avenue (mailing address: P.O. Box
  960); (303) 486–1418
Rooms: 37, including 6 suites; all with private bath.
Rates: $35 to $65, single or double. Includes continental breakfast.
  Well-behaved pets allowed. No air conditioning (not needed: eleva-
  tion 10,152 feet!). No-smoking rooms available. MasterCard and
  Visa accepted.
Open: All year.
Facilities and Activities: Breakfast served to hotel guests only. No lunch.
  Dinner served 7 days a week. Bar in dining area. Fruit baskets in all
  rooms. Reduced-rate ski-lift tickets available. Nearby: local tours,
  museums, shopping; complete recreation complex including Olympic pool, whirlpool, gym, indoor track; fishing, hiking, horseback
  riding, river rafting, downhill and cross-country skiing.

The Historic Delaware Hotel celebrated its one-hundreth
birthday in 1986. Despite its having had its share of hard times,
vacancy, and vandalism over the years, it has now come full
circle back to "the good old days," actually to "*better* than the
good old days." The entire building has been beautifully refur-

bished, every room has a private bath, and the dim gas lights have been replaced with electric replicas.

Several shops open off the small, old-fashioned lobby, including an ice cream parlor, an old-time photography studio, and a variety of gift and clothing stores.

Each guest room is different, and every one is truly charming. ☛ Old handmade quilts hang above the period brass, iron, and oak beds, while tiny take-home gift sachets sit on each antique dresser. I chose the Rose Green Suite, named after a prominent Leadville woman and fittingly appointed with thick rose-colored carpet and elegantly carved, green velvet–upholstered chairs and chaise lounge.

As I sat in this spacious corner room, ☛ strains of a classical piano melody floated down the hall and into my sanctuary. The evening's entertainment had begun in the intimate second-floor dining room, aptly called The Second Floor Restaurant.

David Bedillion is the Chef de Cuisine, and a more skilled kitchen master would be hard to find. The menu changes according to whatever is available ☛ fresh from the sea, the butcher shop, and the garden. Nothing is frozen, nothing is canned.

I had chicken Jerusalem, a chicken fillet cooked to perfection in a sauce of veal stock, heavy cream, shallots, garlic, and white wine and served with artichoke hearts, glazed carrots, and new potatoes. A relish tray comes with every meal, as does an individual loaf of hot bread.

Now, I could have stopped right there. But did I? No, and I'm very glad I didn't because the dessert was cheese cake Grand Marnier, fantastically flavored with liqueur and sprinkled with coconut. Oh my, if this keeps up, I'll soon be *rolling* from inn to inn!

How to get there: From I–70, take exit 195 south onto Highway 91 and proceed 24 miles to Leadville. Hotel is on Harrison Avenue, Leadville's main street.

Sylvan Dale Ranch
Loveland, Colorado
80537

Innkeepers: The Jessup family: Maurice, Tillie, and Susan
Address/Telephone: 2939 North County Road 31 D; (303) 667–3915
Rooms: 24; 14 in Wagon Wheel Barn, 1 suite in lodge, 9 cottages; all
    with private bath.
Rates: $25.50 per person, double occupancy, for Bunk and Breakfast
    (EPB). $245 single, $470 double, AP, all-activities 3-day pkg; $465
    single, $910 double, AP, all-activities 6-day pkg. "No tipping" policy.
    No pets. Wheelchair accessible. No TV. No air conditioning (not
    needed; elevation 5,325 feet). Credit cards not accepted.
Open: All year.
Facilities and Activities: BYOB. Heated outdoor pool, tennis courts,
    horseback riding, trout fishing in river and stocked pond, hiking,
    evening entertainment, children's program, farm animals and ac-
    tivities, square dancing. Nearby: white-water rafting, golf, lake
    fishing, boating; Rocky Mountain National Park.

Maurice and Tillie have operated their working guest ranch
for more than forty years. Maurice conducts the farm tours, Tillie
does all the baking, and daughter Susan is general manager and
hostess. These are good people, dedicated to the pleasure of their
guests.

You can 🖙 watch cattle being branded or play a set of tennis; help clean the barn or swim in the heated outdoor pool; take a tour of the haying operation or fish the river and stocked lake. Or how about a hayride, overnight pack trip, an authentic Fourth of July cattle drive, square dancing, or an ice cream social?

Keep in mind that while all these activities are available, there is no pressure to participate. For one entire day, I chose 🖙 the luxury of doing absolutely nothing. I sat for a long time beside the sparkling clear river that ripples through the property and watched this year's crop of frisky colts frolicking in the meadow across the way while shadows lengthened on the red, rocky cliffs in the distance. I was sure I'd never want to move . . . until I heard the dinner bell!

Picnic tables piled high with barbecued chicken, corn on the cob, baked beans, and homemade bread brought on colossal appetites, lively conversation, and nary a frown to be seen. Farm-style breakfasts, including Tillie's outstanding cinnamon rolls, are served in the two antique-filled dining rooms or out on the porch by the river.

I stayed upstairs in the main lodge in a lovely corner suite where the windows opened wide and 🖙 the river below sang me to sleep. Other accommodations are in pretty yellow cabins and in the Wagon Wheel Barn, a for-real barn renovated nicely for people occupancy.

🖙 The children's program is particularly noteworthy. No sitting in circles, cutting and pasting. No siree, "pahdner." Depending on ages, 🖙 the little buckaroos are allowed to help groom the horses and soap the saddles, take off on accompanied nature hikes and scavenger hunts, float on inner tubes on the pasture ponds, fish, pan for gold, or take a farm tour. Next time, I'm going disguised as a kid!

How to get there: From I–25, take exit 257-B west onto Highway 34 and proceed 9 miles. Ranch is on the right.

Peaceful Valley Lodge
and Guest Ranch
Lyons, Colorado
80540

Innkeepers: Karl and Mabel Boehm
Address/Telephone: Star Route; (303) 747–2881
Rooms: 50; all with private bath.
Rates: Winter: $51.50 to $72.50, single, EPB; $58 to $79, double, EPB; $60 to $94, per person, AP. Summer: $51.50 to $72.50, single, EPB; $58 to $79, double, EPB; $86 to $120, per person, AP, includes all activities; $577.50 to $805, per person per week, AP, includes all activities. Six-day week and children's rates also available. No pets. Wheelchair accessible. TV in sitting room only. No air conditioning (not needed; elevation 8,474 feet). All major credit cards accepted.
Open: All year.
Facilities and Activities: BYOB. Swimming pool, tennis court, riding arena, horseback riding, square dancing, jeep tours, trail rides, hiking, fishing, climbing, cross-country skiing. Complete children's program. Sunday services in alpine chapel. Nearby: Shopping in small mountain towns.

    Austria without jet lag—that's Peaceful Valley Lodge. ☞ Red hearts and edelweiss, Tyrolean music and dirndls, window boxes full of geraniums, and, high on a hill, an awe-inspiring, alpine-style chapel complete with "onion" steeple. I was sure, any minute, Julie Andrews and her brood would come swinging across the meadow singing "The hills are alive . . ."!

This is ☛ probably the most extensively equipped inn I've ever been to. That's not to say that it is excessively large or impersonal. It isn't. It's homey, quaint, and authentically European, and yet it ☛ offers everything imaginable: swimming pool, tennis court, indoor riding arena, lessons in horsemanship, square dancing, jeep tours to ghost towns and abandoned mining camps, trail rides, hiking, fishing, climbing, cross-country skiing, coffee shop, two dining rooms, a Western shop, gift shop, sport shop, family room and lounge, and beautiful guest rooms.

Mabel comes from Kentucky, has a degree in sociology, and is a marvelous cook. Karl is from the Austrian Tyrol community of Tarrenz and has a master's degree in foreign affairs. They have owned their inn for more than thirty-three years. Their daughter and son-in-law, Debbie and Randy, help keep things running smoothly, and Grandma Boehm, affectionately known as "Oma," adds her own element of old-world charm.

At one time, Mabel did all of the cooking; but now that Chef Oskar Berger, from Krems, Austria, has been added to the staff, it's a joint effort, and the result is ☛ some of the best European-inspired cuisine to be found. Apple pancakes with apple syrup; *bircher muesli,* a Swiss oatmeal made with fresh fruit and fruit juice; and *rouladen,* thin slices of beef rolled around carrots and dill pickle and served with gravy are only a few of the specialties you will find here.

How to get there: From I–70, north of Denver, take exit 243 west onto Highway 66 and proceed to Lyons. From Lyons, take Highway 7 southwest to the lodge.

✹

D: *I was joking about Julie Andrews, but this is sort of a* Sound of Music *story. Karl's family fled Austria to escape the Nazis, and he came to America to attend school. He later became a member of the distinguished U.S. 10th Mountain Division.*

Gray's Avenue Hotel
Manitou Springs, Colorado
80829

Innkeepers: Tom and Lee Gray
Address/Telephone: 711 Manitou Avenue; (303) 685–1277
Rooms: 10; 3 with private bath, 7 share 2 baths.
Rates: $35 to $54, single; $40 to $60, double; EPB. No pets. TV in library only. No air conditioning (not needed; elevation 6,412 feet). Smoking not allowed in common rooms. Exceptionally well-behaved children only, please. MasterCard and Visa accepted.
Open: All year except January.
Facilities and Activities: Complimentary afternoon refreshments. Picnic lunches. BYOB. Nearby: Pikes Peak, cog railroad, Air Force Academy, Will Rogers Shrine of the Sun, Cave of the Winds, Royal Gorge, museums; shopping; hiking, fishing, cross-country skiing.

More like an inn than a hotel, this shingled Queen Anne Victorian sits back off the street on a nicely landscaped, woodsy lot. As for security, a 350-pound concrete lion guards the steps to the wide, front veranda, and a green gargoyle grimaces from atop a ball-shaped porch lamp. Just think how safe and comfortable you will feel here with those two standing sentinel!

The front parlor is beautifully furnished with antiques, including a circa-1725 Pennsylvania Dutch dowry chest and an 🖝 elaborately carved settee and chair from the Iolani Palace in Hawaii. Tom is descended from Hawaiian royalty, and these two pieces have been in his family since the early nineteenth century. They are thought to have been made in England and brought around Cape Horn to the islands. The Koa bench on the upper floor landing is another interesting piece.

The guest rooms fan off from a white spindled staircase that rises splendidly through the center of the inn, and they are tastefully furnished with an assortment of brass beds, Indian rugs, oversized window seats, and a sprinkling of antiques.

Breakfast is served buffet style and might be ham and pancakes; if you are here on Sunday, though, you will be treated to Lee's special quiche made with heavy cream and nutmeg. In addition, there's always juice, fresh fruit, muffins or pastry, and herbal teas and coffee. In the afternoons, you will find wine, soft drinks, and 🖝 lemonade made with Manitou Springs sparkling mineral water.

Lee also packs a 🖝 first-class picnic lunch, which is especially welcome because there is so much to do outdoors in this area. She will lend you a wicker basket filled to the brim with stone-ground wheat bread, choice cold cuts and cheeses, veggies, fruit, crackers, and dip.

No other meals are served, but the Stagecoach Inn, directly across the street, proffers fine continental cuisine, with a very special rendition of Cornish game hen. Or you might try Adam's Mountain Café just one-half block down the street. You can't miss if you order either the walnut casserole or the Tibetan cashew chicken.

How to get there: From I–25, take Exit 141 west and proceed 4 miles to Manitou Avenue exit. Go west on Manitou Avenue for 1 mile. Inn is on the left.

Ponderosa Lodge
Salida, Colorado
81201

Innkeeper: Bud Geistlinger
Address/Telephone: 9010 County Road 240; (303) 539–2730
Rooms: 18 in lodge, 8 cabins; all with private bath.
Rates: $28 single, $35 double, during summer; $40 single, $46 double,
   during winter; Cabins start at $40, single or double, summer or
   winter; EP. Group rates available. Pets allowed in cabins only.
   Wheelchair accessible. TV in bar only. No air conditioning (not
   needed; elevation 8,400 feet). MasterCard, Visa, American Express
   accepted.
Open: All year.
Facilities and Activities: Full-service dining room. Bar. Cats, dogs,
   ducks, and horses. Horseback riding, chuck-wagon rides, overnight
   pack trips. Nearby: Continental Divide, ghost towns; hiking, fishing,
   river rafting, downhill and cross-country skiing.

   This rough-cedar lodge is ideally ☛ located just far enough
from civilization to feel isolated and just close enough to make it
easy to get to. Nestled all snug and secure at the base of 14,229-
foot Mt. Shavano, the Ponderosa offers year-round outdoor activities but exudes no pressure to participate.
   ☛ Fishing is terrific; brookies, rainbows, and browns are

stocked in the stream that crosses the property, and cutthroat trout crowd the nearby lakes and creeks. Bud can arrange for white-water rafting trips; and horses stand under the trees down by the barn patiently waiting to take you on trail rides, pack trips, and chuck-wagon rides. During winter, there's Nordic and alpine skiing on more than 300 inches of light powder at the Monarch ski area, only ten miles away.

The main lodge has two floors of wood-paneled, nicely furnished guest rooms, some with lofts for storage or extra sleepers. There's a cozy bar; and the red-carpeted, red-linened ☛ dining room, with its massive expanse of windows, looks out on a duck pond with arched footbridge, wooded hills, and breathtaking mountain peaks.

The mood here is so relaxed, ☛ it is not unusual to see folks come to breakfast in their robes and slippers. Or you can do as I did: Pitter-patter down to the dining room and bring a cup of early morning coffee back to your room, watch the ducks slicing a path through the mirrorlike pond, and see the sun break over the distant hills. Perfect peace!

That evening, my dinner choice was a tasty fillet mignon with mushrooms and onions, beef-barley soup, and just-baked rolls. The pan-fried trout looked mighty good, too, and came with a *heated* lemon slice. All the while, melodic strains of Straus waltzes wafted through the air, and I watched as the outdoors turned from gold to pink to mauve.

Need a getaway back to nature? This just could be the right place.

How to get there: From Highway 50, between Salida and Gunnison, take the North Fork Road (#240) north at Maysville. Lodge is only a short distance up the road on the right.

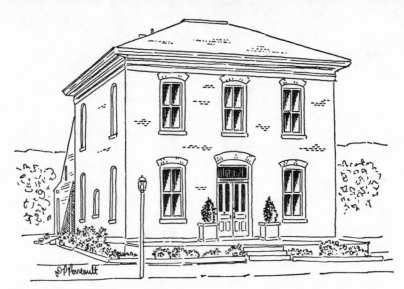

The Poor Farm Country Inn
Salida, Colorado
81201

Innkeepers: Herb and Dottie Hostetler
Address/Telephone: 8495 County Road 160; (303) 539–3818
Rooms: 5; 2 with private bath, 3 share 2 baths.
Rates: $39 to $49, single or double, during summer; $29 to $39, single,
$39 to $49, double, during winter; EPB. No pets. TV in parlor only.
No air conditioning (not needed; elevation 7,000 feet). No smoking
in guest rooms. MasterCard and Visa accepted.
Open: All year.
Facilities and Activities: BYOB. Turn-down service, mints on pillows,
complimentary drink in evening; private fishing. Nearby: Salida
Hot Springs Pool, ghost towns; hiking, fishing, white-water rafting,
jeep tours, downhill and cross-country skiing.

How many times have you thought for sure you were going
to "end up at the poor farm"? Well, now you can do just that, and
enjoy it!

From 1892 to 1943, for more than fifty years, this sturdy
red-brick building loomed over the landscape, a threat to all who
might fall victim to adversity. Young and old lived here, and those
who were able worked the farm for a few pennies to save for an
uncertain future.

Ah, but alas, sometimes even poor farms see better days, and, thanks to Herb and Dottie, ☞ this one has blossomed into a beauty, now listed on the National Register of Historic Places. The parlor is furnished in antiques and has a library complete with sliding ladder for reaching books on high shelves.

The guest rooms are country comfortable, with all the touches that make them homey: lace-curtained transoms, brass and white iron beds, hand-crocheted doilies, bed covers of ruffled gingham with white eyelet skirts, and ☞ unique door stops called Cockleburs. They are made by Herb's 91-year-old grandmother and are best described as patchwork, three-dimensional snow-flakes.

Don't miss the pastoral view of valley and mountain peaks from the east end of the dining-room table. Other specialties of the house are: the ☞ original outdoor fire-escape slide leading from the second floor to a wisely placed box of sand for a soft landing; a skylight-lit, fourteen-bed, cozy, and very inexpensive third-floor loft; a one-fourth-mile stretch for private fishing on the Arkansas River; and a stocked pond for the kids.

Morning brings a full, country-style, all-you-can-eat breakfast of Belgian waffles with fresh fruit and cream, eggs Benedict, twenty-four-hour omelet, or special quiches. The Hostetlers don't serve any other meals, but you are only two miles from town and several good eating places.

I recommend the Palace Restaurant. The décor is turn-of-the-century and the cuisine is European. I had a boneless cut of chicken flamed with Amaretto and topped with toasted almonds and a touch of cream. Fantastic.

How to get there: From Highway 50 at Salida, turn at Salida Hot Springs Pool. Go north on Holman, right onto Poncha Blvd., left onto Grant, left onto Crestone. Go past the golf course. You are on County Road 160. The inn is on the right.

Sweet Adeline's
Salida, Colorado
81201

Innkeepers: Bob and Adella Schulz
Address/Telephone: 949 F Street; (303) 539–4100
Rooms: 3; 1 with private bath, 2 share bath.
Rates: $29 to $49, single; $39 to $49, double; EPB. No pets. TV in side
parlor and Briar Rose Room only. No air conditioning (not needed;
elevation 7,032 feet). No smoking. Well-behaved children over age
8 only. MasterCard and Visa accepted.
Open: All year except for 1 week at Christmas.
Facilities and Activities: Lunch and dinner available. BYOB. Complimentary refreshments, champagne for special occasions; bicycles.
Nearby: Salida Hot Springs Pool; restaurants, antique shops; hiking, excellent river and stream fishing, white-water rafting, downhill and cross-country skiing; jeep tours, ghost towns.

As I walked up the front steps of this lovely delft blue Queen
Anne, a bicycle built for two leaned against the front railing, and
the porch swing swayed in the breeze. Adella met me at the door
wearing a rose-colored Gibson Girl dress with long skirt, high-
topped button shoes, and the sort of smile that makes you *know*
you're welcome. I was immediately convinced that I'd like to
spend the night.

The formal front parlor lends itself to reading and quiet conversation, while the side parlor, with fireplace, player piano, television, stereo, and comfy furniture laden with crazy-quilt pillows and handmade afghans, inspires congenial camaraderie.

☛ Everything has a just-scrubbed look, homespun without being cutesy, ☛ with all the little things that make a place special: framed needlework, ceiling fans, towels and pillow cases edged in lace, lemon slices in ice water, doilies under coffee cups, fresh flowers, and homemade mints.

The guest rooms are "country" at its best. My choice, the Briar Rose Room, is done in off-white and rose with a king-size bed, grandfather clock, quilt rack with extra covers, and a tiny forty-eight-inch claw-footed bathtub.

The sunporch, decked with white wicker, looks out onto a fenced backyard where, amid apple, cherry, and pear trees and raspberry and lilac bushes, guests engage in rousing games of croquet and horseshoes.

Meals here are very special. Breakfast begins with juice, coffee, and fresh fruit followed by either flaky biscuits and sausage gravy, scrambled eggs and hash browns, or French toast, bacon, and homemade chokecherry syrup. ☛ Adella is of Czechoslovakian descent, and she acquired marvelous baking skills from her mother. Her breads are the star attraction: light and fluffy *kolaches* made with fresh rhubarb, cherries, or blue plums; sweet and nutty hot-from-the-oven pecan rolls; raspberry-almond muffins; and heavenly lemon-poppyseed bread, all made with real butter and real cream.

Lunch consists of homemade soup, hot bread, and, perhaps, peach-custard pie. For dinner, one might have tender, browned steak smothered with onions, special seasonings, and brown gravy; rice; vegetable; salad; and lemon or hot apple pie. You must arrange for lunch and dinner in advance, and I highly recommend that you do.

How to get there: From Highway 50, go northeast on F Street for approximately 6 blocks. Inn is on the right.

D: *Considering all the goodies that come from Adella's kitchen, it is really no wonder that Bob has such a pleasant disposition!*

Inn of the Black Wolf
Twin Lakes, Colorado
81251

Innkeepers: Carolyn Slater and John Slater
Address/Telephone: Highway 82, Twin Lakes; (303) 486–0440
Rooms: 14 share 4 baths.
Rates: $39, single or double; EP. Pets permitted. TV in bar only. No air
   conditioning (not needed; elevation 9,200 feet). No smoking in guest
   rooms. All major credit cards accepted.
Open: All year.
Facilities and Activities: Full-service dining room. Bar, gift shop, cross-
   country ski rentals. Genuine European featherbeds. Many special
   events such as: Annual Colorado v. Texas Tomato War, Lovers Only
   Valentine Weekend, and Hooker's Ball. Nearby: hiking, excellent
   fishing, downhill and cross-country skiing, ice fishing.

Named by a former owner who kept her pet wolves on the
property, ☛ this inn has been a refuge for both the famous and
infamous. Built in the 1860s as a stagecoach stop along a line
owned by Kit Carson, it became a brothel for a while, was the
setting for three murders during the last century, served as an
overnight stop for outlaw Doc Holliday, and, during the time it
was owned by movie actor Andy Devine, was frequented by such
Hollywood notables as John Wayne and Loretta Young.

The guest rooms are upstairs, the larger ones having been dorms for the stagecoach travelers. The others, those formerly used by the "tainted ladies," are quite small but very cozy, with dormer windows and sloped ceilings enhanced by Victorian print wallpapers. Incredibly high featherbed puffs, imported from Europe, grace the iron beds; fringed lampshades from New Hampshire hang from above; and marble-topped washstands and diamond-dust mirrors add to the charm.

Carolyn and John are mother and son, John having worked at the inn for several years before Mom decided to get in on the fun. A good team, they provide ☞ an outstanding inn with a German *Gasthaus* atmosphere.

German and American cuisine are served in the dining room. Both are excellent, but my advice is not to miss the chance to try some ☞ exceptionally fine German cooking. The homemade breads and soups, apple pancakes, *rouladen* (slices of veal first rolled and then braised in brown gravy), and sauerbraten (marinated, braised beef) are outstanding. Or you can have bratwurst and sauerkraut *mit ein Glas Bier* in the Biergarten. Carolyn has a dessert chef who makes rich, wondrous chocolate fantasies. A specialty is ☞ *Schwarzwalder kirschtorte,* a chocolate layer cake filled with cream and cherries and flavored with cherry brandy. It alone is worth the trip.

When I last talked to Carolyn, she had just returned from a buying trip to Europe, where she purchased handknit sweaters, woolen mountain-climbing attire, and all sorts of fascinating items to stock the shelves of her gift shop. I can't wait to check that out!

How to get there: From I–70, west of Denver, take Highway 91 south to Leadville. From Leadville, take Highway 24 to the junction of highways 24 and 82. Go west on 82 for 6 miles to Twin Lakes.

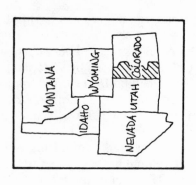

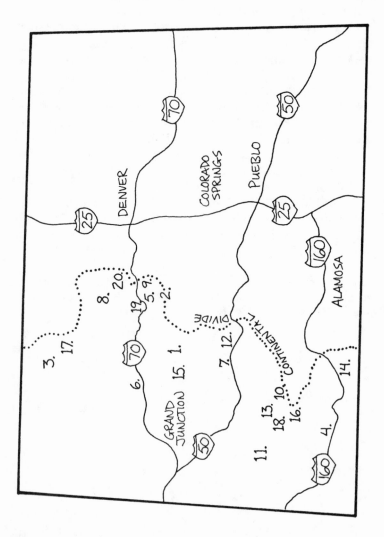

Colorado: The Western Slope

Numbers on map refer to towns numbered below.
Dotted line on map indicates Continental Divide.

1. Aspen,
    Alpine Lodge................70
    Hotel Jerome................72
    Hotel Lenado.......... 74
    Little Red Ski Haus....... ...76
    Molly Gibson Lodge 78
    Sardy House 80
2. Breckenridge, Fireside Inn.... ...82
3. Clark, The Home Ranch.........84
4. Durango,
    The General Palmer House......86
    The Strater Hotel 88
    Victorian Inn.................90
5. Frisco, Mar Dei's Mountain Retreat .92
6. Glenwood Springs,
    The Hotel Colorado...........94
    Talbott House 96
7. Gunnison,
    Waunita Hot Springs Ranch.....98
8. Hot Sulphur Springs,
    Historic Riverside Hotel 100
    Stagecoach Stop 102
9. Keystone, Ski Tip Ranch 104
10. Lake City, The Crystal Lodge.....106
11. Norwood, Back Narrows Inn 108

12. Ohio City, Gold Creek Inn 110
13. Ouray,
    Baker's Manor Guest House....112
    House of Yesteryear 114
    St. Elmo Hotel...............116
    The Western Hotel 118
14. Pagosa Springs,
    Davidson's Country Inn 120
15. Redstone, The Redstone Inn 122
16. Silverton,
    Fools Fe S2 Gold Inn 124
    The Grand Imperial Hotel......126
    Smedley's 128
    Wingate House 130
17. Steamboat Springs, Harbor Hotel. .132
18. Telluride,
    Johnstone Inn...............134
    The New Sheridan Hotel 136
    Skyline Guest Ranch..........138
19. Wildernest,
    Silverheels Country Inn 140
20. Winter Park,
    Millers Inn..................142
    Woodspur Lodge.............144

Alpine Lodge
Aspen, Colorado
81611

Innkeepers: Hans and Sharon Rieger
Address/Telephone: 1240 East Highway 82; (303) 925–7351
Rooms: 7; 4 with private bath. 4 cottages.
Rates: $25 to $30, single or double, during summer; $30 to $40, single
   or double, during winter; EP. Package plan available during winter
   includes 7 nights lodging, 7 breakfasts, 5 dinners; phone for rates.
   No pets. TV in cabins only. No air conditioning (not needed; elevation 7,908 feet). No smoking during meals. Credit cards not accepted.
Open: All year.
Facilities and Activities: Full breakfast and dinner available during winter at additional charge. BYOB. Hot tub, outdoor barbecue, ping-
   pong. Nearby: restaurants, shopping, art galleries, summer music
   festivals; hiking, fishing, river rafting, excellent downhill and cross-
   country skiing, ice skating.

📨 For those who have traveled in Germany and stayed at a
family-run Gasthaus, entering this inn is going to bring back
fond memories and whiffs of déjà vu. The moment I saw the
Zimmer Frei ("vacancy" in German) sign out front, I knew this
inn wouldn't be quasi-cutesy Bavarian. It just had to be for real.
It was.

From the *stammtisch*, a table for repeat guests who traditionally sit in one particular place, to the windows filled with geraniums, from the authentic Blue Pots and cowbells to the wood carvings and beer mugs, the inn is truly Deutschland, à la Bavaria. And then there's Hans, who hails from Garmisch, West Germany; you can't get much more Bavarian than that. Although Sharon grew up in Kremmling, Colorado, and is Irish, to be sure, ☛ she cooks genuine German: goulash with spätzle, bratwurst, wiener schnitzel, smoked pork chops, and a wunderbar rum coffee cake called *gugelhupf*.

Breakfasts are ample, with sausage and eggs or, perhaps, pumpkin pancakes. No meals are served during the summer months, but ☛ downtown Aspen is within walking distance, and, with more than seventy restaurants, there is no shortage of places to eat.

I awoke all snug under a patchwork quilt, hand-stitched by Sharon's grandmother, in a room with balcony, private bath, and a red, stylized heart, marked with number "3," on my door. The rooms have quality antiques, thick carpeting, old-fashioned porcelain doorknobs, and white, textured stucco walls, again very European.

The first-floor sitting room centers on an ☛ Austrian Kachel Ofen, a beautiful, ceramic-tile stove, first introduced during the Middle Ages. It is wood-burning and decorative, and it holds heat up to twenty hours. I have seen these on display in the castles of Europe but had never before seen a working one. They are very unusual, and someday, when I get my very own castle . . .

About once a week, ☛ Hans brings out his zither, and sometimes a friend or two will drop by with an accordion and a violin. Add to this a glass of wine, and you have the sort of evening from which memories are made.

Reserve far in advance for a room at this inn.

How to get there: From Main Street, turn south onto Original Street. Go 3 blocks to Cooper Avenue. Turn left onto Cooper and proceed about 3½ blocks. Inn is on the left.

Hotel Jerome
Aspen, Colorado
81611

Innkeeper: Mr. Jean F. Loubat
Address/Telephone: 330 East Main Street; (303) 920–1000
Rooms: 27 suites; all with private bath.
Rates: $90 to $350, single or double, during summer; $225 to $500, single or double, during winter; EP. No pets. Wheelchair accessible. All major credit cards accepted.
Open: All year.
Facilities and Activities: Full-service restaurants. Bar. Complimentary wine in rooms, concierge service, room service, twice-a-day maid service, Jacuzzi in every suite, valet/laundry service, some non-smoking rooms, complimentary newspapers delivered to rooms, cribs available. Nearby: many restaurants, shopping, art galleries, summer music festivals; hiking, fishing, river rafting, excellent downhill and cross-country skiing, ice skating.

To sit in the lobby of the historic Hotel Jerome is to feel very elegant indeed. There's no reason not to. Fresh roses adorn pink marble-topped tables, and a huge matching bouquet graces the mantel of the ornate fireplace. Intricately carved twin staircases, covered with luxurious carpeting, lead from the lobby to the upper floors, where 🖙 expansive hallways lined with magnificent antiques become second and third lobbies.

The Grand Parlour Suite, on the main floor, is the *crème de la crème*. Double doors open onto an entryway, parlor, and bedrooms, where the televisions are discreetly hidden in armoires; and the settees, fainting couch, massive bed, marble floors, and rose-colored tile fireplace all contribute to the grandeur of the suite. Other rooms, though smaller, are 🖙 masterpieces of Victorian splendor as well.

It has not always been so for the Jerome. Built in 1889, it was for several years *the* place to stay, as was the Jerome Bar *the* place for successful miners to whoop it up. After silver was demonetized and long before Aspen became a world-class ski resort, however, the hotel fell on hard times. Neglect and indifference took over, and its opulence was soon a thing of the past.

Enter the present owners Dick Butera and Julie Anthony, who breathed new life into the Jerome along with more than $5 million. The entire hotel was refurbished; the original atmosphere was re-created; and modern niceties such as whirlpool baths, wet bars, and phones at bedside, on writing tables, and in bathrooms were added.

Besides the Jerome Bar, there are three hotel restaurants: Jacob's for breakfast, lunch, and Sunday Brunch; the Tea Room for breakfast, afternoon tea, and sumptuous desserts; and The Silver Queen Room for 🖙 candlelight and crystal-chandelier ambiance. This dining room offers, among other possibilities, a one-price, four-course dinner featuring your choice of appetizer, such as Brie cheese in puff pastry with raspberry sauce; two soups; and several entrées, including grilled swordfish sauce béarnaise. After this comes a silver cart with a superb array of sinful but fabulous desserts.

Yes, it's very easy to feel elegant here.

How to get there: Hotel Jerome is on Aspen's main street, on the corner of Main and Mill Streets.

Hotel Lenado
Aspen, Colorado
81611

Innkeeper: Jayne Poss
Address/Telephone: 200 South Aspen Street; (303) 925–6246
Rooms: 19, including several suites; all with private bath.
Rates: $95 to $135, single or double, during summer; $145 to $335,
single or double, from December 15 to April 5; EPB. No pets. No air
conditioning (not needed; elevation 7,908 feet). No smoking in
common rooms. All major credit cards accepted.
Open: All year.
Facilities and Activities: Breakfast only meal served. Many restaurants
within walking distance. Bar, with complimentary hor d'oeuvres.
Hot tub on sundeck, large-screen TV, VCR screening room, library,
whirlpool baths. Wet bars and refrigerators in some rooms. Heated
ski-boot lockers. Nearby: shopping, art galleries, summer music
festivals; hiking, fishing, river rafting, excellent downhill and cross-
country skiing, ice skating.

This inn's neo-modulated exterior challenges you to discover
what lies behind these cream-stucco walls and this lofty roof
chopped into gables and pyramids of red. You won't be disappointed.

The atmosphere is at once warm and "refined ski lodge." A

fire roars in the cement-and-redrock fireplace. French doors open into a well-stocked library, and, beyond, identical doors give way to stone steps leading to a lovely park. The hunter green carpet, an Axeminster from Scotland, features gracefully scattered, long-stemmed red roses; and bent-twig lobby furniture, stuffed with puffy, down-filled, plaid cushioins, envelops you like a giant security blanket. Clean lines, cushiony comfort, and the creative use of many kinds of wood make this inn unusual and unsurpassed.

The hotel is named after an 1880s lumber town located eighteen miles away in Woody Creek Canyon. *Lenado* is the Spanish word for "wooded," and the inn reflects its name in every respect: lodgepole pine support posts; cherry-wood bar; bent-willow couch; hickory chairs; pine and fir armoires; carved applewood and twig ironwood beds; and end-cut hemlock floors.

The energy and enthusiasm of the staff is definitely contagious. Guests' needs are their number-one priority. Amenities abound: chocolates on pillows, room service, complimentary mountain-appetite breakfasts, bedtime turndown service, and morning newspapers. Some rooms even have tiny black stoves to heat your toes and warm your heart.

Breakfast is served in Markham's, and the staff actually vies for working on Sundays so they can partake of chef Linda Smisek's Sunday special: Belgian oatmeal waffles. I can personally vouch for her "Super Scramble," a Smisek specialty consisting of eggs, scallions, cheddar, and Monterey Jack cheese. In the evening, Markham's, named for a poet who once lived in the town of Lenado, magically changes from breakfast room to congenial bar.

 Rated four-star by *Mobil Travel Guide,* the Lenado has earned the designation "Outstanding—worth a special trip."

How to get there: Inn is one block south of Main Street on Aspen Street.

❈

D: *Whether you languish in the rooftop Jacuzzi, lounge before a warm fire, leisurely sip wine in Markham's, or snuggle under a down comforter, there's much to make you happy here.*

Little Red Ski Haus
Aspen, Colorado
81611

Innkeepers: Jim and Marjorie Riley
Address/Telephone: 118 East Cooper; (303) 925–3333
Rooms: 21; 4 with private bath, 17 share 8 baths.
Rates: Vary, divided into 4 seasons. On the average a single is $37, a double is $40 to $68. Best to call for exact rates. EP in summer, with continental breakfast included; EPB in winter. No pets. No TV. No air conditioning (not needed; elevation 7,908 feet). Smoking in parlors only. No credit cards accepted.
Open: Mid-June to October 1 and mid-November to mid-April.
Facilities and Activities: Breakfast only meal served. Many restaurants within walking distance. BYOB. During winter months, once-a-week, hot-spiced-wine, get-acquainted parties. Ski movies. Coffee, tea, and cocoa always available. Nearby: shopping, art galleries, summer music festivals; hiking, fishing, river rafting, excellent downhill and cross-country skiing, ice skating.

This inn is so 🐾 popular with skiers in winter and musicians during the summer music festivals, there are times when the sitting room is wall-to-wall people. Noisy and a bit hectic? Yes. Fun and exciting? Absolutely! The décor is an eclectic mix of antiques, primitives, and memorabilia, with velvet settees likely to be sharing space with a homemade table suspended from the ceiling by heavy chains. Or a room with a delicate brass bed and dainty rocker might be neighbor to one with shake walls and handmade bunks.

You get the feeling that, structurally, this inn just sort of happened: a room added here, a hallway there. At the front of the house a narrow, winding stairway leads to three little rooms, all with private baths. The guest rooms in the back part of the house are less fancy and share baths.

☛ Marge is as diversified as her inn. A school teacher for many years, she and her twin sister, Norma Dolle, who lives next door and operates a small bed and breakfast, were also professional singers and dancers. In the days of Shirley Temple, the bouncy curlyheads ☛ had a contract with MGM, sang on the Tom McNeil Breakfast Club radio show, and later became one of the famous sets of Toni Twins, of home-permanent fame. They are so identical that, when they were babies, their mother sometimes fed the same twin twice; and, when in college, they would switch dates while jitterbugging on the dance floor and get away with it!

Marge skis three times a week with her guests, helps them with their plans, and serves a full breakfast in winter, sometimes to as many as fifty. In summer, the morning meal is continental-plus. There are more than seventy restaurants within a few blocks, and Marge will help you find the sort you are hungering for. For inexpensive barbecued ribs, an active, energy-packed bar, and a chance to meet the locals, I recommend Little Annie's Eating House; for fine dining in a restored Victorian homestead, there's Poppie's; and for innovative and traditional French cuisine, it's Charlemagne's.

How to get there: From Main Street, turn south onto Aspen and right onto Cooper. Inn is on the right.

Molly Gibson Lodge
Aspen, Colorado
81611

Innkeeper: David Jones
Address/Telephone: 120 West Hopkins Avenue; (303) 925–2580
Rooms: 20; all with private bath.
Rates: $65 to $139 single, $69 to $139 double, during summer; winter
rates are divided into three seasons and range from $79 to $269;
best to phone. Includes continental breakfast. No pets. No air conditioning (not needed; elevation 7,908 feet). MasterCard, Visa,
American Express accepted.
Open: All year.
Facilities and Activities: Bar. Hot tub. Heated, outdoor pool. Complimentary champagne and wine-tasting parties. Nearby: restaurants,
shopping, art galleries, summer music festivals; hiking, fishing,
river rafting, excellent downhill and cross-country skiing, ice skating.

Molly Gibson ran a boarding house for miners back in the
1880s, when Aspen was a silver-mining boom town. She was
known for her generosity, and legend has it she was so well
thought of that the largest-producing silver mine in the area was
named after her. And Molly has a present-day namesake as well:
the exquisitely appointed Molly Gibson Lodge.

David describes his inn as Aspen-mining-town-rustic. Perhaps that's a valid description of the exterior, but inside it is immediately apparent that much thought has gone into the 🖝 precision blending of color, texture, and design. When you enter the fireside lounge and Molly's Bar, you are met with soft classical music, muted colors, and comfortable couches. The resulting atmosphere is warm and hospitable.

The guest rooms are strikingly modern with custom-made furniture; hand-picked artwork; 🖝 sunken, oversized Jacuzzi bathtubs wrapped in mirrors; hand-blown, Italian milk-glass lamps; down comforters; VCRs; and greenhouse windows.

The outdoor pool and hot tub are nicely landscaped amongst tall trees and more than forty species of plants.

Arriving guests will find a fruit basket with Toblerone chocolate waiting in their rooms. Breakfast includes European custard pastries, three juices, coffee, and twelve different kinds of tea. 🖝 On Sunday evenings there is a champagne get-together; on Monday nights, it's a wine-tasting party; and Tuesday through Saturday, during ski season, one finds appetizers and special hors d'oeuvres in Molly's Bar, all complimentary.

David goes out of his way to help provide information on local shopping, art galleries, restaurants, and special events. I took his suggestion and tried Guido's for Swiss- and German-style dining. The veal cordon bleu is exceptional and the schnitzel is terrific! But do save room for the chocolate fondue, a seemingly endless array of nuts, fruits, bits of this, and bits of that dipped into a smooth, rich sauce. Fun *and* delicious!

How to get there: From Main Street, turn south onto Garmisch. Go one block, turn right onto Hopkins. Inn is on the right.

Sardy House
Aspen, Colorado
81612

Innkeeper: Jayne Poss
Address/Telephone: 128 East Main Street; (303) 920–2525
Rooms: 20, including 5 suites; all with private bath.
Rates: $80 to $260 single, $95 to $275 double, during summer and fall; $150 to $350 single, $165 to $365 double, during winter and early spring; EPB. No pets. No air conditioning (not needed; elevation 7,908 feet). No smoking in common rooms. All major credit cards accepted.
Open: Mid-June to mid-October and late November to mid-April.
Facilities and Activities: Full gourmet breakfast served to inn guests; no lunch; dinner every night; Sunday brunch. Bar. Heated outdoor pool, sauna, Jacuzzi. Most rooms have whirlpool baths. VCR, stereos, dry bars in suites. Nearby: many restaurants, shopping, art galleries, summer music festivals; hiking, fishing, river rafting, downhill and cross-country skiing, ice skating.

If your taste leans toward mansions, perhaps this is the inn for you: ☛ a red-brick Victorian masterpiece with original oak staircases and sliding parlor doors, round reading rooms tucked away in a turret, gourmet breakfast and afternoon tea set upon ivory linen centered with real roses, and fine dining in the evenings as well.

Soft plum carpeting with pale pink roses, made in Ireland especially for the Sardy, is used throughout the building, and wallpaper of subdued gray cloaks the walls. The guest rooms have thick terry robes, ☞ heated towel racks, down comforters with Laura Ashley duvets, and televisions hidden in walls or armoires. Except for those units with antique tubs, all have ☞ whirlpool baths.

I have a thing about carriage houses, and that is where I chose to stay, in a beautifully appointed complement to the main mansion. My room had a vaulted, many-angled ceiling; natural wicker table, chairs, and writing desk; a cherry-wood, high-off-the-floor bed with feather-filled comforter and five fluffy pillows; and ☞ a bay window that looked out on Aspen Mountain and the ski slopes. The almond-scented lotion, shampoo, and bath gel were another nice touch. Just don't add the bath gel to your whirlpool bath unless you want to disappear in a myriad of boundless bubbles! (Who would do such a crazy thing? I'll never admit to it!)

An ☞ authentic, hand-carved huntboard, thought to be from Bavaria and used in Victorian times as a buffet table for serving meat and game from the hunt, distinguishes the front parlor. Lace curtains, stained-glass window, rich brown love seat and chairs, and a two-foot, sterling-silver tray atop the coffee table complete this room.

My breakfast was a Brie-cheese omelet topped with sautéed cinnamon apples, nut bread, a garnish of fresh fruit, coffee, and orange juice. Crabtree & Evelyn preserves from London were on every table.

The evening meal included enticing entrées such as filet mignon in shallot butter and prawns à la Florentine, an extensive wine list, unusual hors d'oeuvres, and fancy desserts.

How to get there: Sardy House is on the corner of Main and Aspen Streets in downtown Aspen.

Fireside Inn
Breckenridge, Colorado
80424

Innkeepers: Jean and Jack Wells
Address/Telephone: 200 Wellington Street (mailing address: Box 2252); (303) 453–6456
Rooms: 9; 4 with private bath. 1 large dorm with bath, 4 small dorms share two baths.
Rates: $45 to $110 single, $45 to $113 double, $14.50 to $20 dorm, EP, during ski season; $24 to $48 single, $29 to $48 double, $11 dorm, EP, during summer. No pets. No air conditioning (not needed; elevation 9,600 feet). No smoking in dorms or dining room. MasterCard and Visa accepted.
Open: All year.
Facilities and Activities: Full breakfast, $3. Traditional Thanksgiving and Christmas dinners. Dinner available throughout the year for groups of 10 or more. BYOB. More than 30 eating places, from gourmet cuisine to doughnut shops, within walking distance. Downhill and cross-country skiing, free shuttle stops at door. Free buses to other ski areas. Carriage and sleigh rides. Alpine slide. Ice skating, tennis, river rafting, fishing, golf.

Innkeepers Jean and Jack Wells have been quoted as saying, "We have but one goal: to help you get the most out of the time you spend with us." Considering the hospitality, comfort, reasonable rates, and special little extras I found in this pretty Victorian inn, I'd say the Wellses have reached their goal.

A cozy parlor, three dining areas, hot tub, ski lockup, and bicycle storage all contribute to the many advantages provided here. Jean even came to the rescue of one gentleman, who had split his britches on the ski slopes, by sewing up the rip so he could return to his skis the following day. Bicyclists and hikers themselves, Jean and Jack can tell you of innumerable routes to take and will sometimes even join you if you wish.

An all-you-can-eat breakfast is available for just $3. And, believe me when I tell you, it is exactly that. ☛ Those platters of French toast, pancakes, and eggs keep coming until you have no choice but to go outdoors and get some exercise.

Evening meals are not offered daily, but Jean will cook family-style dinners for groups of ten or more if requested ahead. She also cooks traditional Thanksgiving and Christmas extravaganzas for guests. Sometimes as many as thirty-seven festive visitors are seated around the dining-room tables for holiday meals, and, according to Jean and Jack, "It's like having a very large, happy family."

Want to know my fantasy? I want to spend the Christmas holidays in the Wellses' ☛ Brandywine Suite with its bright sitting room, a bedroom with shiny brass bed and oak dresser, an outside entrance, and a private circular stairway to the hot tub. (Those staying in the Brandywine Suite have time set aside each day for exclusive use of the hot tub.) For days before Christmas, the aroma of pies baking fills the house. I would awake on Christmas morning, smell the turkey cooking, go downstairs to Jean's *stollen*, made from her mother's recipe, and, later in the day, join some thirty other merrymakers for Christmas dinner. If you decide to live out my fantasy, make reservations early in order not to be disappointed.

How to get there: From I–70, take exit 203 onto Highway 9, south, to Breckenridge. Turn left on Wellington and go two blocks to Fireside Inn.

DPPerreault

The Home Ranch
Clark, Colorado
80428

Innkeeper: Ken Jones
Address/Telephone: 54880 County Road 129 (mailing address: P.O. Box
    822); (303) 879–1780
Rooms: 7 cabins; all with private bath.
Rates: $275 to $316, double, per day; $1,890 to $2,172, double, per
    week. Children 5 years and younger are free. AP. No pets. No TV.
    No air conditioning (not needed; elevation 7,200 feet). No smoking
    in dining room. MasterCard, Visa, American Express accepted.
Open: June 1 to October 1 and mid-December to April 1.
Facilities and Activities: BYOB. Private hot tub on porch for each unit.
    Heated outdoor pool, sauna, children's program, hiking, fishing,
    cross-country skiing, sleigh rides—all on ranch property and on
    adjacent National Forest land. Guides and instructors available for
    all activities. Nearby: river rafting, lake fishing, ice fishing, downhill
    skiing.

Ken humbly refers to his accommodations as "cabins," giving an entirely new connotation to the word.
    If beautiful little log dwellings, set among groves of aspen
trees and enhanced with designer furniture; down comforters;
hand-woven, wool-blend bedspreads; hardwood floors; authentic

84

Navajo rugs; small wood-burning stoves; and ☛ private Jacuzzi hot tubs on individual decks qualify as "cabins," then I am compelled to add "luxurious" and "splendid," because they are that and more. Soft terry robes hang in the closets; the baths have the thickest towels I've ever seen; and ceramic baskets hold Scottish Pine toiletries. Coffee, tea, imported cheeses, honey, crackers, and a ☛ jar of homemade cookies (refilled every day) are also provided.

The main lodge is a beauty, too, with its antique grand piano, a 32-foot-high stone fireplace, brown leather chairs and couches, and more Navajo rugs. Just off the sitting room, one finds a small glassed-in sun porch with inviting window seats, a loft library, and a sunny, sweet-smelling greenhouse.

Ken plays the guitar and bass fiddle, and he takes music and performing abilities into account when hiring staff. ☛ Impromptu music is not uncommon during the evenings.

Ken describes his dining as "family gourmet," which translates to nonstuffy but ☛ fantastically prepared cuisine like peach-filled German pancakes, a nine-vegetable minestrone soup, shrimp Macademia on wild rice, and raspberry Bavarian pie with chopped almond–pastry crust. The one responsible for all these gastronomic delights is Jodi Calhoun, who has been ranch chef for five years.

☛ Children are especially welcome here. In the recreation building, I found an intriguing toy box, a doll house, lots of books, and a ping-pong table. There are special horses for youngsters to ride, and, for those who would rather pretend, there's a brightly painted, antique carousel steed that has been made into a rocking horse strong enough for the biggest kids among us.

How to get there: From Highway 40, northwest of Steamboat Springs, turn north (toward Clark) onto County Road 129. Ranch is on the right.

೦ಾ

D: *The Home Ranch has the distinction of being* ☛ *listed in the prestigious, French-based* Relais and Chateaux, *a directory of 347 outstanding lodgings and restaurants including castles, manor houses, and grand estates from 30 nations.*

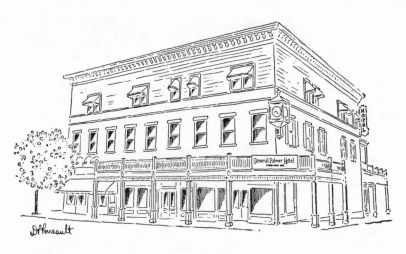

The General Palmer House
Durango, Colorado
81301

Innkeeper: Carolyn Rector
Address/Telephone: 567 Main Avenue; (303) 247–4747, (800) 824–2173
within Colorado, (800) 523–3358 outside Colorado
Rooms: 39; all with private bath.
Rates: $40 to $95, single; $45 to $95, double. Includes continental
breakfast. No pets. Wheelchair accessible. All major credit cards
accepted.
Open: All year.
Facilities and Activities: Breakfast for inn guests only. Lunch Monday
through Friday, dinner nightly. Quiet Lady Tavern. ☛ AAA four-
diamond rated. Basket of toiletries in each room. 2 suites have
Jacuzzis. Nearby: narrow-gauge passenger train, hiking, fishing,
river rafting, downhill and cross-country skiing; Mesa Verde National Park.

Durango is one of my favorite little mountain towns, but,
even if it were not, I'd come here anyway just to stay at The
General Palmer House.

Classical music floats through the handsome lobby and into
the small library with its heavy wine-colored drapes and rich
green velour settee, chairs, and rocker. There is something very

comfortable, very elegant, and very English about the dark wood paneling, etched glass, and exquisite light fixtures, some with crystal teardrops, others with silk or fluted glass shades.

Do help yourself to the fresh coffee, served in china cups from a silver pot, and take it into the solarium, a veritable jungle of plants, antiques, and comfy couches.

Many of the guest rooms overlook the historic round-house and train yard used by the Silverton–Durango narrow-gauge passenger train that chugs and puffs its way through the San Juan Mountain range.

My room was called the Murphy Suite. Three guesses why. No, not because my cat is named Murphy, but because it has an old-fashioned Murphy bed. During the day, this room is a pleasant parlor with love seat, period table and chairs, wet bar with stemmed glassware, and a large window dressed in apricot sheers and ripe-peach drapes.

After a memorable dinner of steak McMahon, a New York sirloin sauced and topped with grilled onions, and Turkish-coffee-ice-cream pie smothered in butterscotch sauce and whipped cream in the Palace dining room, I returned to my third-floor room via the tiny European-style elevator, and, remembering all those old movie scenes where would-be snoozers are suddenly flipped backward into the wall, I gingerly crawled into bed . . . and had one of the best night's sleep I've had anywhere.

When I awoke (the bed still safely grounded), I went down to a breakfast of tasty blueberry muffins, orange juice, and cof-fee.

How to get there: Both Highway 550 (north–south) and Highway 160 (east–west) lead directly to Durango. Hotel is on the main street of town.

✳

D: *Built in 1898 and recently refurbished, this grand hotel deserves a caring innkeeper like Carolyn. She's always cheerful, and her concern for her guests' contentment is apparent in the behavior of her entire staff.*

The Strater Hotel
Durango, Colorado
81302

Innkeeper: Rod Barker

Address/Telephone: 699 Main Avenue (mailing address: P.O. Drawer E); (800) 247–4431 nationwide, (800) 227–4431 within Colorado

Rooms: 94; all with private bath.

Rates: $56 to $98 single, $62 to $98 double, during summer; $45 to $98 single, $49 to $98 double, during winter; EP. No pets. Wheelchair accessible. All major credit cards accepted.

Open: All year.

Facilities and Activities: Two full-service restaurants. Diamond Belle Saloon. Gay Nineties theater. Hot tub, turn-down service, valet. Nearby: narrow-gauge passenger train, hiking, fishing, river rafting, downhill and cross-country skiing; Mesa Verde National Park.

John F. Kennedy stayed here. And so did Gerald Ford, Will Rogers, and Tom Thumb. Louis L'Amour wrote many a chapter of his best-selling western novels in Rooms 222 and 223.

In continuous operation since it was built in 1887, this hotel is one of the finest examples of Victorian opulence I have ever seen. The guest rooms are so elaborately furnished, staying here seems ☞ more like being in a grand old mansion rather than a ninety-four-room hotel.

Instead of a large lobby, there are a front and a back parlor, each intimate and beautifully appointed. The upstairs hallways are done in scarlet carpeting and crimson walls, accented by an abundance of pure white woodwork. The hotel has been in Rod's family since 1926. He grew up here and remembers the fun he and his sister had racing through the corridors.

The Strater is said to have ☞ one of the largest collections of American–Victorian era antiques under one roof in the entire world. Incidentally, Room 110 has a most interesting bed. Rod found a ☞ secret compartment hidden in the foot board! There is also a concealed drawer in the dresser in Room 207.

For formal dining, try the Columbian Room; for something more casual, make it the Opera House Restaurant. The same menu serves both dining rooms; only the atmosphere is different. An excellent dinner choice would be the Johnny Walker strip steak, which is sautéed in butter, lemon, mushrooms, and peppercorns and deglazed in Johnny Walker Scotch. There are many other imaginative entrées as well.

It's impossible to ignore the strains of honky-tonk piano coming from the Diamond Belle Saloon, where it's Gay Nineties all the way. Scantily dressed cancan girls wait tables, and sleeve-gartered bartenders hold court at the gold-leaf filigree back bar. The décor is faithful to that of the original saloon, from the half-balcony to the red-flocked, gold-foil wallpaper imported from England.

During the summer, the Diamond Circle Theatre, voted one of the top three theaters of its kind in the country by *Time* magazine, presents authentic, turn-of-the-century plays.

The Strater definitely deserves the AAA ☞ four-diamond rating it has had for many years.

How to get there: Both Highway 550 (north–south) and Highway 160 (east–west) lead directly to Durango. Hotel is on main street of town.

Victorian Inn
Durango, Colorado
81301

Innkeeper: Karen Peters
Address/Telephone: 2117 West Second Avenue; (303) 247–2223
Rooms: 6; 4 with private bath, 2 share 1 bath.
Rates: $40 to $45 single, $50 to $55 double, during summer; $35 single,
$45 double, during winter; EPB. No pets. TV in sitting room only.
No air conditioning (not needed; elevation 6,512 feet). No smoking
inside inn. MasterCard and Visa accepted.
Open: All year.
Facilities and Activities: Box lunches available. BYOB. Hot tub (sea-
sonal), large yard, lawn games, barbecue, bicycles. Nearby: Durango
and Silverton Narrow Gauge Railroad, Mesa Verde National Park,
ghost towns. Hiking, fishing, white-water rafting, downhill and
cross-country skiing, sleigh rides.

If this inn were mine, I might call it The Teddy Bear House.
The little critters are everywhere. Handmade bears lounge around
the parlor, decorate the dining area, and hang on the fireplace.
There are also extensive collections of antique dolls, little Chinese figurines, and wooden nutcrackers from Europe.

The breakfast room, bright and cheery, has wooden tables
and chairs, a wide expanse of windows, and many straw

baskets. ☛ The meal itself is a minor feast. It might be cinnamon coffee cake and quiche with fresh-from-the-garden vegetables; or it could be very special French toast dipped in a batter of eggs, cream, cinnamon, and vanilla and served with locally made cinnamon-honey spread, choke-cherry syrup, and smoked ham. There's also yogurt, juices, coffee, and milk.

The guest rooms are attractively furnished with antiques, the front upstairs room being my favorite. You ☛ share this cozy chamber with an antique rocking horse and a rag doll that has made herself at home amongst the four pillows on your bed. An old-fashioned bowl and pitcher on a period dresser, a beautiful armoire, and a red velvet settee complete this room. One reaches the shared bath via a narrow, slope-ceilinged private hallway. Even the doorway is slanted to fit the unique space.

The extra-large yard is perfect for a game of croquet; and there are ☛ picnic tables under shade trees, a brick patio with grill, a hot tub, and several bicycles for guests' use, including a tandem and one that is kid-size.

When you arrive, you are greeted with lemonade, iced tea, or a hot drink. Karen likes to cook, is happy to pack you a box lunch, and is thinking about offering Southwestern dinners during the winter months. For out-on-the-town dining, she recommends Father Murphy's, across the street from the narrow-gauge-train station, where you can eat in the garden and enjoy, among many other items, homemade soups and breads. She also suggests the Lost Pelican for great steaks and lobster.

How to get there: The inn is located 1 block off of Main Avenue, on the corner of West 2nd and 21st streets.

Mar Dei's Mountain Retreat
Frisco, Colorado
80443

Innkeepers: Martha Elliott and Deidre Wolach
Address/Telephone: 221 South 4th Avenue (mailing address: P.O. Box 1767); (303) 668–5337
Rooms: 5, including 1 suite and 1 4-bed dorm; 2 have private bath, 3 share 1 shower and 2 water closets.
Rates: $27 to $45 summer, $38 to $70 winter, single or double. Christmas holidays slightly higher. Dorm ranges from $15 to $27 per person depending on season. Includes continental-plus breakfast. No pets. Wheelchair accessible. No air conditioning (not needed; elevation 9,400 feet). Well-behaved children only, please. Credit cards not accepted.
Open: All year.
Facilities and Activities: BYOB. Complimentary wine and snacks; bicycles. Nearby: Frisco Historic Park, Lake Dillon, Nordic Ski Center. Hiking, wildflower searching, biking, fishing, boating, excellent downhill and cross-country skiing, snowmobiling.

This is a "make yourself at home" sort of place. One finds vases of wildflowers in every room during the summer and popcorn and wine in front of the fire in winter. Other nice touches are: filled candy dishes; ☞ a sunning deck that is great for summer *and* winter tans; a VCR for "a night at the movies"; fireplaces in both the living and dining rooms; shaded picnic tables in the front yard; the heady essence of fir trees; fresh mountain air; and bikes for wheeling down to the lake.

The large Garden Level Suite has a sitting room, queen-size waterbed, and private bath. On the second floor, two smaller rooms with sloped ceilings, down comforters, and lace curtains share a shower and two water closets with a four-bedded dorm. The fifth guest room has ☛ its own private stairway and balcony, a small fireplace, king-size bed, and complete bath. All rooms have sinks.

Snuggled amongst eighty-four towering Douglas fir trees, the inn is within walking distance to shopping, restaurants, and nightlife and is ☛ ideally located as close as seven miles to and no farther than twenty-four from five major Colorado ski resorts, including Vail.

Breakfast is a generous continental meal with a wide variety of home-baked goodies. Cinnamon rolls, bran muffins, banana bread, special biscuits, and homemade bread for toasting are only a few of the items that might appear along with fresh fruit, granola cereal, fruit juice, coffee, and tea.

Frisco has many restaurants for other meals. For dinner, I recommend that you try the ☛ Blue Spruce Inn, a quaint log cabin with gourmet selections. The filet béarnaise, a crab-filled fillet of tender beef topped with what the house calls "perfect sauce," can't be beat. The breads, pies, and ice cream are made daily on the premises, and the hot apple pie à la mode is a must.

How to get there: From I–70, take exit 203 to Highway 9. Go south on Highway 9 for 1 mile to Frisco. Turn right onto Main Street and left onto 4th; proceed 2 blocks. The inn is on the right.

❦

D: *An off-road, black-topped path leads from Frisco to Vail (24 miles) and Breckenridge (9 miles) and is perfect for biking, jogging, or just plain strolling in summer and Nordic skiing in winter.*

The Hotel Colorado
Glenwood Springs, Colorado
81601

Innkeeper: Ron Droegmyer
Address/Telephone: 526 Pine Street; (303) 945–6511
Rooms: 128; all with private bath.
Rates: $55 to $195, single; $60 to $200, double; EP. No pets. Wheelchair accessible. No air conditioning. MasterCard, Visa, American Express, Carte Blanche, Diners Club accepted.
Open: All year.
Facilities and Activities: Devereux Dining Room, Palm Court Bar and Grill; Nautilus, Jacuzzi, Finnish sauna, tanning booth, traditional and Far East massage. Nearby: world's largest hot-spring swimming pool across street from hotel, alpine and cross-country skiing, hiking trails, fishing in Colorado River, Vapor Caves, Doc Holliday's grave site.

It's surprising to find a 128-room grand hotel that is intimate, warm, and friendly, but this one is. No doubt it is because of the staff, from Art, the assistant innkeeper, who treats every guest like a much-respected friend, to bell captain–historian Michael Reilley, who delights in telling stories about former hotel guests (including presidents), gangsters, ghosts, and teddy bears.

And ☞ speaking of teddy bears, this is where the little critters are said to have originated. It seems that after one of President Teddy Roosevelt's many hunting expeditions, he returned to the hotel, tired and empty-handed. The maids, hoping to lift his spirits and also wanting to tease a little, gathered some towel scraps and stitched together a cloth bear. They ceremoniously presented it to President Roosevelt that evening during dinner. A newspaper reporter wrote up the incident and coined the name "Teddy Bear"; soon after, a toy manufacturer began making the stuffed animals.

Built by mining engineer Walter B. Devereux in 1893 and styled after Villa de Medici in Rome, the hotel is a comfortable blend of modern amenities and turn-of-the-century ambiance.

The elegant dining room, with sparkling chandeliers and live dinner music, serves fine gourmet meals. The house salad is prepared table-side, and all the other courses are served from a cart wheeled to your table. My dessert was a tortuffo: an amaretto chocolate, ice cream ball, rolled in chocolate chips and nuts and centered with a cherry. Incredibly good!

All the rooms are large and partially furnished with antiques. The second-floor Presidential Suite is gorgeous and boasts of having had six presidents as occupants. But the *crème de la crème* are the two Bell Tower Suites. Total luxury. A television and Jacuzzi are the only modern touches; the rest is wall-to-wall, priceless antiques. A circular stairway leads from the parlor to ☞ your very own bell tower, a private balcony, and a view of forever. This suite is definitely worth saving your pennies for.

How to get there: From I–70, take exit 116 into Glenwood Springs. The Hotel Colorado overlooks the Hot Springs Pool.

Talbott House
Glenwood Springs, Colorado
81601

Innkeeper: Cherry Talbott
Address/Telephone: 928 Colorado Avenue; (303) 945–1039
Rooms: 4 rooms share 2 baths; carriage house, with private bath, sleeps 5.
Rates: $24, single; $36, double; $50 to $80, carriage house; EPB. No pets. TV in game room only. No air conditioning (usually not needed; elevation 5,700 feet). Smoking allowed in common rooms only. MasterCard and Visa accepted.
Open: All year.
Facilities and Activities: "One pot" dinners available during winter if requested ahead. Complimentary seasonal beverages during afternoons. BYOB. Hot tub. Baby crib available. Nearby: hot-springs pool and Vapor Caves, restaurants, dinner theater, summer theater, shopping. Hiking, fishing, river rafting, horseback riding, jeep tours, golf, downhill and cross-country skiing.

After chatting in Cherry's kitchen for more than an hour, I began to feel a little guilty relaxing on a bar stool as she scurried from cupboard to stove preparing dinner for seventeen; but she continued to carry on an animated conversation and never missed a beat. Energetic, intelligent, and outgoing, she *expects* you to make yourself at home and welcomes you like an old friend. At the rear of the house, her door mat reads, "A back door guest is always best." Sort of reveals the tone here, I think.

Cherry has traveled extensively throughout Europe and Central and South America, and her inn is ☛ filled with collectibles from many countries. Fascinating wood carvings are showcased in every room and hallway.

Brass and iron beds, writing desks, thick carpets, and white, ruffled curtains combined with homey touches of embroidery and lace decorate the upper level. Downstairs, guests gather in the front room for conversation or reading, in the game room for television or a rowdy bout of checkers, and in the back yard for a soak in the redwood hot tub.

An all-you-can-eat breakfast of, say, French toast, sausage, fried potatoes, raspberry wheat muffins, juice, fruit, and coffee, served on a long, oval dining table set with Cherry's white Wedgwood wedding china, gets your morning off to a good start. During the winter months, Cherry serves ☛ "one pot" evening meals if asked ahead of time. These are hearty affairs consisting of beef stew or chicken casserole with home-baked bread, salad, and a light dessert.

Or you might want to try the Gypsy J, just around the corner from the Talbott, for Hungarian cuisine at its best. I recommend either the chicken paprikash, in a spicy cream sauce, or the meaty Gypsy goulash.

The ☛ world's largest, mineral hot springs–fed swimming pool is just a few blocks away, and Cherry has some pool towels she will lend you. She will help with dinner, theater, jeep tour, and river-rafting arrangements as well.

How to get there: From I–70, take Highway 82 south at Glenwood Springs. Turn right onto 10th Street and right onto Colorado Avenue. Inn is on the right.

Waunita Hot Springs Ranch
Gunnison, Colorado
81230

Innkeepers: Rod and Junelle Pringle
Address/Telephone: 8007 County Road 887; (303) 641–1266
Rooms: 22; all with private bath.
Rates: $495 per week, per person. Children's rates available. AP. No
    pets. TV in TV room only. No air conditioning (not needed; eleva-
    tion 8,900 feet). No credit cards accepted.
Open: May 20 to September 30 (complete dude-ranch program), Octo-
    ber 15 to November 15, December 15 to April 15.
Facilities and Activities: No alcohol allowed on premises. Children's
    activities, part-time child care, teen rides. Hot springs–fed swim-
    ming pool. Nearby: fishing, 4 × 4 trips, downhill and cross-country
    skiing; Black Canyon of the Gunnison National Monument, Great
    Sand Dunes.

How about pan-fried trout, cowboy beans, and apple fritters
cooked over an open fire? Or corn chowder, grilled steak, angel
biscuits (that's right, they're perfect in every way), and fresh
strawberry pie? That's the kind of fare you will find at this ranch.
Junelle is thinking of publishing a cookbook, and she should.
    The guest rooms are large, pine-paneled, and located in both
the main ranch building and an attractive annex with full-length

veranda and porch swings. You probably won't want to spend much time in your room, though, because there is so much to do here: hayrides, breakfast and dinner rides, square dancing, fishing in the Pringles' private lake stocked with rainbow trout, and side trips to the Great Sand Dunes, the Black Canyon of the Gunnison, and to the ski village of Crested Butte. And then there's the outdoor pool, a ☞ gigantic (30' × 90') hot springs–fed, mineral-water oasis. Even bathing is special here because your ☞ bath water is supplied by the mineral hot springs, too.

As you cross the little bridge heading toward the barn and corral, pause to see the ducks swimming in the creek and the turkey pen just beyond. Look closely. There are apt to be lambs, baby goats, piglets, and perhaps a colt or two. Inside the barn, a small green-and-red wagon waits for the next children's hayride, and a ☞ fringed surrey is ready to be pulled by two Shetland ponies. Can you imagine a better opportunity to get truly special photos of children?

Upstairs in the loft, there is square dancing on Tuesday nights; on Friday evenings, ☞ live, Western music is provided by the Pringle sons and their wives. And, believe me, they can really get the place rockin'.

This is a family-run ranch, with all members having a hand in the operation. Whether it's riding, cooking, cleaning, or caring, one of the Pringles will be there. And from Rod and Junelle on down to their grandchildren, who share the toy box with small guests, the hospitality is unsurpassed.

How to get there: 18 miles east of Gunnison, on Highway 50, turn north at the Waunita Hot Springs sign. Continue on for 8 miles to the ranch.

Historic Riverside Hotel
Hot Sulphur Springs, Colorado
80451

Innkeeper: Abraham Renta

Address/Telephone: 509 Grand Avenue (mailing address: P.O. Box 22); (303) 725–3589 or (303) 725–9996

Rooms: 20; 1 with private bath, 19 share 4 baths and 3 separate showers.

Rates: $20, single; $26 to $32, double; EP. Well-behaved pets allowed. Wheelchair accessible. TV in sitting room only. No air conditioning (not needed; elevation 7,670 feet). Credit cards not accepted.

Open: All year.

Facilities and Activities: No breakfast served. Lunch available during summer. Dinner served Tuesday through Sunday. Bar. Nearby: Rocky Mountain National Park, museum; hot-springs mineral baths (usually open only during summer months), hiking, fishing, downhill and cross-country skiing, snowmobiling.

According to Abe, an innkeeper must have "sleeves with buttons that come off quick." In other words, more times than not, you'll find Abe hard at work with his sleeves rolled up to the elbows. And it shows. From the sparkling-white café curtains in the traditional dining room to the shimmering clean windows, ☞ this inn is spotless.

Preservation of the past through the restoration of old structures is very important to Abe, and he has put a lot of work into his vintage 1903 hotel.

The Riverside is not quaintsy-cutesy. It offers ☛ simplistic, down-home comfort. The guest rooms all have old-fashioned round sinks, antique oak dressers, electric heat, and painted iron beds with good mattresses and pretty covers. A different woman's name is above each door—Mae, Elizabeth, Audrey, Patsy—leading one to speculate as to other possible uses the old building has endured. A more respectable explanation is the rumor that a previous owner persuaded each of his female employees to paint one room for the privilege of having it named after her.

Overstuffed chairs and couch form a half-circle before the stone fireplace in the mountain lodge–style lobby. The small barroom is separate and features a cherry-wood bar with brass footrail.

The two dining rooms are dressed in white linen, one with a free-standing wood stove and the other with a stone fireplace. Soft classical music and ☛ a view of the tumbling Colorado River add a dignified, restful ambiance to the River Room.

The meals are best described as ☛ good home cooking with a touch of finesse: Canadian flounder with sauce Español; breaded pork chops, German style; baked chicken with oven-roasted potatoes or Puerto Rican rice. And then there's home-made wild-cherry pie or Abe's special bread pudding. Dinner here is a must.

How to get there: From I–70, take Granby exit north on Highway 40 past Winter Park and Granby to Hot Sulphur Springs. Hotel is one block off of Highway 40.

DPlenault

Stagecoach Stop
Hot Sulphur Springs, Colorado
80451

Innkeeper: Jean Crouch
Address/Telephone: P.O. Box 181; (303) 725–9990
Rooms: 9; 5 with private bath, 4 share.
Rates: $14 to $18, single or double; EP. Pets allowed. TV in bar only. No
air conditioning (not needed; elevation 7,670 feet). MasterCard and
Visa accepted.
Open: All year.
Facilities and Activities: No breakfast served. Lunch Monday through
Friday. Dinner Monday through Saturday. Restaurant closed on
Sundays. Bar. Nearby: Rocky Mountain National Park, museum,
cafés; hot-springs mineral baths (usually open only during summer
months), hiking, fishing, downhill and cross-country skiing,
snowmobiling.

This Western Victorian inn hasn't changed much over the
years since it was ■ a stagecoach stop on the line from
Georgetown to the settlement of Troublesome. It was built in
1875 by one Captain Dean, a soldier with the Confederate
Army, back in the days when the local hot springs were a big
draw for recreation and medicinal purposes. Teddy Roosevelt is

said to have stayed here during one of his many journeys out West.

The guest rooms are small, as was the custom in the captain's day, but they are adequate for the outdoorsy type of visitors who frequent this inn. One of the most ornate brass beds I've seen is in Room Nine, along with a lovely antique oak chest of drawers with a beveled-edge mirror. Jean has refinished many of the old wooden pieces in the inn, and her expertise is especially apparent in the fine old dressers she has placed in each room.

Jean's son, ☛ William Crouch, is an accomplished wildlife artist using a combined medium of watercolors and pen and ink, and his works are displayed on the lower level of the inn.

The dining room, with its green and beige linens, serves both American and Mexican cuisine, the specialty being the south-of-the-border variety. The *fajitas* are outstanding and consist of marinated chicken or beef strips grilled with green bell peppers, onion, and tomatoes and served piping hot with *pico de gallo,* rice, beans, and fresh flour tortillas. And do try the ☛ deep-fried ice cream for dessert! This is vanilla ice cream covered with a crunchy coating, delicately deep-fried, and topped with Mexican chocolate and whipped cream. Unique and very good!

Meet the locals around the pool table and potbellied stove in the inn's bar. Nice on a winter's eve.

How to get there: From I–70, take Granby exit north on Highway 40 past Winter Park and Granby to Hot Sulphur Springs. Inn is three blocks off of Highway 40.

❋

D: During the summer months, the ☛ *local museum sponsors several day-long guided excursions along the old stagecoach road, with an orientation before starting out and many stopping points along the way. Grand County Museum, (303) 725–3939.*

Ski Tip Ranch
Keystone, Colorado
80435

Innkeeper: Maria Schnekser
Address/Telephone: Montezuma Road (mailing address: Box 38); (303) 468–4202
Rooms: 13; 9 with private bath.
Rates: $95 single, $121 double, MAP, during ski season; $65 single, $95 double, EPB, late spring, summer, early fall. No pets. No TV. No air conditioning (not needed; elevation 9,300 feet). No cigars or pipes in dining room. All credit cards accepted.
Open: All year.
Facilities and Activities: Lunch available at extra charge; gourmet dinner available all year but not included in room charge during summer. Tea hour from 3:00 P.M. to 5:00 P.M. daily. Pub lounge. On premises: cross-country ski center, directed by Olympic-medal winner Jana Hlavaty; tennis courts; and free shuttle to nearby Keystone Resort. Available via shuttle: downhill skiing, sailing, river rafting, horseback riding, balloon rides, golf.

It seems as if innkeeper Maria Schnekser and her agreeable staff have been waiting for weeks in eager anticipation of your arrival, for that is the sort of welcome you receive as you pass through the low, rounded-top, Hansel and Gretel doorway into the Ski Tip Ranch.

This former stagecoach stop, built in 1869 and operated as an inn since 1949, has 🖝 the amenities of a ski lodge with the warmth of a country inn. What a combination!

The large, heavy-beamed living room, with log walls and huge stone fireplace, is furnished with antiques and lit with electric lights, flickering candles, and kerosene lamps.

On your way into the lounge, notice 🖝 the door handle made from a broken ski tip. Long ago when locks were unnecessary, all doors at Ski Tip were fitted with this type of grip. Hence, the lodge's name.

The windows of my room, Number Seven, swung open onto a Bavarian-style balcony with a breathtaking view of tall evergreens and cross-country ski trails, which begin just steps from the inn's front door.

For breakfast, I recommend either the hot porridge with your choice of brown sugar, coconut, granola, and raisin toppings or the banana pancakes and sausage patties—a hearty beginning for you skiers and a satisfying start for the dedicated shoppers among you as you head for the many attractive boutiques at nearby Keystone Resort.

While you are outdoors in the brisk, mountain air, Chef Peter Murphy is busy in the kitchen preparing homemade soup, crisp salads with inventive toppings, four entrées, and fantastic desserts. I had the New England clam chowder, 🖝 fresh grilled trout topped with Alaska king crab in pecan-butter sauce (a taste sensation I will never forget), and pumpkin-cheese cake in graham-cracker crust. I have it on good authority that the shrimp scampi, sautéed in garlic butter, tomatoes, and green onions and served over a bed of fettuccini, was equally terrific. With a fire burning in the corner fireplace, fresh flowers and candles on all the tables, and gracious waiters clad in plaid shirts and suspenders, this truly was a memorable dining experience.

How to get there: From I–70, take exit 205 (Dillon). Turn left onto Highway 6 and continue through Keystone to Montezuma Road. Turn right onto Montezuma and proceed one mile. Ski Tip Ranch is on the right.

D: Chef Peter Murphy's recipe for rolled, boneless breast of chicken, was requested by Bon Appetit *magazine.*

The Crystal Lodge
Lake City, Colorado
81235

Innkeepers: Harley and Caryl Rudofsky
Address/Telephone: (P.O. Box 246); (303) 944–2201
Rooms: 14, plus 4 cottages; all with private bath.
Rates: $50 to $80, single or double; EP. No pets. No TV. No air conditioning (not needed; elevation 8,637 feet). No smoking in restaurant or bar. Well-behaved children only, please. Credit cards not accepted.
Open: Usually all year; best to phone.
Facilities and Activities: Full-service restaurant, closed on Tuesdays. Bar. Heated outdoor pool. Nearby: Alferd Packer site, quaint shops, restaurants; hiking, great fishing, horseback riding, jeep touring, cross-country skiing, snowmobiling.

Hidden away in a narrow valley surrounded by the San Juan Mountain Range, The Crystal Lodge offers ☛ gourmet dining at its best. Extraordinarily good things come from Caryl's kitchen, including her homemade soups, sauces, breads, and desserts. ☛ Her recipe for hot apple cake with caramel rum sauce appeared in *Bon Appetit* magazine along with raves about the restaurant's other fare.

In the dining room, Harley, a soft-spoken man of Russian

and Polish descent, greets his guests at the door wearing Marithe Gerboud originals (a blousy, tight-ankled trouser imported from France) and escorts them to their tables with ceremony and flair. Such fun!

My dinner was a fabulous experience. The food was, without a doubt, among the very best I've ever eaten. First I tried Harley's own "The American Intelligence," a nonalcoholic, refreshing blend of sparkling mineral water, sparkling apple cider, and fresh lime served in a copper mug. Next, I chose the herb-roasted chicken with homemade pasta and stir-fry vegetables. My dessert was Grenoble tart, a wickedly wonderful sweet layered with a cookie crust, caramel, pralines, semi-sweet chocolate, and whipped cream. My room was only a few steps away, but after all this indulgence, I'd have been better off if I'd had to walk two miles to reach it!

The overnight accommodations are large and neatly furnished in contemporary mountain-lodge décor. Each has a deck with a magnificent view. Colorful umbrella tables and lounging chairs are scattered about the heated outdoor pool nearby.

☛ Lake San Cristobal is only one and one-half miles away; excellent stream fishing is but a few strides from the front door; and numerous hiking trails begin at the lodge.

How to get there: From Highway 50, a few miles west of Gunnison, turn south on Highway 149 to Lake City. Inn is on the right, 2 miles south of town, on 149.

D: *Guests are encouraged to use the jars of crayons on the dining-room tables to draw on the white paper tablecloths. The sight of adults gleefully executing brightly colored designs and figures with stubby little crayons is entertaining to the nonartists in the crowd as well.*

J.A.Perreault

Back Narrows Inn
Norwood, Colorado
81423

Innkeepers: Terre and Joyce Bucknam
Address/Telephone: 1550 Grand Avenue (mailing address: P.O. Box 156); (303) 327–4417
Rooms: 11; 2 with private bath, 9 share 3 baths.
Rates: $18 to $23, single; $21 to $27, double; slightly higher during holidays. Includes continental breakfast. Pets are permitted. TV in some rooms. No air conditioning (not needed; elevation 7,014 feet). MasterCard and Visa accepted.
Open: All year.
Facilities and Activities: Dinner served Thursday through Sunday. Bar. Antique shop. Rare books and book-search service. Nearby: hiking, fishing, wind sailing, gold panning, mountain climbing, downhill and cross-country skiing, ice fishing. Many summertime festivals in nearby Telluride.

Sitting all snug and secure at the western edge of the San Juan Mountain Range, the Back Narrows Inn is the ☞ perfect base camp for fishing the nearby river and reservoir, hiking the hills, skiing the slopes, or gliding along on skinny skis through national-forest or high-country ranchland. Or, it's a great destination for just reading and loafing.

The guest rooms are filled with brass, iron, and oak beds; old steamer trunks serve as lamp tables; and antique rockers are scattered about. Low ceilings and handmade quilts add to the coziness.

Dinner is served in two small dining rooms. A potbellied stove sits against one barn-wood wall; shelves filled with old books, pinecones, and dried flowers line another; and a third is honored with vintage photographs by master photographer Edward S. Curtis (well known for his photographs of early American Indians).

The menu includes chicken and dumplings served with Joyce's homemade soup or a dinner salad, vegetable, and warm fresh-baked bread. And folks come from miles around to partake of the Mexican specialties. Terre and Joyce tell me that ☞ the absolute favorite is *Flautas de Pollo:* crisp, deep-fried flour tortillas filled with chicken, cheese, and green onions and covered with tomato cream sauce, more cheese, sour cream, and guacamole. *Olé!*

Breakfast is continental and consists of coffee, tea, and homemade doughnuts made next door at The Bakery. For a more extensive breakfast and also for lunch, I suggest the Sweetie Pie Bakery and Cafe, next door to the inn in the opposite direction.

Joyce has a small antique shop just off the sitting room, and ☞ Terre is a connoisseur of old books. He has collected many rare editions and operates a book-search business, helping people all over the country find the out-of-print books they are looking for.

I think ☞ you will like the little town of Norwood. It's the sort of place where the gas-station attendant strikes up a conversation; the local veterinarian picks up an injured dog and nurses him back to health without first checking to see if the owner will be able to pay; and complete strangers say "Good Morning." I like that.

How to get there: From Highway 550, between Durango and Montrose, turn west onto Highway 62 at Ridgeway. At Placerville, turn west onto 145 to Norwood. Inn is on the left.

Gold Creek Inn
Ohio City, Colorado
81237

Innkeeper: Joe Benge
Address/Telephone: (P.O. Box HH); (303) 641–2086
Rooms: 2; share 1 bath.
Rates: $25, single; $40, double. Includes continental breakfast. No pets.
No TV. No air conditioning (not needed; elevation 8,595 feet).
MasterCard and Visa accepted.
Open: All year.
Facilities and Activities: Dinner served Wednesday through Saturday
during summer; during winter, Friday and Saturday. Sunday
brunch served all year. Bar. Complimentary champagne and flowers
for special occasions. Nearby: ghost towns; hiking, fishing, biking,
cross-country skiing, snowmobiling.

Who would ever expect the tiny town of Ohio City, Colorado
(pop. 44), to have 🖝 one of the most sought-after gourmet restaurants to be found?

First built as a general store in 1890, the unobtrusive
building now ensconces a dining room with chinked log walls,
blue plaid carpeting, and open-hearth fireplace where a black,
🖝 cast-iron pot simmers over red coals. Chef/innkeeper/
owner/manager Joe Benge attended New York State's Culinary

Arts Institute of America and does most of the food preparation on a cooking surface set up in front of the copper utensil–festooned fireplace. It is a treat, indeed, to watch his pot-and-pan proficiency while anticipating a mighty delicious meal.

Dinner choices are displayed on a chalkboard menu. Joe enjoys creative cooking, and his New York strip steak comes two ways: "with fresh sautéed mushrooms or prepared at the chef's inspiration." Let him go for it—You won't be disappointed. There's also a very special roast game hen blessed with a sauce of red plums and gooseberries. Reservations are always recommended, but for the Sunday Brunch, they are a must. There are three seatings, and they are always filled in advance. No wonder, with specialties like shrimp, cod, and scallop seafood crêpes with creamy champagne sauce and quiche Sacramento, an extravaganza of crab, artichokes, tomatoes, and mushrooms.

Yes, there are guest rooms here as well, but only two, so, again, reserve ahead. Tucked into the gabled roof, they are snug and comfy, with brown enameled iron beds, nice period pieces that originally belonged to Joe's grandparents, embroidered table scarves, wallpaper, and beaded tongue-in-groove wainscoting. Each room has a private outdoor entrance.

Unspoiled by developers, Ohio City is a low-key, picturesque community, perfect as a jumping-off place for exploring nearby ghost towns or photographing wildlife such as elk and Rocky Mountain sheep.

How to get there: From Highway 50, between Gunnison and Salida, turn north at Parlin to Ohio City. Inn is on the right.

Baker's Manor Guest House
Ouray, Colorado
81427

Innkeepers: Ivan Rudd and G. E. Mahan
Address/Telephone: 317 Second Street; (303) 325–4574
Rooms: 6; share 1 bath and a separate shower.
Rates: $26, single; $28, double. Includes continental breakfast. No pets.
   No TV. No air conditioning (not needed; elevation 7,700 feet). No
   cigars or pipes, please. Well-behaved children over age 8 only, please.
   Credit cards not accepted.
Open: All year.
Facilities and Activities: BYOB. Nearby: swimming in hot-springs pool,
   narrow-gauge passenger train, horseback riding, hiking, fishing,
   jeeping, trails for 4-wheeling, downhill and cross-country skiing, ice
   climbing, snowmobiling.

Nicely located just one block from Ouray's main street, this inn is 🖛 well away from the din of traffic and crowds and yet conveniently close to all activities.

The front door is flanked by panels of beautifully stained glass, and two Victorian parrot benches, painted white with brown slats, stand on the front porch, inviting all comers to sit awhile and enjoy the quiet neighborhood and mountain vistas.

The guest rooms are on the second floor and lead off from an open hallway surrounding a center stairwell. ☞ Staying here feels somewhat like spending the night in the home of a favorite relative. Quaint without being cutesy, the rooms are furnished with antiques; pretty spreads cover very comfortable beds; windows open to fresh mountain air; and walls are papered with posies.

A continental breakfast, served in the downstairs entry hall, consists of juice, coffee, fruit, and homemade muffins baked by Ivan in the antique Chambers gas range in the kitchen. You can pad down the stairs and take your morning repast back to your room or stay and exchange plans for the day with other guests as you munch a muffin and sip your coffee.

Ivan is originally from Kent, England, and has a marvelous accent. He and G. E. have planted many flower bulbs around the house, and the yard is lovely from early spring until the first frost of autumn. And after the flowers are gone, ☞ snowflakes and icicles make the inn a particularly cozy wintertime haven.

Always busy upgrading, these two gentlemen are adding "gingerbread" to the exterior and plan to have additional guest rooms with private baths in the future.

There are many eating places in Ouray. Ivan recommends The Bon Ton for terrific pasta and sinfully good desserts and The Western Hotel for fabulous Mexican cuisine. I, too, can heartily vouch for both of these restaurants.

How to get there: Ouray is north of Durango and south of Montrose on Highway 550. The inn is one block west of Main Street, between Third and Fourth avenues.

House of Yesteryear
Ouray, Colorado
81427

Innkeepers: Ray and June O'Brien
Address/Telephone: 516 Oak Street (P.O. Box 440); (303) 325–4277
Rooms: 8; 2 with private bath, 6 share 3 baths.
Rates: $25 to $45, single or double, continental breakfast included. No
  pets. TV in common room only. No air conditioning (not needed;
  elevation 7,700 feet). No pipes or cigars. Credit cards not accepted.
Open: Mid-June to October 1.
Facilities and Activities: Hosts will make tour and restaurant reservations. BYOB. Nearby: swimming in hot-springs pool, horseback
  riding, hiking, fishing, jeeping, narrow-gauge passenger train,
  downhill and cross-country skiing, ice climbing, snowmobiling.

I liked this place the moment I put my foot in the front door.
The parlor, with priceless antiques lining all four walls, is outstanding. Lovely old pieces decorate the guest rooms, too, one of
Ray's favorites being the ornate brass bed in the Columbine Room.
The Cascade Room caught my fancy. It features a heavy,
sleek ☛ Russian walnut sleigh bed with peach-and-beige comforter; green upholstered, high-back chairs; sparkling chandelier; and ☛ a fine view of Cascade Falls plunging hundreds of
feet down the mountainside.

114

For breakfast, Ray serves his fresh-baked muffins, fruit, orange juice, and coffee while 🖝 Alfie, the canary, sings his cheery morning song. Notice the magnificent buffet bought at auction many years ago by Ray's parents. It was formerly owned by the Adolph Coors family of Coors beer fame. Also of interest are the four North Wind chairs; the face of the puffy-cheeked character is exquisitely carved into the back of each chair.

For dinner, I walked to the Alpine Cafe and had an 8-ounce rib-eye steak, cut five-eighths of an inch thick. It had been marinated and then dusted with coarse black pepper and garlic and grilled to perfection.

The O'Briens will make reservations for mine and jeep tours (Ouray is touted as the jeeping capital of the world), arrange transportation on the Silverton–Durango narrow-gauge passenger train, and suggest several excellent restaurants within walking distance. Ray summed up their idea of hospitality when he told me, "We try to answer 'Yes' to all requests."

A recent guest came to spend the night and stayed for two weeks. On the morning of his departure, he informed Ray and June that he was "adoptable." It's that hard to leave this lovely inn.

How to get there: Ouray is north of Durango and south of Montrose on Highway 550. From Main Street, take 7th Avenue west. Turn left onto Oak Street. Inn is on the right.

╰∽╮

D: *No matter what the nighttime temperature is in this mountain town, you* must *sleep with your window at least a little bit open. Just snuggle deep under your quilt and be lulled by the steady and comforting sound of the Uncomphgre River, less than 100 yards from the inn.*

St. Elmo Hotel
Ouray, Colorado
81427

Innkeepers: Dan and Sandy Lingenfelter
Address/Telephone: 426 Main Street (mailing address: P.O. Box 667);
  (303) 325–4951
Rooms: 11; 7 with private bath, 4 share 2 baths.
Rates: $36 to $62, single or double; includes continental-plus breakfast.
  No pets. TV in parlor only. No air conditioning (not needed; elevation 7,700 feet). MasterCard and Visa accepted.
Open: All year.
Facilities and Activities: Full-service gourmet restaurant, featuring
  continental cuisine. Weekend champagne brunch. Outdoor patio
  dining. Sauna. Bar. Nearby: swimming in hot-springs pool, horseback riding, hiking, fishing, jeeping, narrow-gauge railroad, downhill and cross-country skiing, ice climbing, snowmobiling.

No doubt Kitty Heit would be mighty proud if she could see
her St. Elmo Hotel as it is today, all gussied up with new Victorian wallpapers, polished furniture, and the same brand of hospitality that she was famous for.

Hard-working, with one small child to support, Kitty came to
Ouray in the 1880s and went to work at the Bon Ton Restaurant
on Main Street. Before long, she bought the restaurant, and, in

1898, she built the St. Elmo Hotel next door. Never one to say no to "down on their luck" miners and their families, "Aunt Kitty" was quick with a room and a handout for those in need.

The exterior of the building has a sort of sleepy look resulting from the dark green awning "eyelids" on two of the front windows. Inside, plush new carpets and pretty printed walls enhance color schemes that are so well done that the 🖝 rooms seem to glow with warmth. Fine antiques grace the guest rooms, parlor, and dining room, where Sandy and Dan serve a buffet-style morning repast of juice, fresh fruit, homebaked breads, coffee, and tea. Sometimes a delicous fruit salad awaits guests as they tumble from their beds, and the luckiest visitors will be at the St. Elmo on the mornings when the aroma of 🖝 Sandy's very special strawberry bread rises to meet them as they descend the stairs.

During the evening, as I sat sipping a glass of excellent house wine in the Bon Ton, I didn't care if my meal ever came. The 🖝 ambience of this cellar café, with its stone walls, period furniture, and subdued lighting, was so romantic, so "just right." However . . . when I got a glimpse of my fettuccini St. Elmo, tossed in a pesto sauce of garlic, fresh basil, pine nuts, and Parmesan cheese, I quickly remembered my reason for being here. I also sampled the beef Wellington. It was superb. My dessert was *zuccotto,* an Italian upside-down sponge cake soaked in liquor and filled with vanilla ice cream, a thick chocolate sauce, crushed macaroons, filberts, and bits of milk chocolate. I'll be back!

How to get there: Ouray is north of Durango and south of Montrose on Highway 550. Inn is on main street of town.

The Western Hotel
Ouray, Colorado
81427

Innkeeper: Roberta Peterson
Address/Telephone: 210 7th Avenue (mailing address: P.O. Box 25);
   (303) 325–4645
Rooms: 12; 1 with private bath, 11 share 4 baths and 2 shower rooms.
Rates: $20 to $45, single or double. Includes continental breakfast. No
   pets. TV in upstairs parlor only. No air conditioning (not needed;
   elevation 7,700 feet). Well-behaved children only, please.
   MasterCard and Visa accepted.
Open: Mid-May to mid-September.
Facilities and Activities: Saloon. Nearby: hot-springs swimming pool,
   narrow-gauge passenger train, ghost towns, mine tours. Hiking,
   fishing, horseback riding, bird watching, rock hunting, mountain
   climbing, jeeping, four-wheeling.

   Looking for all the world like a Western-movie set, The
Western (what else?) Hotel sits on a side street bordering the
edge of what was once Ouray's red-light district.
   The three-story white structure was built in 1891 and opened
in the spring of '92. The unforeseen silver crisis one year later
forced it to close its doors, and there followed many owners and
many closures. Finally, in 1916, a colorful husband-and-wife team

named Floro and Maria Flor came along, and under their guidance The Western became a successful boarding house for miners. Mrs. Flor, known for her kindness and generosity, was christened Mother Flor by her tenants. She ran the hotel until well into the 1940s, and it is said that no one, no matter how destitute, ever went away from her door hungry. Since that time the hotel has changed hands several times, spent a short while as a museum, and finally in 1982 was purchased by five partners dedicated to bringing it back to the lovely Victorian it once was.

During my night here, the parlor, furnished in good quality period pieces, was quiet and sedate; the linen-and-china-bedecked dining room was humming with contented diners; and the saloon was rocking as any good western bar should be.

The Western serves a wide selection of ☞ down-home, stick-to-the-ribs-type chow. The *rellenos* and enchiladas are especially good. Or you could order a 16-ounce Western-cut rib steak; settle for a 7-ounce filet mignon; or try "Ouray's Revenge," a zesty burger garnished with creamed horseradish and bacon.

A steep, narrow stairway leads to the guest rooms. Small in size, as was the custom when the hotel was built, a typical room will have an iron bed with good, comfortable mattress and velvet patchwork spread; a time-worn, antique dresser; and oriental rug. The décor is not fancy; but ☞ if you are into true Old West flavor, you'll find it here.

The cozy parlor on the second floor opens onto a wide front veranda. Complimentary fruit juice, sweet rolls, and coffee are brought upstairs each morning; and ☞ it is particularly nice to sit out on the balcony, sip your coffee, and imagine what it was like here a hundred years ago.

How to get there: Ouray is north of Durango and south of Montrose on Highway 550. From Main Street, turn west onto 7th Avenue. Hotel in on the right.

Davidson's Country Inn
Pagosa Springs, Colorado
81147

Innkeepers: Evelyn and Gilbert Davidson
Address/Telephone: P.O. Box 87; (303) 264–5863
Rooms: 9; 1 with private bath, 8 share 4 baths.
Rates: $42, single; $48, double. Includes continental-plus breakfast.
   Well-behaved pets considered. TV in solarium only. No air conditioning (not needed; elevation 7,079 feet). Smoking outside only.
   MasterCard and Visa accepted.
Open: All year.
Facilities and Activities: Picnic lunches available with advance notice.
   Alcohol not permitted. Sun deck, solarium, library; horseshoes, outdoor barbecue and picnic area, children's play corner and sand box.
   Gift shop with handmade country items. Nearby: restaurants, hot springs; hiking, fishing, hayrides, downhill and cross-country skiing, snowmobiling, sleigh rides.

   When you come to stay at the Davidsons', be sure to make friends with every guest so you can take a peek into all their rooms. I wandered up and down the hallways on all three floors and couldn't decide on a favorite. High on my list, though, is the dainty Hummingbird with its ☛ quilt wall-hanging, brass bed, two old kerosene lamps, and antique dresser. For contrast, there's the third-floor Mountain Man Country, which feels like a frontier cabin, with wooden-spoked wagonwheels hanging from the ceiling and snowshoes tacked to the walls. This hideaway is the only room with a water bed, and I'm not sure what a mountain man would think of that; but being an adventurous sort, he'd probably love it.

Each room is tastefully decorated with family heirlooms, valuable antiques, carefully chosen country touches, and fine pieces of handmade furniture. This would be a good place to pick up some excellent home decorating ideas.

All the quilts were made by Evelyn's mother and 90-year-old grandmother. And there's a stuffed-goose doorstop and a calico pig that I would like to have in my own menagerie. One thing is for sure; when I go back, I'm going to allow time to look up the gentleman who made the wooden rockers and see if I can order one. They are really special.

Breakfast is fun at the Davidsons' because Evelyn serves a large helping of cheeriness along with her special apple kringle, fresh fruit, cereals, juice, coffee, homemade jellies, and farm-fresh honey. Stay a second day, and you may get to try her strawberry muffins. Coffee, iced tea, and hot chocolate are always available.

Evelyn will pack box lunches for hikers and fishermen; or she recommends The Pie Shoppe for sandwiches, homemade breads, and pies and the Old Miner's Steak House for good, hearty dinners.

How to get there: Inn is on south side of Highway 160, 2 miles east of Pagosa Springs.

✱

D: *This inn has a solarium with* *a children's corner that is guaranteed to delight the small tykes. A doll bed filled with "babies," a school desk, play church, doll house, books, and child-size cupboard, sink, and stove are sure to keep the little ones busy.*

The Redstone Inn
Redstone, Colorado
81623

Innkeeper: Nancy Lambert
Address/Telephone: 0082 Redstone Boulevard: (303) 963–2526
Rooms: 35; 32 with private bath, 3 with half-bath.
Rates: $30 to $65, single; $35 to $65, double; EP. No pets. Wheelchair
accessible. No air conditioning (not needed; elevation 7,180 feet).
MasterCard, Visa, American Express accepted.
Open: All year.
Facilities and Activities: Breakfast, lunch, dinner served in dining room.
Lounge, library, music room; hot tub, tennis court. Nearby: White
River National Forest; good fishing in Crystal River, cross-country
skiing, hiking trails, horseback riding, jeep tours, sleigh rides, hay-
rides, guided tours through Osgood's Castle, 1 mile from the inn.

I can't help but think how pleased John Cleveland Osgood
would be if he could see his inn as it is today. Mining magnate
Osgood built the inn in 1902 as bachelor quarters for unmarried
miners, and its amenities were luxurious for the day: electricity,
steam heat, baths, barber shop, and shoe-shine parlor. He also
built a double row of Victorian cottages along the main street for
miners with families. Osgood's wife, Alma, known as Lady Boun-
tiful because of her yearly trips to New York City to Christmas

shop for the local children, often went into the community to care for the sick. Her portraits hang in the sitting room and reveal a kind and beautiful woman.

☛ Listed in the National Register of Historic Places, this is a truly lovely inn with delicate floral wallpaper, creamy white woodwork, an abundance of antiques, and a staff that is genuinely delighted when you express pleasure with "their" inn.

Magnificent fireplaces grace the public rooms. A white spindled staircase leads to the second and third floors, where hallways twist and turn on their way to antique-filled bedrooms. Much of the furniture is turn-of-the-century Gustav Stickley Mission Oak with a few original pegged and slotted miners' pieces.

In the gourmet dining room, you are immediately served a loaf of homemade bread, hot from Chef Dina Larkin's oven. I had ☛ albondigus soup, something I had never tried before. I am still experimenting, attempting to duplicate this marvelous concoction. It seems to be a cross between a vegetable and minestrone, with just the right spices added, including chili powder, I think.

There are many enticing entrées on the menu, including roast duckling à l'orange, with a glaze made of fresh oranges and a hint of Grand Marnier, and a seafood crêpe with a generous amount of crab and shrimp in a "flavored just right" white sauce. Absolutely wonderful!

Yes, there is no doubt. John C. and Alma surely would be pleased.

How to get there: From I–70, take exit 116 onto Highway 82 east, through Glenwood Springs, for 10 miles. At Carbondale, turn right onto Highway 133 and go 18 miles to Redstone. The inn overlooks the main street.

༚

D: *Notice the tapestry, original to the inn, above the fireplace in the lounge. Its proverb translates, "Don't sell the hide before you kill the bear." I wonder if this preceded "Don't count your chickens . . ."*

Fools Fe S2 Gold Inn
Silverton, Colorado
81433

Innkeeper: Ann Marie Wallace
Address/Telephone: 1069 Snowden Street (mailing address: P.O. Box 603); (303) 387–5879
Rooms: 4; 1 with private bath, 3 share 1 bath.
Rates: $30 single, $40 double, shared bath; $60, private bath; EPB. Well-mannered pets accepted. No TV. No air conditioning (not needed; elevation 9,318 feet. Bring your snuggies!) Smoking in parlor only. MasterCard and Visa accepted.
Open: All year.
Facilities and Activities: Dinner available to guests only on Thursday, Friday, and Saturday evenings. Box lunches. BYOB. Complimentary coffee, tea, juice available at all times. Sherry before dinner hour. Cooking seminars. San Juan Geotours. Nearby: shopping; narrow-gauge passenger train, hiking, fishing, horseback riding, tennis, downhill and cross-country skiing.

I found Ann Marie sitting in the dining-room bay window working at her rug loom, a cup of coffee to one side. Her greeting was so warm, I knew at once I had chosen the right place to visit. And a walk through the parlor and upstairs bedrooms, each named for the particular mountain seen through its window, made me want to stay forever.

I found family-heirloom, antique furniture tucked under sloped ceilings, lace-curtained closets, patchwork and crazy quilts, crocheted afgans, kimonos for the down-the-hall bath, and handmade soaps from Maine made especially for this inn.

My very favorite corner in the whole house was the ☞ little nook at the top of the stairs. Lit by a dormer window and just big enough for one, it is perfect for reading or for writing letters home to tell about the perfect inn you've found in the Colorado high country.

Ann Marie conducts ☞ cooking seminars: intense, three-day culinary experiences in which she shares her expertise in the field with those wishing to learn her creative secrets.

But if you merely want to taste and enjoy her kitchen ingenuity, make a reservation for one of her outstanding ☞ candlelight dinners. Staged in the formal dining room with no light except that from candles, these romantic affairs feature entrées such as French roast beef braised in red-wine sauce and filled with diced ham, mushrooms, black olives, and herb dressing.

Breakfast is brunch style and might be crêpes filled with mushrooms with a sherry sauce or scrambled eggs with sausage, mushrooms, and a dash of sage. All breads are baked from scratch on the premises and include moist, flavorful banana bread, blueberry muffins, and cinnamon coffee cake.

Ann Marie also sponsors ☞ San Juan Geotours, an opportunity to learn about the intricacies of the mountains, their formations, their metal deposits, and the reasons for their many colors. A two-day-minimum, six-person-maximum event, the package includes all housing, meals, and transportation in and around Silverton. Call for rates and scheduled dates.

How to get there: Silverton is north of Durango and south of Montrose on Highway 550. The inn is 2 blocks from Greene Street (main street of town), on the corner of 11th and Snowden.

The Grand Imperial Hotel
Silverton, Colorado
81433

Innkeepers: Ken and Mary Helen Marlin
Address/Telephone: 1219 Greene Street (mailing address: P.O. Box 57); (303) 387–5527
Rooms: 40, including one 3-room suite; all with private bath.
Rates: $35 to $46, single or double; $90, suite; EP. No pets. No air conditioning (not needed; elevation 9,318 feet). MasterCard and Visa accepted.
Open: Mid-March to October 1.
Facilities and Activities: Full-service restaurant. Saloon. Live music. Nearby: ghost towns, shopping; narrow-gauge passenger train, hiking, fishing, horseback riding, tennis, downhill and cross-country skiing.

When I entered this grand old hotel, it was midday, ☛ the honky-tonk piano was going full blast in the Hub Saloon, the chandeliers were aglow, a life-size portrait of Lillian Russell smiled coyly from one wall, and Ken extended a warm welcome from behind the magnificent front desk. I knew immediately that coming here just might become a habit; one look at my room and the "might" became a certainty.

My haven included dusty-peach woodwork; soft pink, rose-bedecked wallpaper; antique brass bed; brocade settee; and 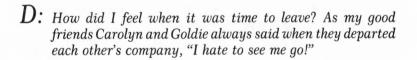 a genuine crystal chandelier that once had held candles and now was outfitted for electricity. The bath was special, too, with oak appointments and even ☞ an oak, pull-chain-style commode. I peeked into several other unoccupied guest rooms and found them just as lovely.

The cherry-wood back bar in the saloon was made in England, brought around Cape Horn on a windjammer to San Francisco, and then hauled overland to Silverton. It is now in splendid condition, but during Prohibition, it lost a little of its dignity. First, previous owners painted it for use in the restaurant, and then it fell victim to a jealous admirer of one of the local "girls." The story goes that he found her flirting in the dining room, aimed his gun, missed his target, and hit the bar instead. ☞ The bullet hole can still be seen in the scrimshaw work on the left column of the bar.

The Gold King Dining Room is truly elegant with its plum-colored wainscoting; burgundy, rose, and gray wallpaper; silk flowers; and three etched-glass light fixtures that make the tin ceiling glitter. Amid all this splendor, I had some of the best home-style cooking I've ever eaten; huge portions, prepared and served just like Sunday dinners used to be.

Breakfast had that same homey taste. I chose a waffle topped with blueberries and sprinkled with powdered sugar, instead of the usual mound of fluff that always cools your waffle too fast. I also tasted the bacon-and-walnut waffle and wished I could spend another day.

How to get there: Silverton is north of Durango and south of Montrose on Highway 550. The hotel is on Greene Street, the main street of town.

❉

D: How did I feel when it was time to leave? As my good friends Carolyn and Goldie always said when they departed each other's company, "I hate to see me go!"

Smedley's
Silverton, Colorado
81433

Innkeepers: Fritz Kline and Loren Lew
Address/Telephone: 1314 Greene Street (mailing address: P.O. Box 2);
    (303) 387–5713
Rooms: 3 suites; all with private bath.
Rates: $29, single; $39, double; EPB. No pets. No air conditioning (not
    needed; elevation 9,318 feet). All major credit cards accepted.
Open: All year.
Facilities and Activities: BYOB. Kitchen facilities, clock radios, TV with
    HBO, coffee and coffee makers, in-room phones available. Nearby:
    narrow-gauge passenger train, shopping, jeep rentals, ghost towns;
    hiking, fishing, horseback riding, tennis, downhill and cross-country
    skiing. Many scheduled events: cross-country ski races, World
    Speed Skiing Championship, Hardrocker's Mining Contests, Great
    Western Rocky Mountain Brass Band Festival.

    Behind Smedley's Victorian exterior and above the old-fashioned ice cream parlor, ☛ immaculate, contemporary guest rooms offer the latest in amenities with just the right ☛ touch of Victoriana. With separate sitting room, bedroom, kitchenette, and private bath, each unit sleeps up to four people without crowding. Room One has an 1870 Empire Revival green velvet settee, oak dresser, and ornately carved, circa 1870, cherry-wood bed covered with a patchwork quilt. All rooms have clock radios, color television with HBO, coffee and coffee makers, and some kitchen utensils. Room phones are available.

Downstairs, Smedley's Ice Cream Parlor presents made-on-the-premises ice cream in elegant turn-of-the-century style. Bentwood chairs encircle small, round tables; fluted lamps hang from the shiny tin ceiling; red posts support the filigree woodwork above the serving area; and, over to one side, red-and-white candy-stripe wallpaper surrounds the irresistible candy counter.

A breakfast of bacon, eggs, hash browns, and toast is complimentary for Smedley's lodgers and is served next door at The Pickle Barrel. If you choose, you may substitute other menu items for this standard breakfast and pay the difference in price.

For lunch or dinner, I suggest ☞ The French Bakery Restaurant, owned by innkeepers Fritz and Loren and located in the Teller House Hotel. The restaurant, a Silverton landmark and one-time grocery store and meat market, dates back to 1917 and retains its original floors, walls, and ceiling. The glass-fronted back bar came from a barbershop in Ouray, Colorado: and the large oak ice box has been restored, insulated, and turned into a cooler for beer and wine. Breakfast and lunch are served here daily, and dinners are available during the summertime; but the bakery is the big draw. Pies, cakes, pastries, and rolls are all made fresh daily, and it's hard to think about ordering anything else after you've walked past the baked-goods counter.

How to get there: Silverton is north of Durango and south of Montrose on Highway 550. The inn is located midtown, on Silverton's main street.

Wingate House
Silverton, Colorado
81433

Innkeepers: Fritz Klinke and Loren Lew
Address/Telephone: 1045 Snowden Street (mailing address: P.O. Box 2); (303) 387–5713
Rooms: 4 share 2 baths.
Rates: $29, single; $39, double; EPB. No pets. TV in parlor only. No air conditioning (not needed; elevation 9,318 feet). No smoking inside inn. All major credit cards accepted.
Open: All year.
Facilities and Activities: BYOB. Kitchen for guest use. Nearby: restaurants, shopping, narrow-gauge passenger train, ghost towns; hiking, fishing, horseback riding, tennis, downhill and cross-country skiing.

This 1886 mansard-roofed Victorian has been 🖝 meticulously restored to its former grace and also has a few added amenities such as clock radios in all guest rooms, Bradbury and Bradbury wallpapers, television and coffee maker in the parlor, and a new, modern kitchen.

My room was upstairs and featured a majestic oak, Eastlake-style four-poster, beautifully handcrafted by Loren. Tiny blue and rust flowers dance across the peach wallpaper; lace curtains drape the windows, and a marble-topped table resides in the corner. Some of the rooms have sitting alcoves and magnificent views of 13,000-foot Kendall Mountain, and one has a dresser that once belonged to one of the leading ladies from Silverton's former red-light district.

In the late afternoon ☛ I sat for a while in a white wicker love seat on the front porch, watching through a fringe of gingerbread railings and eave trim as the narrow-gauge train came and went amid loud chugs and huge puffs of steam. From my vantage point I could see the town's church spires and a conglomeration of houses, many dating back to the 1880s.

Breakfast is complimentary and is only a short walk away at one of Fritz and Loren's two restaurants, The French Bakery. Anything with the word *bakery* sounds good to me, so in the morning I merrily skipped down the hill and had a ☛ baked-at-that-very-moment cinnamon roll, a perfectly prepared ham-and-cheese omelet, and home-fried potatoes, all served promptly with care.

For other meals, guests can use the Wingate's kitchen facilities or walk the two blocks to Silverton's main street and numerous restaurants. Fritz and Loren will also cater dinners for small groups.

I decided to have dinner at The Pickle Barrel, Fritz and Loren's other restaurant, and it was a wise choice. Rock walls, a fifteen-foot ceiling, extensive use of wood, and lots of plants provide an atmosphere of pleasant rusticity. I had an excellent prime rib, crab salad, baked potato, and homemade cherry pie. This is a happy place. The help is friendly, and the food is superb.

How to get there: Silverton is north of Durango and south of Montrose on Highway 550. The inn is 2 blocks from Greene Street (main street of town), just off of 11th on Snowden.

Harbor Hotel
Steamboat Springs, Colorado
80477

Innkeeper: John Mitchell
Address/Telephone: 703 Lincoln Avenue (mailing address: P.O. Box
    774109); (303) 879–1522, (800) 334–1012 inside Colorado, (800)
    543–8888 outside Colorado
Rooms: 60, including several suites; all with private bath.
Rates: $30 to $38, single; $36 to $44, double; $56 to $70, suites, during
    summer. Winter rates are divided into four periods and range from
    $46 to $72; best to phone. Children 18 years and under, sharing
    room with parents, free in summer. Children 12 years and under,
    sharing room with parents, free in winter. All include continental
    breakfast. No pets. Wheelchair accessible. All major credit cards
    accepted.
Open: All year.
Facilities and Activities: Saloon. Two hot tubs, sauna, steam room.
    Complimentary wine-and-cheese parties in winter. Storage for skis.
    Nearby: sports park, restaurants, shopping, rodeo; natural-hot-
    springs pool and water slide, hiking, fishing, tennis, rafting, kayak-
    ing, downhill and cross-country skiing.

In the '40s, the *Denver Post* proclaimed the Harbor ". . . the
finest hotel between Denver and Salt Lake City." Then the lean
years came, and it developed into nothing more than a "cheap

sleep" for unaffluent skiers. A slow upward climb in the early '70s progressed until, today, it is once more 🖝 a first-class hotel and the pride of Steamboat Springs. Long-time desk clerk Martha Ursich said it best: "She's been up, and she's been down; but through it all, she's remained a mighty sweet old girl."

The lobby, small and intimate, has red brick and dark-stained walls; a maroon, tufted leather couch; a ceiling fixture that flickers like a gas light; and a curved window that looks out on the main street. All the antiques in the building came from one gigantic shopping spree in England, and they are elegant, indeed.

A continental breakfast is served in the pretty back parlor. Be sure to see the fainting couch in the side parlor and 🖝 check out the ornate chair with green velvet seat in the main room. It is a commode, well disguised and uniquely designed.

It was difficult to decide on a room in this hotel because every one is furnished differently and every one is extremely beautiful. Number 342 has to be one of the best, though. 🖝 Its sitting room is directly above the lobby, so its corner window, framed in champagne-colored draperies, is also curved. What a lovely place to sit! The carpet is Kelly green. Some of the walls are papered and others are paneled, giving them an English library look. The bedroom is light and airy and has an elaborate headboard and dresser.

The hotel restaurant, The Cove, features Chinese cuisine and has a wonderfully complete menu with thirty-four entrées. I suggest you begin with Fountain of Youth soup and finish with mandarin orange cheese cake.

The hotel's Hatch Bar is 🖝 the oldest saloon in Steamboat Springs and a local cowboy hangout—country-western music, lots of action, lots of fun.

How to get there: Steamboat Springs is on Highway 40, 166 miles northwest of Denver. The Harbor Hotel is on the main street.

Johnstone Inn
Telluride, Colorado
81435

Innkeepers: Mike and Christine Courter
Address/Telephone: 403 West Colorado Avenue (mailing address: P.O. Box 546); (303) 728–3316
Rooms: 8; 1 with private bath, 7 share 3 baths.
Rates: $22 to $35, single; $30 to $35, double, in summer. $30 to $50, single; $45 to $50, double, in winter; higher during holidays and festivals. Includes continental-plus breakfast. No pets. TV in TV room only. No air conditioning (not needed; elevation 8,745 feet). MasterCard, Visa, American Express accepted.
Open: Mid-May to mid-October and mid-November to mid-April.
Facilities and Activities: Complimentary après-ski refreshments. Nearby: world-renowned festivals including those honoring film making, dance, jazz, bluegrass, chamber music, hang gliding, river rafting, wine tasting, ballooning, and mushrooming. Restaurants, shopping; hiking, fishing, golf, horseback riding, mountain climbing, excellent downhill and cross-country skiing.

About as Victorian as you can get, the lavender-trimmed-in-violet Johnstone Inn boasts a peaked roof, stained-glass windows, and a gracefully spindled railing on the approach staircase and lengthy veranda.

Built in the early 1890s, the inn first operated as a hotel for local silver miners. Now, after being locked up for more than thirty years, it is completely renovated and provides all the comforts of home plus ☛ an ideal location close to restaurants, shops, and recreational activities. It is only two blocks from the new Oak Street Ski Lift and three blocks from the Coonskin Lift. A free shuttle stops in front of the inn and services all ski areas.

Guest rooms have either brass or oak antique beds, roomy closets, and extraordinary views of the mountains. All the woodwork and stained glass are original to the house. Most rooms share baths, but this has an advantage in this inn. ☛ Tucked away at the end of the hall on the second floor is an oversized cooper tub with oak rim. Now, the best way to enjoy this room to its fullest is to bring along some bubble bath (optional for guys), a candle, and a glass of wine. The copper seems to keep the water warm forever, and this goes a long way toward erasing the kinks resulting from many hours on the slopes or hiking trails. (The wine helps, too!)

The small parlor adapts well both to quiet reading or spirited conversation and to the enjoyment of hot cider, cookies, and popcorn served après-ski during the wintertime.

Breakfast is brought to individual tables in the dining room and consists of homemade English or bran muffins; raspberry, peach, or blueberry crumb cake; juice; cereal; and coffee, tea, or hot chocolate. Hot beverages are always available on the sideboard. Full breakfasts can be arranged for groups, and picnic lunches can be had with prior arrangement.

For dinner, I suggest the Silver Glade for good Cajun cooking. The popcorn shrimp are outstanding.

How to get there: Take Highway 145 into Telluride. Highway 145 becomes Colorado Avenue, Telluride's main street. Inn is on the left, just before the center of town.

The New Sheridan Hotel
Telluride, Colorado
81435

Innkeeper: Wendy McFadden
Address/Telephone: 231 West Colorado Avenue (mailing address: P.O. Box 980); (303) 728–4351
Rooms: 30, including 1 suite; 9 with private bath.
Rates: $30, single; $32, double; $100, suite, during summer. $36 to $66, single or double; $120, suite, during winter; EP. No pets. Wheelchair accessible. No air conditioning (not needed; elevation 8,745 feet). MasterCard, Visa, American Express accepted.
Open: All year except from April 15 to May 15.
Facilities and Activities: No breakfast served. Lunch served in summer only; dinner 7 days a week. Bar. Nearby: restaurants, shopping; summer chamber music, jazz, bluegrass, and film festivals. Hiking, fishing, horseback riding, mountain climbing, 3 blocks to alpine ski lifts, cross-country skiing out the front door.

The New Sheridan Hotel, thought to have been named after a prosperous local mine, was built in 1895. Though "new" no more, it is still the cornerstone of this bustling little mountain town of first-rate winter skiing and internationally known summer festivals.

The lobby is small and sparsely furnished, but its large windows face Telluride's main street and provide the best spot in town to be on the lookout for celebrities and to just plain people-watch.

Most of the rooms are simply furnished, with a smattering of antiques. The finest is the William Jennings Bryan Suite, so named because that presidential candidate stayed in these rooms in 1902 while politicking in the West. During my visit the suite was occupied by Jimmy Stewart, who was in town for the annual film festival.

Just past the front desk and down a short hallway, I found a delightful courtyard and bar. It was in this saloon that several scenes from the movie *Butch and Sundance: the Early Days* were filmed. Incidentally, the real Butch Cassidy made his first unauthorized bank withdrawal just one block down the street. And three blocks over once stood the Senate bordello, where Jack Dempsey washed dishes for a living.

Julian's, the hotel restaurant, specializes in northern-Italian cuisine and features seven kinds of spaghetti dishes along with other pastas, veal, chicken, and shrimp.

I spent two wonderful hours in Julian's, indulging first in an antipasto of mozzarella alla marinara: little cheese chunks breaded, fried, and served with marinara sauce. Next, Chef Wayne Gustafson really outdid himself in preparing my filetto di manzo, a tender fillet of beef sautéed with walnut, gorganzola cheese, cream, and all the right herbs and spices. Along with this came Tuscan flat bread and a dinner salad. A cup of cappuccino, and I was in heaven.

How to get there: Take Highway 145 into Telluride. Highway 145 becomes Colorado Avenue, Telluride's main street. Hotel is on the left.

D: *The staff is friendly and accommodating. The hotel may not be as lavish as it was at the turn of the century, but it has retained its charm. And if it's good enough for Jimmy Stewart, it's plenty good enough for me!*

Skyline Guest Ranch
Telluride, Colorado
81435

Innkeepers: Dave and Sherry Farny
Address/Telephone: P.O. Box 67; (303) 728–3757
Rooms: 11 in ranch house, 5 cottages; all with private bath.
Rates: $610 per person per week in ranch house; AP. Cottage occupants
    may choose EP, EPB, MAP, or AP; EP only in winter; phone for
    rates. No pets. No TV. No air conditioning (not needed; elevation
    8,745). No smoking inside buildings. No credit cards accepted.
Open: Cottages, all year; ranch house, late spring through early fall.
Facilities and Activities: Dude-ranch activities in late spring, summer,
    and early fall only. Happy hour; for the rest of the time, BYOB. Hot
    tub, sauna. Horseback riding, hiking, fishing, rock climbing, jeep
    trips, river rafting, trips to Mesa Verde National Park, downhill and
    cross-country skiing.

    The dirt road winds gently through a grove of aspen and
pine, past a mirror-like pond, and up to the weathered ranch
house where Dave meets you with a sincere greeting and a firm
handshake and Sherry treats you like an old friend.
    Rustic, picturesque cottages are scattered amongst the trees
and around the pond. The ranch-house bedrooms have wood
walls covered with burlap (quite effective); they also have 🖝 little

niceties like gingham-wrapped soap made especially for Skyline Ranch and a tiny tube of lip gloss for protection from the high-altitude air and sunshine.

Dave took me on a tour, first up to the high plateau where the horses graze, then to a lake with so many fish, I could actually *see* them swimming below the surface.

Meals are served family style at tables set with blue-and-white woven table covers, blue bandana napkins, and bowls of wild flowers. Dinner included wonderfully tender Colorado beef, gravy, stuffed baked potatoes, green beans, garden salad, home-made Sherry bread (a cracked wheat, whole grain wonder named for Sherry Farny, not the beverage), and fresh peach cobbler with real cream. Who would have thought that I'd be hungry enough the next morning to eat my share of homemade granola with sour cream, scrambled eggs and bacon, and apple coffee cake! Blame the appetite on the pure mountain air!

The Farnys have ☛ a superb stable of saddle horses, with animals available for all levels of riding ability. Hiking, rock climbing, river rafting, and jeep trips to ghost towns and Mesa Verde National Park are only a few of the many activities here.

Or you could do as I did: find the old swing located amid a mass of wildflowers and white-barked aspen trees. I must have stayed for more than an hour, watching hikers return for supper and savoring a view of the ranch lands, winding brook, and mountains beyond. Did I? You bet! I swung like a kid, my feet not touching the ground, and I managed to ignore the bewildered looks a chattering chipmunk kept sending my way.

How to get there: Ranch is 8 miles south of Telluride on Highway 145. Watch for sign atop log planter on west side of road.

Silverheels Country Inn
Wildernest, Colorado
80435

Innkeeper: Jo Ann Rouse

Address/Telephone: 81 Buffalo Drive (mailing address: P.O. Box 367, Dillon, CO 80435); (303) 468–2926

Rooms: 10; all with private bath.

Rates: $50 to $60, single; $65 to $80, double, during summer. $70 to $80, single; $85 to $100, double, during winter. Includes continental-plus breakfast. No pets. TV in game room only. No air conditioning (not needed; elevation 9,800 feet). Children under 12 stay free. MasterCard and Visa accepted.

Open: All year except first 2 weeks of May.

Facilities and Activities: Dinner served every day, breakfast to inn guests only, no lunch served. Lounge, game room, deck, indoor sauna, outdoor hot tub. Nearby: many restaurants, shopping; hiking, fishing, tennis, downhill and cross-country skiing.

All the while I stayed at this inn, 🖝 I had the distinct feeling of being in a tree house. And I loved it! Perhaps it was the narrow, spiral staircase I climbed to reach my room. Maybe it was the way my windows looked out in three directions to a forest. Or could it have been the little covered walkways leading here and there, from room to room, reminiscent of the captivating Ewok village in the movie *Return of the Jedi?* And waking to the rustle of pine trees, the cawing of crows, and the chatter of a scolding squirrel surely had something to do with it.

My room, number nine, was delightfully decorated in sea green and dusty rose, from the solid green carpet and matching chairs to the wee pink flowers on the bedspread, drapes, and wallpaper. Some of the rooms have stone fireplaces, and all have large, well-lighted mirrors and ample luggage and closet space.

☞ Elegant dining in the European tradition is featured in the Columbine Room. You enter the dining area through the immaculate kitchen and thus are privileged to a glimpse of what is to come. I paused to admire five golden-glazed roast ducklings and several pans of bread ready for the oven.

My choice of soup was the *crème dame blanche,* a chicken-based cream soup garnished with sautéed, blanched almonds and a touch of sherry. Hearts of Bibb lettuce with a creamy dill dressing made up my salad; and my entrée was a tender, tasty pork loin Normandy, stuffed with apples and onions and flavored with Riesling wine. I followed this with a fluffy lemon soufflé and vowed to skip breakfast (I didn't).

Following an after-dinner walk along the quiet mountain road, plus a nightcap of cognac in the intimate lounge, I was ready to climb back up to my tree house. Whoops, I mean my lovely room.

How to get there: From I–70, take exit 205 onto Colorado 9 and proceed north for a short distance. Turn left onto Wildernest Road and drive to the Wildernest Center. Road name changes to Ryan Gulch Road at Center. Continue on Ryan Gulch Road for 6 miles. Inn is on the right.

Millers Inn
Winter Park, Colorado
80482

Innkeeper: Nick Teverbaugh
Address/Telephone: 219 Vasquez Road (mailing address: P.O. Box 53);
   (303) 726–5313, (800) 824–8438 outside Colorado
Rooms: 19, including 4 suites. 5 cottages.
Rates: $25 to $40, single; $30 to $45, double, in summer; EP. $56 to
   $62, single; less for those sharing rooms in winter; MAP. Cottage
   rates on request. No pets. No air conditioning (not needed; elevation 9,110 feet). MasterCard, Visa, American Express accepted.
Open: All year.
Facilities and Activities: Dining room closed from April to mid-November. Breakfast and dinner served mid-November through March.
   No lunch. Service bar for guests. Hot tub, Finnish sauna. Nearby:
   hiking, fishing, horseback riding, white-water rafting, tennis, golf,
   downhill and cross-country skiing, snowmobiling, tubing, sleigh
   rides.

   Innkeeper Nick Teverbaugh is also mayor of this tiny community of six to seven hundred permanent residents. Soft-spoken
and accommodating, he seems to set the mood for his ☞ laid-
back mountain lodge.
   The guest rooms vary in size, décor, and amenities. Indian

Paint Brush, one of the four corner suites, is particularly pleasing. Windows on two sides open onto giant pine trees and the creek below. A beamed ceiling, one wall made of stone, and a freestanding wood stove accent this room.

Downstairs, at least one of several fireplaces is sure to be glowing, while in the dining room, a corner waterfall feeds the goldfish pond. Out back, ☛ the covered bridge beckons you over the creek to an attractive indoor spa guaranteed to take out the kinks, whether they be from skiing the slopes, hiking the trails, or cruising the many nearby shops in downtown Winter Park.

German pastry chef Wolfgang Wendt is in command of the kitchen during fall, winter, and spring, and the aromas emanating from his little kingdom are something to experience. Blueberry kuchen, vegetable-and-ham quiche, lingonberries, and a wonderful rough-grind, whole grain wheat cereal promise to get you off to a good start. And what's for dinner? How about ☛ lentil soup, *brötchen,* sauerbraten, and one of Wolfgang's special desserts?

During the summer months, when meals are not offered at the inn, I recommend breakfast about a block away at Carver Brothers Bakery. Here, one can sit indoors or out and enjoy a light repast of hot pecan or cinnamon rolls, juice, and coffee. For a more substantial beginning to your day, try The Panhandler, just a few steps farther on, for its Homesteader, an individual casserole teeming with a flavorful blend of crunchy croutons, cheddar cheese, eggs, and bacon served with hot peaches and golden-fried potatoes. This restaurant also has terrific barbecued ribs and a mighty fine pasta made with bacon, hot peppers, and white-wine sauce.

Millers Inn is a comfortable, soothing sort of place—Good beds, great food, and the rippling of Vasquez Creek to lull you to sleep.

How to get there: From I–70, take exit 232 onto Highway 40 and proceed west to Winter Park. Turn left onto Vasquex Road and drive for about 1 block. Inn is on right.

Woodspur Lodge
Winter Park, Colorado
80482

Innkeeper: Hank Kaseoru
Address/Telephone: 111 Hideaway Drive (mailing address: P.O. Box
  249); (303) 726–8417 or (800) 626–6562
Rooms: 30; all with private bath.
Rates: $35 single, $48 double, during summer; includes continental
  breakfast. $65 single, $100 double, during winter; MAP. Special
  rates for groups and children (latter under 5 stay free). Reduced
  rates for off-season. Best to phone. All accommodations are by reservation only. No pets. TV in common rooms only. No air conditioning (not needed; elevation 9,200 feet). No smoking in dining
  room. MasterCard and Visa accepted.
Open: All year.
Facilities and Activities: Bar. Hot tub, Jacuzzi, sauna; recreation room,
  ski storage, van shuttle service. Nearby: restaurants, shopping; hiking, fishing, tennis, racquetball, golf, biking, horseback riding,
  white-water rafting, jeep tours, alpine slide, excellent downhill and
  cross-country skiing, snow tubing, ice skating, snowmobiling, sleigh
  rides.

If you come to the Woodspur during the winter, you are in
for a special treat. ☞ The inn has its own groomed tubing hill. It
is even lit for nighttime tubing and has two lifts, tubes to rent,

and a warming hut with fireplace. For those of you, like me, who haven't learned to stay standing up while sliding downhill on two oversized popsicle sticks, tubing just may be the answer.

Summertime is great here, too, with wilderness trails to hike and mountain streams to fish.

Hank hails from the Estonia section of Russia and is dedicated to his guests' needs and pleasures. He is always familiar with what is going on in the area and willingly makes guest reservations and arrangements for regional activities.

☛ Meals are "all-you-can-eat," served buffet style. Chef Hoppy Hayes makes a terrific breakfast entrée that she calls eggs Woodspur. These are delicate pastry shells filled to the top with eggs, artichoke hearts, crabmeat, and hollandaise sauce. Another of her specialties is honey-butter chicken, baked in, and basted with, a delicious honey-butter sauce and served with rice and vegetables. Hoppy makes all of the breads, pastries, and desserts from scratch, and every dinner includes homemade soup and an extensive salad bar set up in an ice-filled, claw-footed bathtub.

The guest rooms are pine paneled and nicely furnished with either queen- or king-size beds or bunks. Many have magnificent views of the mountains as well.

Antique gaslights and old railroad signal lights illuminate the sitting room, where soft couches are gathered around the freestanding fireplace. Downstairs, the guest bar features rustic wood pillars and walls, a stone fireplace, piano, and television.

The outdoor hot tub is available until 11:00 P.M., and I can think of no better way to appreciate the stars than to sit in that tub about 10 o'clock at night with a glass of wine and good company.

How to get there: From I–70, take exit 232 north onto Highway 40 and proceed to Winter Park. Turn left onto Vasquez and drive for ½ mile, cross the railroad tracks, and turn right onto Hideaway Drive. Inn is up the hill, on the right.

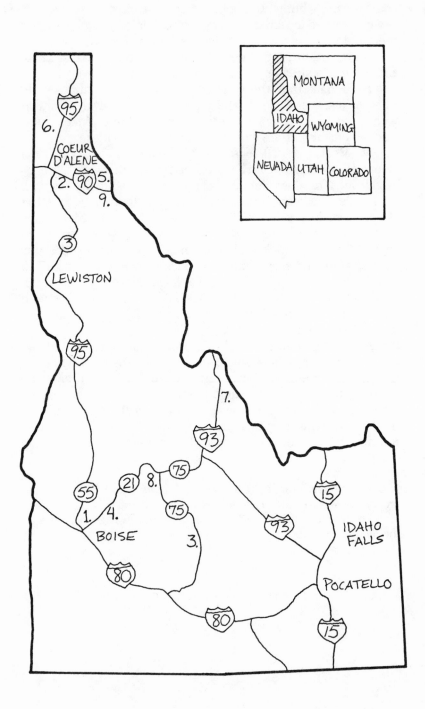

Idaho

Numbers on map refer to towns numbered below.

1. Boise, The Idanha 148
2. Coeur d'Alene,
    The Blackwell House 150
    Cricket on the Hearth....................................152
    The Gables..154
    Greenbriar Inn..156
3. Hailey, The Ellsworth Inn....................................158
4. Idaho City, Idaho City Hotel.................................160
5. Kellogg, Historic Dorsett House 162
6. Laclede, River Birch Farm....................................164
7. Salmon, Heritage Inn...166
8. Stanley, Idaho Rocky Mountain Ranch 168
9. Wallace, The Historic Jameson 170

147

The Idanha
Boise, Idaho
83702

Innkeeper: Ray Stattner
Address/Telephone: 928 Main Street; (208) 342–3611
Rooms: 76; all with private bath.
Rates: $49 to $79, single or double; $95 to $145 suites. Includes continental breakfast. No pets. All major credit cards accepted.
Open: All year.
Facilities and Activities: In house: restaurants, lounge, bar, hairstyling salon, complimentary 1948-Packard-limousine service, access to fitness facilities. Nearby: state capitol, Boise State University, Boise Tour Train, Old Idaho Penitentiary, philharmonic orchestra, opera, ballet, theater, museums, art galleries, parks, zoo. Golf, tennis, jogging, biking, hiking, fishing, downhill and cross-country skiing.

This red-brick, ivory-turreted chateau is ☞ the sort of place you might hope to find in the French countryside. But in the middle of a bustling city in southern Idaho? Astounding!

When it was opened in 1901, it was the state's largest building and the grandest and most expensive hotel in town. It has had many distinguished guests over the years, including Pablo Casals, Ethel Barrymore, and Clarence Darrow.

Idanha is said to be an Indian word meaning "healing waters"; if so, the hotel is well named because a stay here is indeed "healing," in the sense that it is relaxing, comforting, and restful. ☞ To climb the marble steps and enter the beautifully restored lobby is to find the grace and charm of a time long past. ☞ An Art Deco chandelier from New York's famed Astor Hotel glistens from the ceiling, and the room is softly lit by circa-1896 brass statue lamps. The Sun Room is off to one side, and it is here that complimentary sweet rolls, orange juice, coffee, and the daily paper await guests in the morning.

At the opposite end of the lobby is ☞ Peter Schott's Continental Restaurant, sophisticated in Old World style, where Austrian-born Schott, along with Chef Othmar Markt, also from Austria, present ☞ fine gourmet dining amid white linen-over-lace tablecloths and bouquets of red carnations. Black-tied waiters brought me an unforgettable meal of French wine, filet of beef Madagascar, and fresh blueberries Grand Marnier over French-vanilla ice cream. Hot, damp towels for your hands, a French-speaking sommelier, candlelight, and chamber music—truly memorable.

Following dinner and a walk to the nearby state-capitol grounds, I ascended to my castle chamber, commonly known as Room 312. It has a king-size brass bed, elegant writing desk, and, best of all ☞ a tiny sitting area located in the turret with a half circle of lace-covered windows that catch the morning sun. I was reminded of Tennyson's "Elaine the fair . . . Elaine the lily maid of Astolat, high in her chamber up a tower to the East . . ." ☞ It is easy to feel like a princess while sitting in your own private tower and savoring that first cup of morning coffee. When you go, do ask for a turret room.

How to get there: From I-84, take City Center Exit. The hotel is a Boise landmark, easy to spot, on the corner of Tenth and Main streets in the center of the business district.

The Blackwell House
Coeur d'Alene, Idaho
83814

Innkeepers: Kathleen Sims and Elizabeth Hoy
Address/Telephone: 820 Sherman Avenue; (208) 664–0656
Rooms: 8, including 3 suites; suites have private bath; 5 rooms share 2
    baths.
Rates: $40 to $75, single; $45 to $75, double. Includes continental-plus
    breakfast. No pets. TV in TV room only. No air conditioning (not
    needed; nights are usually cool year-round). No cigars or pipes.
    Well-behaved children over age 12 only, please. MasterCard and
    Visa accepted
Open: All year.
Facilities and Activities: Catered dinners available. BYOB. Complimen-
    tary coffee, tea, and cookies or wine and snacks. Music room with
    grand piano. Large yard with gazebo and barbecue. Champagne in
    room for special occasions. Within walking distance to downtown.
    Nearby: Lake Coeur d'Alene, "World's Longest Floating Boardwalk,"
    Tubb's Hill nature trails. Shopping, restaurants; hiking, fishing,
    boating, bicycling, downhill and cross-country skiing, snowmobil-
    ing.

People passing by with no intention of spending the night
cannot resist ringing the doorbell and asking if they can see the
interior of this stately mansion. From the perfectly appointed

parlor to the music room with its 🖙 rosewood grand piano, from the sweeping staircase to the upper floors of absolutely 🖙 picture-perfect guest rooms, this inn is a designer's showcase.

Built by F. A. Blackwell in 1904 as a wedding gift for his son, this magnificent, three-story structure was allowed to deteriorate over the years to the point that, when Kathleen bought it in 1982, it took nine months, one hundred gallons of paint remover, 282 rolls of wallpaper, nineteen tons of sod, and unmeasured amounts of laughter and tears to help bring it around to the masterpiece it is today.

Breakfast is served in the Garden Room, where 🖙 French doors open out onto the patio and spacious lawns. A fire in the fireplace removes the early-morning chill, freshly ground hazelnut coffee warms the tummy, large bowls of fruit center the round, cloth-covered tables, and baskets of huckleberry muffins soon appear hot from the oven. 🖙 Dinner can be catered for two to twenty-five guests and is served in the formal dining room.

The second-floor Blackwell Suite is a pink-and-white dream with oak-spool bed; white wicker settee, table, and chairs; white ruffled curtains with pink tiebacks; white eyelet-trimmed comforter and bed ruffle; pink floral wallpaper; dusty-rose carpet; and 🖙 claw-footed bathtub sequestered in its own little alcove.

But, before you decide on this one, you must also see the former servants' quarters and children's playroom on the third floor. Smaller but ever so cozy, the three rooms share a sitting area with love seat, and they, like the others, are exquisitely decorated.

The hospitality here even extends to your friends, who are welcome to join you for late-afternoon tea and cookies or wine and munchies 🖙 If you haven't yet tried staying at country inns, The Blackwell House would be a great place to start.

How to get there: From city center, go east on Sherman Avenue (main street) for approximately 5 blocks. Inn is on the right.

Cricket on the Hearth
Coeur d'Alene, Idaho
83814

Innkeepers: Jeanne Biner and Vivien Willard
Address/Telephone: 1521 Lakeside Avenue: (208) 664–6926
Rooms: 3; 1 with private bath, 2 share bath.
Rates: $25 to $45, single; $35 to $55, double; EPB. No pets. Smoking in common rooms only. Well-behaved children only, please. Credit cards not accepted.
Open: All year.
Facilities and Activities: Dinner available if requested ahead. BYOB. Dry bar, sun deck, large yard; pool table, croquet, bicycles. Champagne for special occasions. Cookies and snacks. Nearby: Lake Coeur d'Alene, "World's Longest Floating Boardwalk," Tubb's Hill nature trails. Shopping, restaurants, live theater; hiking, fishing, boating, downhill and cross-country skiing, snowmobiling.

Finding a cricket on your hearth is said to be a sign of hospitality and good fortune. Well, I've seen those little critters, and I think I'll settle for the brass variety on Jeanne and Vivien's fireplace hearth.

These two sisters are a perfect innkeeping team, and 🖝 staying here is truly an adventure. The guest rooms are individually designed, and each offers a completely different atmosphere.

In the Geisha Room, ☛ you are magically transported to a lovely villa in the countryside of Japan via the teakwood bed, red-and-black oriental comforter, black-enameled breakfast tray, and black-and-white *shoji* screen. A paper-moon lantern hangs overhead, and an oriental rug covers the floor of the private bath.

Upstairs, ☛ the Casa Blanca Room is another exquisitely decorated fantasy room, with two peacock chairs in a dormer-window alcove and king-size water bed. The Blue Room is smaller, but oh, so cozy with an antique bed and shaving stand and shuttered dormer window. These two rooms share a most unusual little bathroom snuggled under the eaves and a small sitting room perfect for reading.

Breakfast is part of the fun because you never know where you will be seated. Sometimes it's the formal dining room, but it might be on the deck, in the game room, or at the umbrella table in the garden. You will find fresh-squeezed orange juice, just-ground coffee, perhaps a hot apple crêpe, fruit, and an inventive egg dish or maybe Belgian waffles.

I recommend that you reserve ahead for dinner. Not only is the food excellently prepared, it is presented in a marvelously creative fashion. ☛ You might sit on pillows under a Japanese umbrella and cook morsels of chicken, mushrooms, steak, and shrimp over a miniature grill before dipping them in a variety of sauces. Or, in winter, Jeanne and Vivien might serve a ☛ Swiss *reclette* supper before the fire. They also offer an old-fashioned barbecue and picnic lunches, and they will even prepare your catch for the lucky fisherfolk among you.

I'm not convinced that we can give Mr. Cricket all the credit, but this is definitely a hospitable inn, and it will be your good fortune, indeed, if you plan a stay here.

How to get there: From Sherman Avenue (main street), turn north onto 16th Street and proceed 1 block to Lakeside. Inn is on the corner.

The Gables
Coeur d'Alene, Idaho
83814

Innkeepers: Gil and Elizabeth Shadwick
Address/Telephone: 916 Foster Avenue: (208) 664–5121, (800) 325–
    8049 Monday through Friday
Rooms: 3 share 1 bath.
Rates: $35 to $40, single; $45, double. Includes continental breakfast.
    No pets. No air conditioning (not needed; nights are usually cool
    year-round). Smoking on deck only. Well-behaved older children
    only, please. MasterCard and Visa accepted.
Open; February 1 through November 30.
Facilities and Activities: BYOB. Small library, piano, bicycles, compli-
    mentary refreshments; transportation arranged to and from airport,
    ski slopes, and points of interest. Nearby: Lake Coeur d'Alene,
    "World's Longest Floating Boardwalk," Tubb's Hill nature trails.
    Shopping, restaurants; hiking, fishing, boating, downhill and cross-
    country skiing, snowmobiling.

Secret rooms, secret gardens, secret hiding places—there's
always something so intriguing about anything secret.

When Gil was doing some remodeling on the second floor
several years ago, he discovered 🖙 a secret room that had been
sealed off for more than fifty years. A light hung from the ceiling,

a baseball and glove and documents dating from 1898 to 1908 lay on the floor, and an unsmoked cigar wrapped in a 1916 newspaper was stuffed into the rafters. He and Elizabeth installed a window, carpeted the floor, and furnished the tiny room with dolls, doll bed, and highchair, thus transforming it into a playhouse for their grandchildren.

Now that the grandchildren are beyond the doll-playing age, ☞ the playhouse has become an irresistible addition to one of the guest chambers. This guest room has twin beds, a 125-year-old rocker, and an antique, black iron crib. The playhouse is entered by crawling through a low-ceilinged passageway leading from this guest room, and I defy anyone spending the night in this particular room not to be absolutely compelled to enter the small hideaway and, for a little while, feel exactly like Alice in Wonderland.

All guest rooms are done in pleasing colors with antique furnishings and lovely bedspreads. There is a large deck off the kitchen where you can relax with a fresh lemonade or iced tea, and guests are welcome in the tastefully appointed living room and television room with fireplace.

Breakfast, served under a crystal-teardrop chandelier in the dining room, consists of home-baked rhubarb, blueberry or huckleberry muffins, fresh Idaho honey, and endless cups of coffee. If you are into china dishes and Depression glass, you will want to spend hours in this room admiring the treasures in Elizabeth's china closets.

There are many restaurants just a few blocks away. The Shadwicks especially recommend The Cedars on Lake Coeur d'Alene, a floating restaurant specializing in prime rib.

Innkeeping comes naturally to Gil and Elizabeth. Over the years they have had many, many house guests and have now extended their hospitality to include you and me. Elizabeth told me, ☞ "We treat our guests the same way we do our friends." It's true, and they have a guest book filled with nice comments to prove it.

How to get there: From midtown, go east on Sherman (Coeur d'Alene's main street) to 9th. Go north on 9th for 6 blocks to Foster. Turn right onto Foster. Inn is on the right.

Greenbriar Inn
Coeur d'Alene, Idaho
83814

Innkeepers: Kris and Bob McIlvenna
Address/Telephone: 315 Wallace Street; (208) 667–9660
Rooms: 7; 2 with private bath, 5 share 3 baths.
Rates: $25 to $44, single; $25 to $49, double. Includes continental breakfast. Add $5 per person for full gourmet breakfast. No pets. No air conditioning, but ceiling fans in all rooms. Window and portable fans available. TV in TV room only. No smoking. Well-behaved children only, please. MasterCard, Visa, American Express accepted.
Open: All year.
Facilities and Activities: Complimentary 4:00 P.M. high tea with sweets upon request or bedtime snack. Hot tub. Baby-sitting service by advance arrangement. Canoe and bike rentals. Romance weekends with flowers, champagne, and breakfast in bed. Dinner, hay and sleigh rides, dinner/theater packages for groups. Nearby: 4 blocks from downtown and 4 blocks from Lake Coeur d'Alene. Golf courses, hiking, fishing, horseback riding, swimming, water skiing, sailing, downhill and cross-country skiing, snowmobiling.

Perhaps the next best thing to waking up in Dublin or Killarney would be starting your day all snug under one of the Greenbriar's 🖝 down comforters imported directly from Ireland

Add to this pure-linen pillow cases; a hand-crocheted, fisherman's-weave coverlet; and sunlight filtering through white, gossamer curtains, and you might just take Kris up on her offer of a continental breakfast in bed.

However tempting that offer was, I padded down the stairs to the dining room where ☛ a truly gourmet, four-course breakfast awaited me. First came a goblet of cranberry juice with frozen-juice ice cubes, coffee, and an artistically designed fresh-fruit plate. Next, it was eggs, chives, and Swiss cheese in a puff pastry, followed by a raisin tart spread with strawberry jam. Kris mentioned one guest who stayed for four weeks, and she didn't serve him the same breakfast twice. Now, that's what I call creative cooking!

If you plan to take advantage of the many outdoor activities in and near this attractive city, I recommend you make arrangements to have Kris pack you one of her box lunches. She has a menu to choose from and is open to suggestions as well. She also will serve dinners for groups of eight or more.

There is a stack of menus from local restaurants on a shelf in the library. I chose the Osprey, overlooking the Spokane River. Known for its seafood, it also has many beef, chicken, and veal dishes.

This staunch, red-brick inn has had a diversified past. Built in 1908 as a boarding house, it later served as a brothel, a bookie joint, a sanctuary for nuns belonging to a radical offshoot of Catholicism, and an office building. It is now one of the finest country inns in Idaho.

How to get there: From I-90, take Northwest Boulevard exit onto Sherman Street. Turn north onto 4th Street, then onto Wallace. The inn is between 3rd and 4th, on Wallace.

The Ellsworth Inn
Hailey, Idaho
83333

Innkeeper: Sonja Tarnay

Address/Telephone: 715 Third Avenue South (mailing address: P.O. Box 1253); (208) 788–2298

Rooms: 8; all with private bath.

Rates: $55 to $85, single or double; EPB. Well-behaved pets considered. TV in library only. No air conditioning (usually not needed; elevation 5,000 feet). No smoking permitted inside inn. Well-behaved children considered. MasterCard and Visa accepted.

Open: All year except from May 1 to mid-June and from October 1 to mid-November.

Facilities and Activities: Champagne, sherry, and white wine only alcohol permitted. Nearby: Sun Valley Ski Resort, Sawtooth National Forest. Hiking, fishing, horseback riding, tennis, swimming, downhill and cross-country skiing, ice skating.

For quilt fanciers, The Ellsworth Inn is a patchwork paradise. 🖝 Sonja, an internationally known quilter and quilt designer, has been collecting, designing, and stitching masterpieces for more than thirty years. Every bed has one, of course, and the walls are honored with them as well.

Room number five glows with its peach and brown quilt,

dusty-apricot carpet, and pale peach walls. The pattern in the pierced-tin lamps matches that in the quilt, and the stencils on the bathroom vanity are the same design as that in the sofa cover. Lots of attention is given to detail in this inn.

During my visit, I got in on a christening of sorts. Previously, the suite on the second floor was simply referred to as Room 4. But because of special guests—Idaho's Governor and Mrs. John Evans, who had spent the previous night in the suite—it became from that day forth the Governor's Suite.

And fit for a governor it is. The brick fireplace and golden-fir floors in the sitting room, huge tub in the old-fashioned bathroom, antique writing desk, and king-size bed made this corner chamber a special treasure.

The large first-floor parlor and pleasantly small library, each with fireplace, are both popular meeting places for guests. The dining room features an antique oak English officers table, which is set with china, crystal, old silver, and handmade starched and ironed napkins.

Sonja's pastry chef creates marvelous breads and cinnamon rolls. Other breakfast treats include fresh fruits in season and a terrific crab soufflé. Gurney's Restaurant, just down the street, serves a seafood lasagna that is unique. Instead of the usual tomato sauce and beef, this one has noodles layered with crab, shrimp, spinach, and lots of cheese. Gurney's also makes its own soups and desserts.

The Ellsworth sits on two acres of ground, separated from the road by tall trees and a circular driveway. A wide veranda skirts two sides of the building, and for privacy, there is a lovely lattice-work gazebo covered with honeysuckle vines and currant bushes.

How to get there: From I-84 at Twin Falls, take Highway 93 north to Shoshone. At Shoshone, take Highway 75 north to Hailey. Turn right onto Third Avenue South and proceed two blocks. Inn is on the right.

❀

D: *The Ellsworth Inn was recently awarded a Four-Diamond rating by the AAA.*

Idaho City Hotel
Idaho City, Idaho
83631

Innkeepers: Don and Pat Campbell
Address/Telephone: P.O. Box 70; (208) 392–4290
Rooms: 5; all with private bath.
Rates: $24, single; $26, double; $34 for lodging, breakfast, and activity
 package for two; EP. Pets permitted. No air conditioning (not usually needed; elevation 4,000 feet). MasterCard, Visa, American Express accepted.
Open: All year.
Facilities and Activities: No meals served, but restaurants one block
 away. BYOB. Located in center of 1860s mining town designated as
 a National Historic Site. Gift shop. Nearby: Historic buildings, shopping, restaurants. Boise National Forest, Sawtooth National Recreation Area, ghost towns, hot springs, hiking, great fishing, snow
 tubing, cross-country skiing, snowmobiling.

 I expected any minute to see the likes of John Wayne jump
from the upstairs veranda, land on the back of his faithful steed,
and ride off into the sunset. That's how authentically Old West
this little hotel is.
 Built in the 1920s, it is really the "new kid on the block"
compared with its circa-1860 neighbors. The guest rooms are

furnished with white iron beds and antique oak dressers. Room 4 is especially nice, with its ornate bed, ruffled curtains, satin bedspread, and super-large, oak-fixtured bathroom. Mickey the shaggy dog is usually flopped on the front porch; tame ducks frequent the creek out back; and there are five cats that, if invited, will sleep with you.

Don and Pat offer ☞ a package deal that just could be the deal of a lifetime. It includes overnight lodging for two, breakfast at Calamity Jayne's café, passes to the geothermally heated warm-springs pools, admission to the local museum, 10 percent off at the hotel's gift shop, discount coupons for local restaurants, free sarsaparilla at the Sarsaparilla Parlor, and 2-for-1 drinks at Idaho City saloons. The cost? $34 for two!

A rip-snorting gold camp during the 1860s and, for a short time, the largest city in the Pacific Northwest, with more than 6,000 residents, 5,691 of them men, Idaho City is still the county seat of Boise County and remains a nonglitzy, educational, historic site. A self-guided walking tour encompasses eighteen buildings, sixteen of which were built before the turn of the century. These include a hand-hewn 1864 jail, a former schoolhouse, the newspaper office, and Idaho's oldest existing mercantile store.

A variety of gift shops, an ice-cream parlor, and several restaurants and saloons line the boardwalks and dirt streets. I recommend the Golden Nugget for hefty steaks and homemade pies. Or you might try Diamond Lil's for prime rib.

How to get there: From I–84 at Boise, go north on Highway 21 for 38 miles to Idaho City. From Main Street, turn left onto Walulla and drive one block. Hotel is on the corner of Walulla and Montgomery streets.

⌒

D: *To really capture the mood of this once rollicking (and risky!) town, walk up to Boot Hill Cemetery on West Hill. The burial spot contains approximately 200 graves, but local lore has it that only twenty hold those who died of natural causes!*

Historic Dorsett House
Kellogg, Idaho
83837

Innkeepers: Wayne and Joan Dorsett
Address/Telephone: 305 South Division Street; (208) 786–2311
Rooms: 10 share 3 baths.
Rates: $22.50, single; $27.50, double; EPB. No pets. No air condition-
ing. No TV. MasterCard and Visa accepted.
Open: All year.
Facilities and Activities: Full-service restaurant. BYOB. Innkeepers well
versed in area attractions. Nearby: excellent fishing, hiking, boat-
ing, river rafting, golf, gold panning, downhill skiing, snowmobiling.
Municipal swimming pool, District Mine Museum, silver-mine tour,
Old Mission Church at Cataldo.

As you enter the Historic Dorsett House, you are apt to be
met by innkeeper Wayne Dorsett wearing a tall chef's hat and a
big broad smile. Neither the hat nor the grin are just for looks.
The friendliness is genuine; and, after a terrific dinner of butter
basted, stream-salmon steak, a glass of wine, and homemade
custard pie, I was convinced that the cook's hat was also for real.

The Dorsett, a large, three-story structure, was built in 1912
as a boarding house for miners. Later it became a rooming house,
and now, 🖝 the only inn of its kind remaining in the area, it

162

houses an excellent dining facility and offers nine large sleeping rooms.

The furnishings are eclectic. Each guest room has an antique dresser, replica press-back chairs, and various modern pieces. The styles and décor may seem a rather odd mix, but the rooms are squeaky clean, comfortable, and very affordable.

My room had a king-size bed along with a twin bed, a writing desk, an old oak chest of drawers, and two baths right around the corner.

There are two sitting areas on the second floor and another on the third, each with books, magazines, and pamphlets with regional information. There is a total of three baths, two with showers and one with a claw-footed tub.

Be sure to notice the imported crystal chandelier in the dining room. It is original to the house and, along with the antique grand piano, contributes a quality of elegance to the turn-of-the-century-style eating area.

I was given a choice of breakfast items and chose one of Wayne's hot-from-the-oven cinnamon rolls. Never have I tasted better. It was nearly as large as a dinner plate but so light and fluffy, it disappeared without leaving a trace of a crumb. Yes, Wayne definitely wears his chef's hat for good reason.

How to get there: From I–90, take Exit 51 onto Division Street. Go south for ½ mile. Inn is on the left.

＊

D: *In the library, I found an intriguing book called* Jody, *written by Los Angeles Times travel editor Jerry Hulse. I was unable to find time to read it during my stay, so Wayne let me take it along, to be returned when I had finished with it. Such is the hospitality of the Dorsett House!*

River Birch Farm
Laclede, Idaho
83841

Innkeepers: Stacy, Linda, and Rick Cox
Address/Telephone: (P.O. Box 87); (208) 263–4033
Rooms: 3 plus loft share 2 baths.
Rates: $40 single or double; $60, room with loft; EPB. Dog kennel for
    dogs, not allowed out of kennel. No other pets. TV in TV room only.
    No air conditioning. No smoking inside building. Children over 12
    years welcome. MasterCard and Visa accepted.
Open: All year.
Facilities and Activities: BYOB. Package available includes 2 nights
    lodging, float trip, huge picnic lunch, and dinner. No charge for use
    of rowboat and canoe. Nearby: fishing, hiking, hayrides, sleigh rides,
    boating, river rafting, downhill and cross-country skiing.

I'll take a wake-up call from a rooster rather than an alarm
clock any day!

When I was a child, I spent part of each summer visiting my
Aunt Amanda and Uncle Oscar Halgren's farm in Mt. Vernon,
Washington. The River Birch Farm brought back wonderful
memories for me.

Built in 1903, the old farmhouse has since been refurbished
into a first-class inn without sacrificing any of its country charm.

The upstairs bedrooms are tucked under sloped ceilings and feature earthtone carpets, comforters, and small-print wallpapers. The shared bath has a large, step-up, oval tub, romantically draped in ruffles and lace.

A farm-style (and farmer-sized!) breakfast is served in the dining room or on the deck. If you like, ☞ you can gather your own eggs (provided you can convince the hens to share with you). Breakfast fare includes an egg dish; bacon, ham, or sausage; huckleberry pancakes; and, sometimes, pan-fried trout.

For dinner, which is actually an event, by all means go to the Wikel House, only eight miles away in Priest River. The proprietress serves a ☞ seven-course, two-and-a-half-hour, three entrée, gourmet dinner in her own home, including chateaubriand, duck à l'orange, and chicken cordon bleu. Linda or Stacy will make reservations for you. They will also arrange float trips, hayrides, and sleigh rides. Rick, who writes and publishes short stories under the name of Dakota Bear, will delight in telling you tall tales by the fire.

And then there are ☞ the animals: a dog, a cat, chickens, pigs, and cattle. I took a walk through the small orchard of apple, cherry, plum, and peach trees, past a pen of chattering chickens, and found a precocious, nine-day-old, black-and-white calf that insisted on nibbling on my jacket, my notebook, and my shoes. Of course, I could have stepped back, but then I wouldn't have been able to pet his soft, fuzzy coat and gently scratch his ears and look deep into those beautiful brown eyes. I definitely like farms.

How to get there: From Sandpoint, take Highway 2 west. River Birch Farm is on the left, just before Laclede.

Heritage Inn
Salmon, Idaho
83467

Innkeeper: Audrey Nichols
Address/Telephone: 510 Lena Street: (208) 756–3174
Rooms: 5 share 2 baths.
Rates: $18, single; $20 to $35, double. Includes continental-plus breakfast. No pets. TV in parlor only. Some rooms are air conditioned. Smoking on sun porch only. MasterCard and Visa accepted.
Open: All year.
Facilities and Activities: BYOB. Fresh flowers in rooms during summer. Quiet neighborhood. Nearby: restaurants, shopping, ghost towns, municipal swimming pool, hiking, excellent fishing, great river rafting, boating, golf, bowling, downhill and cross-country skiing, snowmobiling.

Don't let the low rates fool you. This is ☛ one of the loveliest small inns with the friendliest of innkeepers you will find anywhere. Salmon is a little off the beaten track, which is a definite plus in my mind, and the ☛ natural treasures in this part of the state are an unintentional secret. If you like small towns with lots of area activities, you ought to swing by Salmon and discover the Heritage Inn for yourself.

Built in 1888, this brick Victorian was first used as lodging and storage for the stagecoach line. Audrey has given it back its dignity, restoring it to the quiet elegance it deserves and filling it with precious antiques. From the parlor, with its bay window, pump organ, and unusually ornate Victorian settee, to the cheerful dining room and charming guest rooms, this has to be one of my favorite inns.

Audrey is the 🖙 type of innkeeper who loans you her iron, her ironing board, and her car vacuum and is apt to send you on your way with a bunch of daisies from her garden. She is always 🖙 cheerful, accommodating, a good listener, and a willing friend, and I wish she lived next door to me. But that would be Salmon's loss. Audrey was born here, and the townsfolk think so much of her, they periodically checked on the renovation of the inn during its restoration and threw a grand surprise party for her when the last starched curtain was hung.

Breakfast is served on 🖙 antique, gold-embossed, Victorian china either in the formal dining room or on the sun porch. Audrey has a marvelous old recipe for bran, date, and nut muffins and willingly pours you endless cups of coffee. Add to this orange juice and, in season, fresh raspberries and cream, and you have a terrific beginning to your day. The inn is located only two blocks from Main Street and many restaurants. I suggest you try the Salmon River Inn for good sandwiches and homemade pies. For an excellent prime rib, try the Shady Nook.

How to get there: At the corner of Main and Church streets, turn south and proceed 2 blocks, then turn right onto Lena Street and drive 1½ blocks. Inn is on the right.

ఌ

D: *Since my notes mention "clean" three times, plus "spotless" and "trim and tidy," I would be remiss if I didn't tell you that this inn absolutely shimmers with cleanliness.*

Idaho Rocky Mountain Ranch
Stanley, Idaho
83278

Innkeepers: Jerry and Joyce Hollander
Address/Telephone: HC64 P.O. Box 9934; (208) 774–3544
Rooms: 16; 3 in lodge, 13 cabin accommodations; all have private bath.
Rates: $40 to $44, single or double, in lodge; $48 to $55, single or
   double, in cabins; EP. No pets. Horses boarded for $3 per day.
   Wheelchair accessible (rough ground, best to reserve lodge room or
   cabin close to lodge). No TV. No air conditioning (not needed; el-
   evation 6,900 feet). No smoking in dining room. MasterCard and
   Visa accepted.
Open: Mid-June to mid-September.
Facilities and Activities: Breakfast, dinner, generous sack lunches
   available. Lounge. Stocked lake, Salmon River on property, hot
   springs–fed swimming pool. Nearby: ghost towns, guided horseback rides, raft trips and white-water rafting, hiking, fishing.

   History and adventure surround the site where this ranch
stands. If it had existed in 1805, guests enjoying their breakfast
on the wide front veranda would have seen Lewis and Clark pass
by only a few yards from where they sat. In 1880, thousands of
gold seekers thronged along the Yankee Fork of the Salmon River,

168

just north of the ranch location. Nearby are the 🖝 ghost towns of Bonanza and Custer, once riotous gold-rush camps.

The ranch remains almost the same today as it was when first 🖝 built as an exclusive hunting lodge more than fifty-five years ago—the walls are chinked log; 🖝 the furniture, from the pole beds and desks to the rush-plaited rockers, is all handmade of indigenous woods; even the original monogrammed china is still used in the dining room.

The attractively furnished lodge rooms have lofts and oakly stone showers; the delightfully pioneerlike cabins have separate dressing rooms, stone showers, fireplaces, and constantly replenished wood piles.

The menu is extensive and moderately priced. For breakfast, you might like a freshly baked scone soaked in strawberry butter and a fluffy ham-and-mushroom omelet. My recommendation for dinner is the tasty trout *meuniere,* a grilled 10-ounce Idaho trout sauced with lemon, parsley, butter, and pecans. You definitely must try the house dessert, a honey-walnut tart all caramelly with a layer of rich chocolate on top.

Be sure, just once, to 🖝 get up at sunrise and watch the crest of the rugged Sawtooth Mountain Range turn glorious pink and rose. It is possible to climb to the highest peak; but if you're not up to a five-hour hike each way, try the fifteen-minute walk to the top of "Nob Hill" and 🖝 see the remains of the cabin where Zane Grey wrote several of his novels. This is a short climb amid sego lillies and wild daisies, and the reward is a breathtaking 360-degree view.

How to get there: From I-84, just east of Boise, turn north onto Highway 21 and proceed to Stanley. At Stanley, turn right (south) onto Highway 75 and drive 10 miles. Ranch is on the left.

❋

D: *After a day of hiking, horseback riding, or pulling trout from the river and stocked lake, slip into the hot springs–fed outdoor pool and watch the darkening sky blossom into a giant bouquet of shimmering stars.*

The Historic Jameson
Wallace, Idaho
83873

Innkeepers: Kay Calkins and Irene Graham
Address/Telephone: 6th and Pine Streets; (208) 556–1554
Rooms: 6 share 2 shower rooms and 2 water closets.
Rates: $32.50, single; $35.50, double. Includes continental breakfast.
   No pets. TV in lounge only. MasterCard and Visa accepted.
Open: All year.
Facilities and Activities: Full-service restaurant; saloon. Complimentary coffee, tea, juice, snacks in the evening. Complimentary champagne for special occasions. Reduced-cost passes to full-service gym, weight room, sauna, Jacuzzi across the street from inn. Nearby: silver-mine tour, Old Mission Church at Cataldo, melodrama theater, museum, shopping; no-charge municipal swimming pool, excellent fishing, hiking, boating, river rafting, golf, gold panning, downhill skiing, snowmobiling.

   This one would be very easy to miss, and that would be a real shame. The vintage 1908, red-brick building sits on a corner amid the business district of this small mining town, looking, perhaps, like a nice place to down a few and have lunch or dinner. But there's more here than meets the eye, for, above the first-level restaurant and bar and the second-floor conference room, I found a 🖛 perfectly charming bed and breakfast inn.

As I climbed the stairs, the overhead skylight beamed down rays of sunshine, spreading a warm glow over the hallway and into the pretty guest rooms. And later, sitting peacefully in the small parlor, I forgot I was in the center of a bustling little town, because the only sound I heard was the comforting ticktock of the pendulum wall clock.

There is something 🖛 very English–country house about this light and airy inn. The guest rooms are furnished with beautiful antique pieces, many of which were attained from an old mansion in Seattle. Each room has an armoire, delightful miniature dresser, luggage rack, ceiling fan, and white-porcelain doorknob with hand-painted pink roses. The beds are all different, every one a gem. I especially liked the one in room eight with the little carved spools that move.

During the evening, it is particularly enjoyable to sit in the parlor and 🖛 listen to Irene tell stories about Wallace's "days gone by." She is a terrific source of information because she grew up in this friendly town of 1,800 inhabitants.

A continental breakfast of croissants, juice, and coffee is brought to the parlor, or you can have it in your room. You are entitled to a discounted full breakfast in the dining room, however, if that is your choice. There is an extensive menu, with eggs Benedict being a specialty. Or you might try the French toast with strawberries and German sausage. Dinner features chicken along with seafood, pasta, and steaks.

The Jameson Saloon is distinguished by a magnificently mirrored back bar and lots of polished brass. After dinner, I suggest you set a spell over a mug of the special Irish coffee, made with John Jameson's Irish Whiskey.

How to get there: The inn is on the corner of 6th and Pine streets, 1 block off the main street.

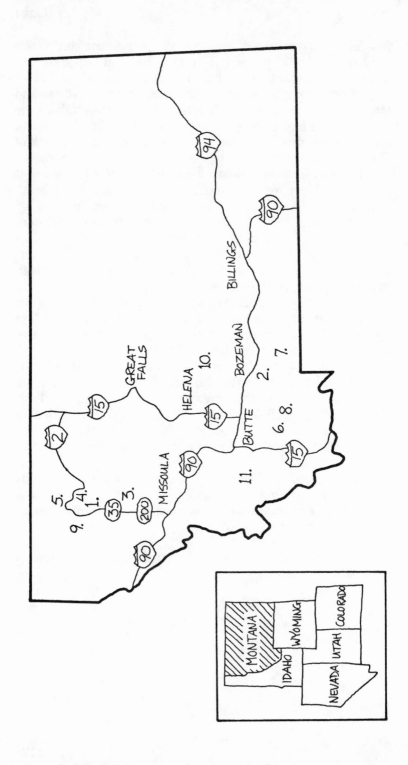

Montana

Numbers on map refer to towns numbered below.

1. Bigfork,
   Averill's Flathead Lake Lodge and Dude Ranch...........174
   Bigfork Inn 176
   O'Duach'ain Country Inn 178
2. Bozeman,
   Crosscut Ranch...180
   The Voss Inn 182
3. Condon, Holland Lake Lodge................................184
4. Essex, Izaak Walton Inn....................................186
5. Lake McDonald, Lake McDonald Lodge.......................188
6. Nevada City, Nevada City Hotel 190
7. Pray, Chico Hot Springs Lodge..............................192
8. Virginia City, Fairweather Inn..............................194
9. Whitefish, Duck Inn...196
10. White Sulphur Springs, The Foxwood Inn....................198
11. Wise River, Sundance Lodge Montana 200

Averill's Flathead Lake Lodge and Dude Ranch

Bigfork, Montana
59911

Innkeepers: Doug and Maureen Averill
Address/Telephone: P.O. Box 248; (406) 837–4391
Rooms: 19 in lodge, plus 16 cottages; all with private bath.
Rates: $763 per adult for 1 week (minimum) stay, double occupancy.
   Special rates for teens and children. All activities included in rate.
   AP. No pets. Wheelchair accessible. No TV. No air conditioning.
   Credit cards not accepted.
Open: May through September.
Facilities and Activities: Saddle Sore Saloon for setups. BYOB. Outdoor
   swimming pool, game room; laundry facilities. Horseback riding,
   breakfast rides, steak-fry rides, hayrides, tennis, hiking, fishing,
   swimming, boating, windsurfing, water skiing, sailing. Nearby:
   Glacier National Park, Swan River, white-water rafting, kayaking.

You don't normally expect a dude ranch to offer many water activities, but at this ranch, the lake provides as much pleasure as the trails and wilderness do.

The family-operated ☛ ranch covers 2,000 acres of sprawling lawns, tree-studded hillside, and remote mountain terrain and ☛ borders on the largest natural lake west of the Great Lakes.

The attractive lodge rooms have log-beamed ceilings and paneled walls, queen- and king-size beds, ruffled curtains, and writing desks. Some rooms have lofts and claw-footed bath tubs. Two- and three-bedroom cottages are also available.

Dining is family style in the large dining room. Long tables are spread with meat-and-potato-type meals that include soups made daily from fresh-from-the-garden vegetables; cheese breads, cinnamon breads, and all kinds of other breads baked in the ranch kitchen; homemade baked beans; 10-ounce steaks; barbecued ribs; and special brownies made from an old family recipe.

After breakfast, lunch, and dinner at this "chuckwagon," you'll be ready for some outdoor activities, and there is no end to things to do. You can participate in ranch chores, learn to rope, take rodeo instruction, help train the new crop of colts, or hit the trail for a long, leisurely ride.

Just about every water spot imaginable is available here, too, including fishing, swimming, sailing, water skiing, and ☛ cruising on the ranch's motorlaunch or fifty-one-foot sailboat.

This ranch is known nationwide, and 60 to 70 percent of its guests are returnees, so it's best to get your reservation in early. ☛ *Better Homes and Gardens* magazine twice named the ranch as the "Outstanding Family Vacation Spot" in the west; *Sunset* magazine featured it in its "Unique Vacations"; *Arco* magazine claims it to be one of the ten best ranches in America; and *Mobil Travel Guide* gave it a four-star rating. Not bad, I'd say.

How to get there: From Highway 35 in northwestern Montana, 1 mile south of Bigfork, turn west onto Flathead Lodge Road. Turn right at the stagecoach that sits beside the road. Inn is at the end of the trail.

D: *In addition to the horses, cows, chickens, steers, goats, cats, and dogs that live on the ranch, deer, bear, and bald eagles are often seen in the pastures or on the mountainside. The National Bison Range, harboring buffalo and elk, is only an hour away.*

Bigfork Inn
Bigfork, Montana
59911

Innkeepers: Bob and Suzie Keenan
Address/Telephone: 604 Electric Avenue (mailing address: P.O. Box
   697); (406) 837–6680
Rooms: 7; 2 with private bath, 5 share bath; all rooms have sink.
Rates: $20 to $30, single and double; EP. No pets. No TV. No air con-
   ditioning. No smoking in guest rooms. MasterCard, Visa, American
   Express accepted.
Open: All year.
Facilities and Activities: Dinner only meal served. Bar. Excellent loca-
   tion in active resort village. Nearby: Flathead Lake, Swan River,
   Glacier National Park, summer theater. Hiking, fishing, boating,
   water skiing, swimming, lake cruises, kayaking, tennis, golfing,
   mountain biking, downhill and cross-country skiing.

When the Bigfork Hotel burned to the ground in the harsh
winter of 1937, the main concern of the unemployed loggers who
were inside at the time was to save the beer. So, as the ashes
cooled, all owner Ernie O'Brien had left were several barrels of
frozen beer. Ernie was not one to give up easily, however, and,
although money was tight because of the Depression, he eventually managed to obtain financing and rebuild. The result was

a ☞ beautiful English Tudor, half-timbered structure that has become a Bigfork landmark and the center of community activities.

The upstairs guest rooms are inviting and simply but adequately furnished with a few antiques mixed with contemporary pieces. All rooms have sinks. ☞ When the local summer theater is in session, you are apt to share the facility with drama majors from around the country. The excitement of those involved rubs off on the other inn guests, and one can hardly wait to go to the evening's performance.

☞ Dinner at the inn is a gourmand's delight. Amidst muslin curtains, brown-and-white checkered tablecloths, and hanging baskets of flowering plants, you will be served some of the best-prepared food you could ever hope for. The inn also has ☞ three private-label wines, two from the Napa Valley and one from Washington State. The wine menu lists thirty-one additional varieties, too, both domestic and imported.

Ah, but let's get back to the food. The entrées run the gamut from beef, chicken, and seafood to pasta. ☞ By candlelight, with fresh wildflowers as a centerpiece, I had salmon, made especially moist and tender by being wrapped in parchment and cooked in butter sauce. A hot loaf of wheat sourdough bread, julienne carrots and zucchini, baked potato, and coffee ice cream Mud Pie completed this memorable meal. The inn's chef puts all his effort into dinners only, and it shows. As for breakfast and lunch, it's only a short walk down the street to either the Breadboard Bakery or the Grand Hotel.

Live Dixieland music rocks the inn's bar on Friday and Saturday evenings, and, whether you dance or simply tap your toes, you are sure to enjoy.

How to get there: Bigfork is on Highway 35 in northwestern Montana. Inn is located at north end of the main street, impossible to miss.

O'Duach'ain Country Inn
Bigfork, Montana
59911

Innkeepers: Tom and Margot Doohan
Address/Telephone: 675 Ferndale Drive; (406) 837–6851
Rooms: 5 share 2½ baths.
Rates: $35, single; $40 to $55, double; EPB. Pets allowed. TV, smoking, in sitting room only. No air conditioning. MasterCard and Visa accepted.
Open: All year.
Facilities and Activities: Gourmet box lunches if ordered ahead. Holiday dinners for inn guests only with advance reservations. Dry bar. BYOB. Hot tub. Area information, shuttle service to airport and lake. Nearby: Glacier National Park, National Bison Range, Historic Jesuit Mission, Bob Marshall Wilderness Area. Shopping, theater; hiking, fishing, sailing, boating, river rafting, golf, cross-country skiing.

Doesn't it feel good when innkeepers come out onto the front porch to greet you? That's the way it is here at the O'Duach'ain, and it is also friendship at first sight. Incidentally, O'Duach'ain is pronounced "oh doo *cane*" and is Gaelic for Doohan.

Both Tom and Margot are good conversationalists, and they are well versed on attractions in their area. They will make theater and dinner reservations and have a ☛ "Komfort Koach" luxury van in which they escort groups of three or more on day-long tours. These jaunts include a ☛ gourmet luncheon of croissants, cheeses, fruit, wine, and other beverages.

My first morning here, I arose and looked out of my garden-level window and came face to face with an inquisitive little guinea hen. Something tells me that she begins each day checking the lower-level guest-room windows to see just who's come to visit. All the animals are friendly, and, believe me, there is quite a menagerie! You'll find geese, ducks, peacocks, finches, parrots, cats, and dogs.

The large sitting room for guests has a stone fireplace, dry bar, VCR and television. The guest rooms are nicely furnished and have special touches such as ☛ satin-covered hangers, bathrobes for use at the outdoor hot tub, a bowl of fresh cherries during season (this is the sweet-cherry capital of the world), a jar of candies, decanters of ice water and sherry, and cookies at bedtime. All these goodies, and I haven't even told you about breakfast yet!

Lace cloth, linen napkins, crystal, silver, and china—then came breakfast Roscommen, named for a county in Ireland. The meal consisted of cranberry juice, cantaloupe, ☛ Irish soda bread, eggs scrambled with cream cheese and chives, potatoes with sausage, and bottomless cups of coffee.

The Doohans have five acres of land, and ☛ a wood borders their yard. I found a path through the trees and wandered onto a Christmas-tree farm. Of course, three Doohan dogs bounded on ahead of me. Well, Winston the English bulldog didn't exactly "bound." He sort of waddled and snortled along; but I couldn't have hoped for better company.

How to get there: From Highway 35, on east side of Flathead Lake and just south of Bigfork, take Highway 209 for about 5 miles to Ferndale Drive. Go north on Ferndale Drive. Inn is on the right.

Crosscut Ranch
Bozeman, Montana
59715

Innkeepers: Dale and Peggy Giem
Address/Telephone: 16025 Bridger Canyon Drive (mailing address: P.O. Box 398); (406) 587–3122
Rooms: 7; all with private bath.
Rates: $36, single or double, summer; $45, single or double, winter; EP. No pets. Wheelchair accessible. TV in TV room only. No air conditioning (not needed; elevation 6,200 feet). MasterCard, Visa, American Express accepted.
Open: All year.
Facilities ⌐nd Activities: Full-service dining room. Lounge. Sauna. Recreation and nature guides, on-site network of novice and professional running trails, hiking, fishing, frisbee "golf," hayrides, wildflower seeking, many photographic opportunities, cross-country skiing, sleigh rides. Nearby: Bridger Mountain Range, Lewis and Clark Caverns, blue-ribbon trout streams, excellent downhill skiing.

The Crosscut began as a military timber camp and sawmill in 1867 and was operated by the U.S. Army 2nd Cavalry Company to provide logs and lumber for the construction of Fort Ellis. ☛ One of the original cabins still stands and is used by ranch personnel.

The guest rooms are large, each with two queen-size beds, a fold-out couch, dressing-table area, and private bath. A shared television room is close by, and a redwood sauna awaits those with trail-weary muscles.

Meals are a special treat. Breakfast can be continental-plus, with huge (and I mean *colossal!*) pieces of homemade blueberry or rhubarb coffee cake, fresh fruit, orange juice, and coffee. Or you can have a traditional ranch-style breakfast of eggs, meat, and potatoes. If you plan to be on the trail at lunch time, Chef Robert Metzger will prepare a sack lunch for you.

☛ Dinners are truly gourmet, with an extensive and varied menu made all the more special because one normally doesn't expect the frills of exquisite cuisine on a ranch. I had Orange Roughy Pompadour: fillets of New Zealand Roughy breaded with Parmesan cheese and herbs, sautéed, and garnished with sauce choron. There is an excellent pastry chef on staff; my poppyseed pound cake with lemon icing was superb.

This ranch has made a ☛ dedicated and successful attempt to combine recreation with environmental appreciation. It offers fun-and-fitness activities along with miles of sightseeing, hiking, and backpacking terrain. A five-kilometer conditioning course, with periodic work-out stations, picnic areas, teepee resting spots, pedal-bike trails, senior walking paths, horseshoe pits, and an eighteen-hole frisbee-"golf" course are only a few of the many open-air amenities here. Dale, an experienced outdoorsman with a deep appreciation for the wonders of the environment, can direct you to the trails and activities that best meet your abilities and needs.

How to get there: From I–90 at Bozeman, take Highway 86 north for 16 miles. Watch for Crosscut Ranch sign on left.

The Voss Inn
Bozeman, Montana
59715

Innkeepers: Ken and Ruthmary Tonn
Address/Telephone: 319 South Willson; (406) 587–0982
Rooms: 6; all with private bath.
Rates: $40 to $50, single; $50 to $60, double; EPB. No pets. TV, smok-
ing, in parlor only. Some rooms have air conditioning; fans available
for others. Well-behaved children only, please. MasterCard and Visa
accepted.
Open: All year.
Facilities and Activities: BYOB. Complimentary nightcap. Nearby:
Lewis and Clark Caverns, Museum of the Rockies, Bridger Bowl
and Big Sky ski areas. Restaurants, shopping; hiking, fishing in
blue-ribbon trout stream, downhill and cross-country skiing.

As meticulously scrubbed, starched, pressed, and polished
as an Easter-morning Sunday School class, ☛ The Voss Inn exudes perfection. Antique beds, private sitting areas, breakfast
nooks, and bay windows all add to the charm of this stalwart,
red-brick Victorian. Every room I peeked into was captivating.
The Sartain Room on the main floor features a provocative tub
and bathing alcove; the front parlor is graced with an ornate,
etched-glass chandelier; the Chisholm Room boasts a magnifi-

cent nine-foot brass headboard; and flowered wallpaper banks the staircase leading to immaculate upstairs guest rooms. I entered my favorite, Robert's Roost, by descending three steps into a bright and cheerful garden of white wicker, deep-green walls sprinkled with tiny white blossoms, white ruffled curtains, and a private balcony. The bed, brass and iron, has a white-eyelet spread and is embellished with dark green, rose-flowered pillows. A miniature bottle of liqueur and two small glasses waited on the bedside table.

Ruthmary tiptoes upstairs and leaves early morning coffee and tea in the hallway. Then, a little later, she brings fresh fruit, orange juice, homemade cinnamon rolls and muffins, and wonderful egg-soufflé dishes to the hall buffet. She has twelve different breakfast entrées that she chooses from, and, even if you stay a week, you will not get a repeat performance. Breakfast is taken to tiny tables in the guest rooms, and that's a definite plus because you'll want to spend as much time as possible in your newly acquired hideaway.

For a variety of inexpensive lunch items, I recommend the Bacchus Pub, only a couple blocks from the inn. For dinner, the nearby Rocky Mountain Pasta Company features pasta extraordinaire. Even if you resort to the old standbys like pasta primavera, as I did, I think you will be pleased with the fine quality.

How to get there: From I–90, take exit 306 into Bozeman. Turn south onto North 7th Avenue, left onto Main Street, and proceed to South Willson. Go south on Willson for approx. 3½ blocks to the inn.

✵

D: *Breakfast rolls are kept hot in a uniquely styled bun warmer built into the circa-1880 upstairs radiator. This type of warming oven is rare, indeed, at least in this part of the country, and The Voss Inn's is only the second one I've seen in all my gypsying about.*

Holland Lake Lodge
Condon, Montana
59826

Innkeepers: Dick and Carole Schaeffer and Howard and Loris Uhl
Address/Telephone: Swan Valley SR, Box 2083; (406) 754–2282
Rooms: 9 in lodge share 2 baths. 5 cottages; all with private bath.
Rates: $30 for lodge rooms, $40 to $65 for cottages, single or double; EP.
  Pets permitted in cottages only. Dining room and 1 cottage are
  wheelchair accessible. No TV. No air conditioning. MasterCard and
  Visa accepted.
Open: All year.
Facilities and Activities: Full-service dining room. Bar Canoe, rowboat,
  aqua-cycle rentals. Volleyball, horseshoes, swimming, fishing, hik-
  ing, backpacking, horseback riding, cross-country skiing on
  groomed trails, snowshoeing, ice fishing, ice skating on lake.
  Nearby: Flathead National Forest, Bob Marshall Wilderness Area,
  Mission Mountain Wilderness.

On the edge of glacier-fed Holland Lake sits a circa-1920
log 🐾 lodge that becomes home the minute you walk through
the door and encounter the friendly innkeepers. Carole greeted
me with "Come in. This is our home, and we're so glad you're
here." And so was I.

The large main room has log walls and ceiling beams, red

carpet, freestanding wood stove, piano, and split-log stairs leading to the guest rooms on the second floor. Under the stairs a toy
box with crayons, color books, puzzles, and all sorts of treasures
waits to be discovered.

The guest rooms are ☞ rustic with a country flavor, very
inviting, and spotlessly clean. The cabins are also immaculate
and are snuggled in amongst tall trees.

Breakfast is a special time of day: A mist slowly rises off the
lake, the sun warms the tops of the Mission Mountains in the
distance, and a plate of delicious baking-powder biscuits, homemade gravy, and Canadian bacon provides energy for the day's
activities. There are many sandwich selections for lunch, including the lodge's famous (infamous?) "Gut Bomb," a half-pound
portion of ground beef, plus ham, bacon, cheese, fried egg, lettuce, tomato, pickle, and mayonnaise. A great idea on the day you
slept in and missed breakfast!

The dinner menu ranges from steaks and seafood to chicken
cordon blue and sweet-and-sour meatballs. Save room for the
inn's special Holland cake, a sour-cream cake smothered in
Kahlua-flavored whipped cream.

Dick and Carole and Howard and Loris were good friends
out in Oregon (Carole was a registered nurse specializing in
gerontology; Loris, a certified occupational-therapy assistant)
who decided to embark on a new adventure. It is amusing and
inspiring to listen to some of the obstacles they have overcome in
their successful attempt to make their inn ☞ a place to which
folks return year after year in order to reassure themselves that
there is more to life than daily routine.

How to get there: From I–90, just east of Missoula, take Highway 200
northeast to Highway 83. Go north on 83 to Condon, then east on Holland Lake Road for 4 miles to lodge.

᪣

*D: If I could spend a week here, I'd make friends with the
mules, hike around the lake, stretch out on a lawn chair at
the water's edge, and just read and snooze.*

Izaak Walton Inn
Essex, Montana
59916

Innkeepers: Larry and Lynda Vielleux
Address/Telephone: P.O. Box 653; (406) 888–5700
Rooms: 30; 9 with private bath, 21 share bath.
Rates: $30 to $40, single; $35 to $45, double; EP. No pets. No TV. No air conditioning (usually not needed; elevation 3,860 feet). MasterCard and Visa accepted but personal checks preferred.
Open: All year.
Facilities and Activities: Full-service dining room. Bar, sauna, laundromat. Amtrak flag stop # E.S.M., train activity, train memorabilia. Cross-country ski rentals. Nearby: Glacier National Park and Bob Marshall Wilderness Area, constituting more than a million acres of wilderness; fishing, hiking, horseback riding, rafting, wildlife viewing, photography, cross-country skiing.

☛ If you are a railroad bluff, you'll never find a more ideal inn. If you are not yet a train enthusiast and you choose to stay here, you may soon be a dyed-in-the-wool fan.

Built in 1939 to accommodate service crews for the Great Northern Railway, whose enormous task it was to keep the mountain track open during winter, the inn is still very much involved in the railroad business. It is here that "helper" engines hook onto lengthy freight trains and help push them over the Continental Divide. The inn is also a designated flag stop, with Amtrak passing through daily. If you decide to arrive via Amtrak, inn personnel will meet you at the platform to help with luggage.

Fifteen to twenty freight trains pass by the front door of the inn each day; and, whether resting in one of the charming guest rooms, playing volleyball in the playfield, or downing a few in the Flag Stop Bar, one is hard-pressed to keep from running outdoors like a kid to watch as the massive trains chug by.

The Izaak Walton is packed with signal lanterns, vintage photographs, and ☞ all sorts of train memorabilia. In the Dining Car Restaurant, you may be seated next to a striped-capped engineer from the train waiting out on the tracks or share a meal and spirited conversation with members of an international rail fan club.

Highlights of my stay at the Izaak Walton: a lovely room facing the train tracks, where, ☞ though engrossed in writing, I could not resist going to the window each time a train passed; a scrumptious, light, and fluffy breakfast crêpe filled to overflowing with huckleberries; a dinner of honey-glazed chicken sautéed with orange slices and onions; ☞ the sighting of whole families of shaggy, beautiful mountain goats zigzagging their way down the hillside to a salt lick; and ☞ spotting a yearling bear cub peacefully munching his way along the side of the road.

How to get there: Inn is ½ mile off of Highway 2, on southern rim of Glacier National Park between East and West Glacier. Watch for sign for Essex turnoff.

*

D: *Wildlife photographers can have the time of their lives here: black bears, mountain lions, mountain goats, 100,000 spawning salmon, and, from early October to early November, a migration of four to five hundred bald eagles. A breathtaking sight, to be sure.*

Lake McDonald Lodge
Lake McDonald, Montana
59921

Innkeeper: Beth Twamley

Address/Telephone: From mid-May to mid-September, mailing address
  and telephone are: East Glacier Park, MT 59434; (406) 226–5551.
  From mid-September to mid-May, mailing address and telephone
  are: Glacier Park, Inc., Greyhound Tower, Station 5510, Phoenix,
  AZ 85077; (602) 248–6000

Rooms: 32 in lodge, 39 cottages, 30 motel units; all with private bath.

Rates: $42 to $59, single; $46 to $66, double; reservations a must; EP.
  Pets permitted. No TV. No air conditioning (not needed; elevation
  over 6,000 feet). MasterCard and Visa accepted.

Open: Mid-May to mid-September.

Facilities and Activities: Full-service dining room. Lounge. Nearby:
  launch cruises on lake, tours via 1936 roll-back-top scenic coaches;
  hiking, fishing, horseback riding, boating, loafing.

    With only thirty-two rooms (there are an additional sixty-
nine individual units discreetly scattered across the property),
☛ this inn has managed to retain its original hunting-lodge
flavor.

    The lobby is open and roomy, with giant log beams, their
bark still intact, supporting second- and third-floor balconies.

☞ A walk-in fireplace dominates one wall, and one can actually sit in a peeled-pole rocking chair within the edifice and read by lights carefully placed so as not to interfere with the cozy atmosphere generated by the crackling fire and glowing coals. An original kettle support remains, a reminder that at one time the massive fireplace operated as kitchen and heat source for the lodge. ☞ Indian-style pictographs painted on the stonework are alleged to be the work of famed Montana cowboy artist Charles Russell.

Guest rooms open off from the upstairs balconies and are pleasantly done in contemporary mountain-lodge décor, with comfy furniture and softly colored walls.

The full-service dining room provides an extensive breakfast buffet. For lunch I had a choice of baked lasagna, sautéed trout, or wrangler stew; dinner featured Montana-style potato skins served with applesauce and sour cream, roast duckling, and a most delicious homemade apple cobbler.

This inn is ☞ ideally situated in the middle of the forest and on the very edge of Glacier National Park's largest lake. Tubs of flowers are everywhere, and pink, purple, and red fuchsia hang from outdoor balconies. I sat for a while in a Papa Bear–sized rocker on the patio facing the lake and watched as the excursion boat approached the dock, bringing waves of emerald green to shore. On the sloping lawn, members of an art class were totally engrossed in capturing the magnificent land and waterscape.

☞ With the sweet scent of cedar and lodgepole pines permeating the air, the chirping of happy birds, and the roar of nearby Snyder Creek, it's no wonder that the woman next to me fell asleep while attempting to write a postcard home. ☞ It would be hard to find a better place to rest and restore.

How to get there: Highway 2 skirts the southern edge of Glacier National Park. From Highway 2 at West Glacier, take the Going-to-the-Sun Road northeast along Lake McDonald to the lodge.

Nevada City Hotel
Nevada City, Montana
59755

Innkeeper: Bruce D. McCallum
Address/Telephone: P.O. Box 338, *Virginia City;* (406) 843–5377
Rooms: 27; all with private bath.
Rates: $34, regular rooms, single or double; $42, large Victorian rooms,
  single or double; EP. Pets allowed. Wheelchair accessible. No TV.
  No air conditioning (not needed; elevation 5,440 feet). MasterCard
  and Visa accepted.
Open: Memorial Day through mid-September.
Facilities and Activities: No meals. Restaurant next door. BYOB. Hotel
  is part of preserved 1860s mining camp. Nearby: railroad museum,
  working narrow-gauge railroad, melodrama theater.

From my room, I could hear ☛ old-time tunes coming from
the mechanical music machines in the Nevada City Music Hall
next door. Mine, number 7, and the one across the hall, number
8, are completely furnished with gorgeous antiques. Each has
two double beds with eight-foot headboards; marble-topped
dressers; velvet-upholstered, high-backed chairs; and gigantic
armoires. The walls and ceilings are made of split logs painted
white; the floors are carpeted in what appears to be wall-to-wall
braided rug. Between these two rooms, and shared with all guests,

is a Victorian parlor with plush chairs and an old Beatty's Beethoven organ. The other accommodations are not done in antiques, but they are country comfortable.

The upstairs veranda, facing the main street, looks across to an old railroad museum with vintage train cars that one can leisurely stroll through.

This hotel is unique in that it is part of a restored open-air museum. A step out the back door, past the two-story outhouse (said to be the most-photographed building in Montana!), brings you to dirt streets and authentic shops and homes from another era. A walk through the wagon barn, with dusty sun rays lighting the way, reveals old buggies, stagecoaches, and a seemingly endless assortment of wagon wheels.

I tiptoed through one old Victorian house and sat on the front porch of another, listened to the screen door softly creaking in the breeze, and imagined petticoated little girls giggling on their way to the school house just two doors away. Behind them, I was sure I saw several rosy-faced boys, dragging their feet to delay submitting to another day of dreaded 3 Rs. Oh my, was that really a frog peeping out from a coat pocket?

Dinner that night was in the patio garden of the Star Bakery, just up the street. I had the char-broiled pork chop, and my guest had linguine and clams. Good-sized portions, nicely prepared and seasoned.

How to get there: From I–90, take Highway 287 south to Ennis, then west to Nevada City. Inn is on right.

ॐ

D: *Allow time to take the narrow-gauge passenger train that chugs along the 1½ miles between Nevada City and Virginia City during the summer.*

Chico Hot Springs Lodge
Pray, Montana
59065

Innkeepers: Mike and Eva Art

Address/Telehone: P.O. Box 127; (406) 333–4933

Rooms: 52 in lodge; 9 with private bath, 43 share 8 baths. 7 chalets, 12 motel units; all with private bath.

Rates: $21 to $29 single, $31 to $42 double, lodge; $95 to $125, chalets; $29 single, $42 double, motel units; EP. Pets permitted ("anything but alligators," according to Mike). Wheelchair accessible. TV in saloon only. No air conditioning (not needed; elevation 5,200 feet). Children welcome; "unattended kids sold into slavery" (Mike again). MasterCard and Visa accepted.

Open: All year.

Facilities and Activities: Full-service dining room. Bar, saloon, snack bar. Hot springs–fed swimming pool, 3 hot tubs, tanning bed, licensed Swedish and Oriental masseurs on weekends; cross-country ski rentals, private trout lake. Nearby: Yellowstone National Park, Yellowstone River; hiking, fishing, horseback riding, cross-country skiing.

Looking as unpretentious as one of the "good ol' boys" in the Chico Saloon, this three-story, clapboard Victorian ☞ hosts many a famous guest. Film stars Ali McGraw, Peter Fonda, Jeff Bridges, Margot Kidder, Dennis Quaid, and others come to soak in the hot-springs pool, ride horseback into the Absaroka Beartooth Wilderness, and sit unnoticed in the barnwood-walled dining room.

The tempo, set by the easygoing innkeepers, is slow and ☛ ultra-casual. Mike is a laugh a minute, while Eve, his perfect complement, exudes grace and charm.

The large sitting room has a Steinway grand piano, an open-hearth brick fireplace, and back-to-back antique writing desks. The smaller, side parlor is elegantly attired in red and burgundy velvets, a 1912 wicker couch, and a parrot named Bruce. Upstairs, numerous hallways ramble in every direction on their way to guest rooms furnished with brass beds, old-fashioned quilts, flocked wallpapers, stained-glass lamps, and bunkhouse chairs. ☛ According to Mike, when he and Eve first moved here, they had to drop bread crumbs in order to find their way around the inn!

The Saloon features country-western music; a bar where folks are encouraged to carve their initials; a scrap sculpture made of old motorcycle parts and entitled "Montana Chopper," a gift from Peter Fonda; and a congenial mix of imbibers.

A peak into the dining room reveals candlelight reflected by sparkling crystal stemware. With ☛ a menu sporting escargots mountainique, oysters Rockefeller, and imported caviar as appetizers, along with several salads and more than thirty entrées, it took two glasses of wine before I could make my choice. Ah, but it was a good one: fillet vin rouge, a sliced roast fillet served with a red-wine sauce and homemade bread. This restaurant has such an outstanding reputation, hundreds of would-be diners are turned away each week. Reservations are a must, and it's a good idea to make them when reserving your accommodations.

How to get there: From I–90, take exit 333 south at Livingston onto Highway 89 and proceed to Emigrant. Exit left at Emigrant and drive to Chico Hot Springs.

Fairweather Inn
Virginia City, Montana
59755

Innkeeper: Bruce McCallum
Address/Telephone: P.O. Box 338; (406) 843–5377
Rooms: 15; 5 with private bath, 10 share 4 baths.
Rates: $22 to $34, single; $28 to $34, double; EP. Pets allowed. Wheelchair accessible. No TV. No air conditioning (usually not needed; elevation 5,604 feet). MasterCard and Visa accepted.
Open: Mid-June to Labor Day.
Facilities and Activities: Wells Fargo Coffee House, an affiliated restaurant, across the street. BYOB. Inn is set in preserved 1860s "boom town." Nearby: shopping, 25 completely furnished circa-1860 business displays, antique-car exhibit, museums, working narrow-gauge railroad, melodrama theater.

Virginia City was the first boom town established in Alder Gulch, the greatest gold deposit in Montana. ☞ The entire town is a Registered Historical Landmark and provides one of the finest collections in the United States of 1860s to early 1870s commercial buildings remaining on their original sites.

The population of Virginia City, according to historian Dick Pace in his book *Golden Gulch, the Story of Montana's Fabulous Alder Gulch,* "is now about 198 counting kids but not dogs." This

194

small community swells considerably during the summer, and 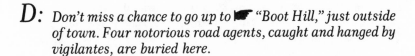 those visitors who want to really experience the Old West stay at the Fairweather Inn, a western Victorian furnished in antiques, some elegant, some timeworn. For me, the elaborate settee, gilded mirror, and red velvet–draped windows in the front parlor were actually enhanced and made more genuinely "old time" by the fact that the once-bright and plush carpet was now faded and worn. It was fascinating to imagine all the miners' boots and high-topped, high-button shoes that must have walked across it over the years.

The back parlor is only for viewing because the antiques displayed here are priceless. The guest rooms are sparingly furnished but intriguing because of their authenticity.

I sat for awhile on the inn's upstairs veranda, contemplating this town of boardwalks and former businesses the likes of Rank's Drug Store, where, according to the Day Book of Register Sales, a Dr. Raymond once bought eight grams of morphine for sixty cents and Fay Harrington purchased a "box of pills" for a quarter. Businesses open for today's customers include Cousin's Candy Shop, where 322 kinds of candy are for sale, and the Bale of Hay Saloon, opened as a miners' bar in 1890.

I had dinner at the Wells Fargo Coffee House and strolled up a few doors to take in a first-rate melodrama at The Virginia City Opera House. Reservations are a must because the actors play to a full house nearly every night.

How to get there: From I–90, take Highway 287 south to Ennis, then west to Virginia City. Inn is on right.

❋

D: *Don't miss a chance to go up to* "Boot Hill," *just outside of town. Four notorious road agents, caught and hanged by vigilantes, are buried here.*

Duck Inn
Whitefish, Montana
59937

Innkeeprs: Ken and Phyllis Adler
Address/Telephone: 1305 Columbia Avenue; (406) 862–3825
Rooms: 10; all with private bath.
Rates: $34 to $40, single; $36 to $48, double. Includes continental breakfast. No pets. Well-behaved children only, please. MasterCard, Visa, American Express accepted.
Open: All year.
Facilities and Activities: BYOB. Hot tub and Jacuzzi. Discounted ski-lift tickets available. Transportation provided to and from airport and Amtrak station. Located on river. Nearby: restaurants; Glacier National Park; hiking, fishing, canoeing, downhill and cross-country skiing, snowmobiling. Winter carnival held ea‸h year in January or February (phone for dates).

To say this inn is "absolutely ducky" is not only accurate but also descriptive. Subtle and always tasteful, artistic duck décor is everywhere: a duck boot-scrape at the 'front door, duck lamps, duck photos, duck paintings, duck dinnerware, ceramic ducks, wooden ducks, duck andirons, and duck fireplace pokers. And the duck phone doesn't ring, it *quacks!*

☛ This place is a beauty. The rough cedar exterior and

brass-accented wood interior boast ten large guest rooms, all with private bath, balcony, and fireplace. Pine armoires, brass and white iron beds with white spreads, and dark cherry carpets add to the loveliness. ☛ Ask for a room overlooking the Whitefish River, and you can watch from your balcony as beaver, otter, geese, and, of course, *ducks* frequent the water below. If you are lucky, you may even catch a glimpse of the eagle that fishes the river beside the inn.

The large stone fireplace, vaulted ceiling, game table and cushy furniture in the sitting room make it very inviting. Down the hall, ☛ the corner hot-tub room has a terrific view of the river. Large, with redwood walls, brick-tiled floor, and wrought-iron chairs, this room is the perfect place to relax after enjoying all the outdoor activities in the area.

A generous breakfast of breads, juices, coffee, and tea is served each morning on pretty china at the ten-foot trestle table in the dining room. The cinnamon rolls, orange rolls, and banana-nut bread are baked fresh each morning at the Little Dog Family Bakery just down the street. Sixteen-year-old Matt Little Dog is in charge of making the orange rolls, and they are special, indeed. Don't pass them up. You'll never find any better.

For excellent Chinese cuisine, I suggest you try Jimmy Lee's Chinese Chow, just a few blocks away. And Ken and Phyllis tell me that La Dump is a fun place with excellent food. Ask Ken for a look at La Dump's dinner menu, and I doubt that you will be able to resist dining there at least once.

How to get there: Whitefish is just southwest of Glacier National Park. From Highway 93 (or Spokane Avenue, Whitefish's main street), at the south edge of town, turn east onto Columbia Avenue and proceed 1 block. Inn is immediately visible next to the river.

D: *The phone number here is 862–DUCK, of course.*

The Foxwood Inn
White Sulphur Springs, Montana
59645

Innkeepers: Shane and Shelley Dempsey
Address/Telephone: P.O. Box 404; (406) 547–3918
Rooms: 14 share 3 baths.
Rates: $19 to $28, single; $23 to $30, double; EPB. Well-behaved pets.
   Wheelchair accessible. No air conditioning (not needed; elevation
   5,280 feet). MasterCard and Visa accepted.
Open: All year.
Facilities and Activities: Full breakfast included. Box lunches and din-
   ner by reservation. BYOB. Nearby: restaurants; excellent fishing,
   float trips, horseback riding, pack trips, downhill and cross-country
   skiing, snowmobiling.

If you happened to grow up in a farmhouse with a comfy
bedroom tucked away down the hall or up the stairs, coming to
The Foxwood Inn will be like coming home.

The unoccupied guest rooms have their doors wide open,
and I was told to choose whichever one I wanted. This was difficult, however, because they were all different and all so attractive. It finally came down to two: the blue room, with baby blue
ruffled bedspread and a sitting alcove with its marble-topped
table and red velvet chair; or the gold room, a bit larger, with

writing desk and dormer window. I opted for the one with the writing desk and ended up spending more time looking out the window than writing.

I watched as day faded to twilight over rain-freshened fields and misty hills. The only sound was that of western meadowlarks settling in for the night. On the wide front lawn, ☞ a black buggy with red wheels waited to be hitched to Fletcher and Dutch for a ride through the countryside.

☞ Breakfast was "farm style," designed for someone who had been up since four, already milked forty cows, and plowed several acres instead of having just rolled out of bed, as was the case with me. I was greeted with fresh, sliced peaches; Shelley's cinnamon rolls; ☞ sourdough waffles with homemade, wild-raspberry jam; eggs; thick slices of bacon; juice; and coffee. If you want a second egg or another glass of milk, you have only to ask. Dinner is available if arranged for in advance.

Conversation was brisk, and Shane joined us after he was convinced that we all had had our limit. His grandfather was sheriff in these parts, and Shane has lived in White Sulphur Springs all his life, so he is an authority on what is available to see and do in the area.

Although built in 1890 as a county poor farm, there is no reminder of the inn's dismal past. The Dempseys, with their children, Tara and Tanner, have made this a happy place with happy sounds and happy feelings.

How to get there: From midtown White Sulphur Springs, head west on West Main for ½ mile to S.W. 10th. Turn left and follow signs for 1 mile.

Sundance Lodge Montana
Wise River, Montana
59762

Innkeepers: Les and Jan Davis
Address/Telephone: Wise River, Montana; (406) 689–3611
Rooms: 10; 5 guest rooms in lodge, 5 cabins; all have private bath.
Rates: $40 to $56, single or double; weekly rates available; EP. Pets
   allowed. Wheelchair accessible. TV in living room and homestead
   house only. No air conditioning (not needed; elevation over 6,000
   feet). Well-behaved children only, please. MasterCard and Visa accepted.
Open: June 1 to end of March.
Facilities and Activities: Full-service dining room. Bar, hot tub. Llama
   treks, horseback riding, hiking, excellent creek fishing, blue-ribbon
   trout streams, fly fishing, groomed ski trails, ski-touring instructors
   and guides, ice skating, ice fishing, sleigh rides. Nearby: sapphire
   mine, Big Hole Battlefield National Monument, Historic Territorial
   Prison Tours, downhill skiing.

As I turned off the road and rattled across the cattle guard,
huge, reddish-brown cows lay in the dusty roadway. Taking their
own sweet time, they slowly lumbered to their feet and, giving
me a long, hard look, stepped to one side so I could pass. A

quarter mile down the road, things got even more exciting. The Sundance herd of llamas sauntered out to meet me. What a sight! Eight to ten shaggy, bright-eyed creatures, their heads held high, had come to welcome the newest arrival. I knew then and there that I was going to like it here.

The hospitality at Sundance is genuine, plentiful without being overwhelming. There is ☞ no limit of things to do, but the activities are not so structured that one feels compelled to participate. I took long walks through the woods and around the pond; I went in search of the llamas, who, incidentally, wait very patiently for slow photographers like me to take their picture; I found horses and chickens and cats and geese and a sweetheart of a dog; and I sat for hours before a warm fire visiting with Les, who is an entertaining conversationalist with lots of stories to tell.

Dinner was *calzones* on this particular night, with minestrone soup, garden salad, homemade bread, and hot apple pie. Other nights you are apt to have Les's special alder-smoked chicken or prime rib, which he smokes over applewood for five hours.

The guest rooms are part of the main lodge building and lead off from a long hallway, giving them ☞ a bunkhouse feeling. In addition, there are four guest cabins and a homestead house to stay in. All accommodations have a private bath and ☞ a cowboy-size seven-foot bed.

There is a pool table in the upstairs recreation room, along with ping-pong and shuffleboard. The dining room and bar are open to the public, so you are likely to meet some locals, which can be the highlight of any vacation.

How to get there: Inn is located in southwestern Montana in the Big Hole Valley, on Highway 43 between the towns of Wise River and Wisdom, 4 miles west of Highway 274.

✸

D: *This ranch has a very real element of authenticity. When you leave, you will have experienced some of what Montana and ranch life are all about.*

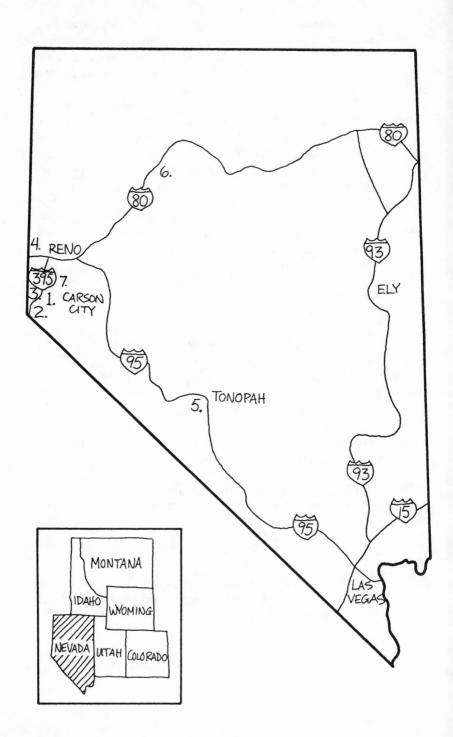

Nevada

Numbers on map refer to towns numbered below.

1. Carson City, Winters Creek Inn 204
2. Genoa,
   The Genoa House Inn 206
   Orchard House..208
   The Taylor House...210
   Walley's Hot Springs Resort..............................212
3. Incline Village, Haus Bavaria...............................214
4. Reno, Wingfield House......................................216
5. Tonopah, Mizpah Hotel......................................218
6. Unionville, Old Pioneer Garden.............................220
7. Virginia City, Edith Palmer's Country Inn 222

Winters Creek Inn
Carson City, Nevada
89701

Innkeepers: Susan Hannah and Myron Sayan
Address/Telephone: 1201 U.S. Highway 395 North; (702) 849–1020
Rooms: 4 (3 plus cottage); all with private bath.
Rates: $75, single or double; EPB. No pets. No TV. No air conditioning. Smoking discouraged. Children age 12 and older welcome in main house; younger children permitted in cottage. MasterCard and Visa accepted.
Open: All year.
Facilities and Activities: Dinner rides to nearby restaurant. Bar. Complimentary wine and hor d'ouevres. Catered weddings and receptions. Beautiful grounds. Hot tub. On property: hiking, horseback riding, fly fishing, bicycling, ice skating, cross-country skiing. Nearby: wildlife preserve, fishing, boating, windsurfing, downhill skiing.

Surrounded by the Toiyabe National Forest and with the Sierra Nevadas as a backdrop, this gracious New England Colonial sits far off the road amid tall pine trees.

Deer, wild turkey, porcupine, eagles, and an abundance of birdlife are often seen along the ranch trails and at the Washoe

Lake wildlife refuge just across the road. The inn has a catch-and-release fly-fishing pond that freezes over for ice skating in winter and a ☞ gazebo-covered hot tub out beside Winters Creek. Or you can ☞ borrow a bike and ride the same country roads that Tour de France winner Greg La Mond uses for training.

Myron, a former airline pilot, restores old farm equipment. A trip to the barn to see his collection and greet the horses is definitely in order.

Susan is the chef, and her creations never fail to bring "ohs" and "ahs" from the guests. She combines ☞ fresh farm eggs and just-picked vegetables from the garden to produce remarkable quiches, does wonderful things with eggs and avocados to come up with what she calls Monterey eggs, and makes fresh apple blintzes with genuine maple syrup. Her apple-nut bread disappears without leaving a crumb, and she generously shares her recipes with anyone who asks. That says a lot, I think.

The guest rooms are beauties. The Colonial Suite has a cherry-wood four-poster, two dormer window seats, fireplace, and dressing room. Across the hall, Oliver's Nook, named after the pen-and-ink sketch of Oliver Twist that hangs on one wall, is done in pinks with a raspberry-colored bedspread, four-poster, and antique commode with sink. The Nevada Suite has a private deck off its sitting room/library, a step-down bedroom, authentic Navajo rugs, and Western antiques. The Gambrel Cottage is attached to one end of the barn and offers a cozy, two-level suite.

After complimentary wine and hors d'oeuvres in the Victorian-furnished living room, ☞ put on your riding duds and take the guided trail ride ("the scenic route," Myron calls it) over to the Cattlemen's Restaurant for a steak to beat all steaks. Let Myron or Susan know ahead of time, however, that you would like to do this.

How to get there: Inn is located on the west side of Highway 395, approximately 20 miles south of Reno and 10 miles north of Carson City.

∽

D: *Twiggy, Myron and Susan's ever-wagging Airedale, will gleefully accompany you on your walks. You won't have to ask twice.*

The Genoa House Inn
Genoa, Nevada
89411

Innkeepers: Bob and Linda Sanfilippo
Address/Telephone: 180 Nixon Street (mailing address: P.O. Box 141);
   (702) 782–7075
Rooms: 2 share 1 bath.
Rates: $50 to $60, single; $55 to $65, double; EPB. No pets. TV in parlor
   only. No air conditioning, fans available. No smoking inside. Children over age 10 permitted if both rooms are taken by same family.
   Credit cards not accepted.
Open: All year.
Facilities and Activities: Dinner with prior arrangement. BYOB. Complimentary refreshments. Jacuzzi. Nearby: museum, Mormon Station State Park, Lake Tahoe, hiking, fishing, downhill and
   cross-country skiing.

According to the proprietress at the Country Store, "Genoa's
population is somewhere around 100—that is, before the school
bus comes into town." So it's a bit of a surprise to find four inns,
each very different from the others but all exceedingly charming,
in this small community. Combined, they make it the "Bed and
Breakfast Capital of Nevada."

Nicely framed with 100-year-old lilac bushes, The Genoa

House Inn is the sort of place that you seem to settle into immediately. The antique-furbished dining room, library, and parlor are all open to guests. Up a steep and winding staircase are two of the prettiest rooms you will ever find. The Blue Room has a queen-size bed, wicker settee, chair and plant stand, and an unusual antique "hip tub" made in London. Ah, but come down the hall and see the masterpiece. This is *the* room for newlyweds and, come to think of it, not-so-newlyweds as well. The sitting area is bathed in glorious color from three antique, cathedral-style, stained-glass windows from New Zealand. The custom-made barnwood, pine, and oak bed is three feet off the floor. It takes a stepping stool to climb into bed at night. Pink roses dance across the wallpaper, a 1906 dark green-velvet fainting couch and a Eastlake dresser share one corner, and ruffled-curtained French doors lead to a private balcony. I could have stayed forever!

Bob and Linda spent several years searching for just the right home for their antique collection and a place well suited for guests. Believe me, they made a good choice.

There's wine in the afternoon, after-dinner brandy can be had before the fire in the library, and mornings bring fantastic breakfasts. Linda is a yeast-bread specialist, and you will be treated to home-baked breads, cinnamon rolls, and hot, sticky, scrumptious pecan rolls along with egg dishes, fruit platters, juice, and coffee. Dinner, with prior arrangement, might be one of Linda's Armenian specialties, something Italian, or wonderfully tender steaks.

How to get there: On Highway 395, just south of Carson City, watch for the "Genoa 4 miles" sign. Turn west at sign onto Highway 206 and proceed 4 miles to four-way stop. Go straight for ½ block. Inn is on the right.

*

D: *Back to the Country Store. This is not the cutesy type. This one is for real, with bulk peanuts "by the cup," hand-dipped ice cream cones, deli, a few gift items, post office, and an honor-system paperback-lending library. Be sure to stop, you hear?*

Orchard House
Genoa, Nevada
89411

Innkeepers: Carl and Hope Falcke
Address/Telephone: 188 Carson Street (mailing address: P.O. Box 77);
(702) 782–2640
Rooms: 2; 1 with private bath, 1 shares hall bath; sleeping room for extra
kids.
Rates: $35, single; $45, double; EPB. Well-behaved pets permitted. TV
in sitting room only. Credit cards not accepted.
Open: All year.
Facilities and Activities: Dinner by prior arrangement for guests staying
several days. BYOB. Outdoor barbecue grill and patio, complimentary evening snacks and beverages. Baby-sitting. Nearby: museum,
Mormon Station State Park, Lake Tahoe, hot-springs resort; hiking,
fishing, downhill and cross-country skiing.

Built in the 1860s, this country home has been in the Falcke
family for four generations. Peach, apple, pear, and plum trees
make up the orchard that surrounds the inn, and it is very special
indeed to look out the large living-room windows and watch as
deer rummage for apples among the fallen leaves.

Breakfast is served in a window-flanked corner nook in
Hope's cheerful kitchen; and ☛ if you like fresh vegetables and

sun-ripened fruit, you're going to love it here. First, I had red raspberries, so firm and sweet, just like those I picked out behind my playhouse when I was a kid. Next, it's French toast and homemade jelly or scrambled eggs, fried potatoes, and sausage, ham, or bacon. I guarantee you will never leave this table hungry.

Guests can arrange for dinner with advance notice if they are staying for several days. It is "pot luck," and I'd take a gamble on this one if I were you. For dining out, Hope suggests The Pink House, a vintage 1855 Victorian only about a block from the inn, where one finds extraordinarily good prime rib. Or wander down the road for a mile and a half to Walley's Hot Springs Resort, as I did, for chicken Chardonnay in cream sauce, parsley potatoes, and flaming Kahlua crêpes topped with chocolate shavings.

☞ Hope refers to her upstairs guest room as "grandma's attic," and ☞ it is indeed a charmer. With knotty-pine walls and ceiling, a queen-size bed, plush brown carpet, and private bath, it is off by itself—very cozy, very comfortable. On the marble-topped antique table, I found a silver tray with a bottle of Chablis and two stemmed glasses. Next to it were fresh flowers, cookies, and candy. Out the window, horses grazed peacefully in the pasture.

☞ Hospitality is first class at this inn. Guests are welcome to share the living room and have a mid-day cup of coffee in the kitchen, and ☞ Hope will even baby-sit for those who would like to get off by themselves for a while.

How to get there: On Highway 395, just south of Carson City, watch for the "Genoa 4 miles" sign. Turn west at sign onto Highway 206 and proceed 4 miles to four-way stop. Turn left and drive for about 1 block. Inn is on the right.

৵৹

D: *If you plan to be in Nevada on the last Saturday of September, also plan to attend Candy Dance, Genoa's annual (since 1919) old-time dance, craft, and homemade-candy festival. Reserve a room well ahead.*

The Taylor House
Genoa, Nevada
89411

Innkeepers: Bob and Charlene Taylor
Address/Telephone: 2383 Jack's Valley Road (mailing address: P.O. Box 16); (702) 782–3932
Rooms: 3; 1 with private bath, 2 share 1 bath.
Rates: $50, single; $60, double; less during the week; EPB. Pet quarters in barn. TV in common rooms and 1 guest room. No air conditioning. No smoking inside. MasterCard and Visa accepted.
Open: All year.
Facilities and Activities: Sack lunches available. BYOB. Wine and flowers for special occasions, late-afternoon snacks and beverages. Nearby: museum, Mormon Station State Park, Lake Tahoe, hot-springs resort; hiking, fishing, horseback riding, downhill and cross-country skiing.

The sprawling English Tudor looks out over Carson Valley, where the pinks of the desert peach and golds of rabbit brush become a veritable artist's palette in spring.

One enters this magnificent inn ☛ through a castlelike door into a stone, turret-style entryway with a pewter chandelier hanging from the domed ceiling. The living-room beams came from San Francisco's old Pier 39, and a massive fireplace made of

Genoa native stone embraces an entire wall. A marvelous reading nook is sectioned off from the rest of the room by circa-1850 two-sided book shelves.

Two downstairs guest rooms open onto the deck that runs the length of the inn. One has a four-poster with blue-and-white quilt and matching shams, while the other displays a king-size brass bed, ivory down comforter, and rich green carpet. The family suite upstairs has a private bath and dormer windows with view.

Charlene serves a ☞ generous country breakfast of bacon, ham, or sausage; eggs; fried potatoes; fresh fruit; juice; and coffee. Even when she has a full house, preparing a large morning meal is no major task for her; she more than paid her dues as a "short-order cook" in the process of raising seven children. She will even pack you a picnic lunch if you ask ahead of time. You'll like Charlene—she is the kind of mellow, agreeable person with whom you feel immediately comfortable.

A short walk away, one finds ☞ a delightful barnyard menagerie of ducks, goats, pigs, and horses. There are ☞ quarters in the barn for guests' pets and private stalls for visitors' horses. This would be a good place to bring along old Trigger because riding trails abound in the area.

Located on eighteen acres of lawn and grasslands, this inn is only ½ mile north of Genoa, within easy walking distance to excellent dining at The Pink House, a restored 1850s Victorian gem.

How to get there: On Highway 395, just south of Carson City, watch for the "Genoa 4 miles" sign. Turn west at sign onto Highway 206 and proceed 4 miles to four-way stop. Turn right and drive for about ¾ mile. Inn is on the right.

❀

D: *The oldest settlement in Nevada, Genoa (pronounced Gen-oh-a) also boasts the "oldest thirst parlor" in the state. Built in the 1850s, it hasn't changed much over the years. I found a mongrel dog asleep in front of the old wood stove, some local residents quaffing a few, and a bib-overalled bartender behind the antique bar. Worth a stop.*

Walley's Hot Springs Resort
Genoa, Nevada
89411

Innkeeper: Spencer Whitted
Address/Telephone: Foothill Road (mailing address: P.O. Box 26); (702) 782–8155 or (702) 883–6556
Rooms: 5; all with private bath.
Rates: $65 to $105, single and double. Includes continental breakfast. No pets. No air conditioning (evenings are usually cool, even in summer). Children are welcome, but state law prohibits children under 12 from being in spa area. MasterCard, Visa, American Express accepted.
Open: All year.
Facilities and Activities: Lunch and dinner served in dining room. Sunday champagne brunch. Bar. Flow-through-hot-mineral-spring pools, swimming pool, weight room, saunas, massages, tennis. Catered weddings and receptions. Nearby: museum, Mormon Station State Park, Lake Tahoe; hiking, fishing, boating, downhill and cross-country skiing.

From Ulysses S. Grant and Mark Twain to Clark Gable and Ida Lupino, the famous and the wealthy have been frequenting this inn since 1862. Thankfully, it is now within the reach of us not-so-famous and not-so wealthy folks as well.

This is 🖝 truly an oasis where one can workout in the well-equipped fitness center, soak in one of several outdoor flow-through-mineral-spring spas, take a dip in the pool, have a massage by a certified masseur or masseuse, play a set of tennis, and indulge in fantastic gourmet meals. Then it's only a few steps to your very own Victorian cottage for a sleep like no other. Or, if you haven't had enough activity for one day, Lake Tahoe and its nightlife and casinos are only twelve miles away. When you finally make your way to your tidy little nest, you'll find a very comfortable bed, cozy wood-burning stove, ceiling fan, and stocked honor bar.

In the morning, at a prearranged time, a continental breakfast of fresh fruit, croissant, juice, and coffee is brought to your room.

Walley's is 🖝 "top of the line" when it comes to hot-springs facilities. Inside out, it is spotlessly clean; all personnel, from Spencer on down, are courteous and helpful; and guests are treated with the same graciousness and hospitality that Walley's has always been famous for.

The tables in the elegant dining room are dressed in pink and white starched linens and bedecked with brass lamps and English china. I had a fantastic Western omelet with ham, cheese, and green peppers garnished with generous slices of melon. And then I made my best decision of the day: I ordered 🖝 coffee-crunch Ice Cream Pie, a brownie pie crust filled with coffee ice cream and almond crunch and topped with meringue and bittersweet hot fudge! This was genteelly served on a frosted glass plate with frosted silverware wrapped in a linen napkin.

If Walley's is booked when you call for reservations, by all means plan at least to spend a day at the spa and enjoy an unforgettable lunch or dinner (preferably both!).

How to get there: On Highway 395, just south of Carson City, watch for the "Genoa 4 miles" sign. Turn west at sign onto Highway 206 and proceed 4 miles to four-way stop. Turn left and travel for 1½ miles. Inn is on the left.

Haus Bavaria
Incline Village, Nevada
89450

Innkeepers: Wolfgang and Annalise Zimmermann
Address/Telephone: Street map provided upon request for reservations
(mailing address: P.O. Box 3308); (702) 831–6122
Rooms: 5; all with private bath.
Rates: $60 single, $70 double for minimum stay of 2 nights; rates slightly
higher for one-night occupancy; advance reservations only; EPB.
No pets. TV in sitting room only. No air conditioning (not needed;
elevation more than 6,000 feet.) Smoking discouraged. Not appropriate for children. Credit cards not accepted.
Open: All year.
Facilities and Activities: BYOB. Complimentary afternoon wine and
snacks. Nearby: Lake Tahoe; tours of Ponderosa Ranch, where TV's
"Bonanza" was filmed; casino's; nightlife. Hiking, fishing, boating,
lake tours, swimming, golf, tennis, downhill and cross-country skiing.

Reading the guest book at this inn is like looking at a geog-
raphy book. Visitors from all corners of the world, including Af-
rican nations, China, and Israel, have been guests here.

It is advertised as a "Deutsche Pension, mit Gemütliche

Unterkunft und gutem Frühstück" (a German Inn with attractive accommodations and good breakfasts). As the name implies, 🖙 the design is Bavarian throughout. German beer mugs line a high shelf in the dining room, Austrian linens grace the tables, and flower boxes full of blossoms skirt the balconies.

When you sit down to breakfast, you think you are in Europe for sure. Platters laden with five to six kinds of cold cuts, all sorts of cheeses, *brot, brötchen*, fresh plum cake, sometimes boiled eggs, and always good, strong German coffee are served in the bright and cheerful dining room.

This inn is 🖙 impeccably clean, with quiet, soft colors and good use of textured fabrics. The structure was built as an inn, so all creature comforts are close at hand. Each room has a private bath and its own entrance to the balcony. The upstairs sitting room is done in knotty pine with windows facing the hills and ski slope. This is where 🖙 guests get together for afternoon wine and snacks, all cozy in big leather chairs before a crackling fire.

Wolfgang and Annalise are particularly accommodating and will assist you in just about any way possible to assure that you have a good stay. They provide their guests with 🖙 complimentary passes to both a private beach and a private pool. They will even lend you their cross-country skis. There is a storage area for your own skis and a refrigerator for guest use.

Although Wolfgang and Annalise will make reservations for you at any one of several area restaurants, I suggest you try the Schweitzer Haus for excellent German and Swiss cuisine.

How to get there: Incline Village is on the north end of Lake Tahoe. From Reno, go south on Highway 395 to Highway 431 turnoff to Incline Village. Turn south into Incline Village at sign reading "Hotel and Business District." When you make your reservations, the Zimmermanns will send you a street map to facilitate your finding the inn.

Wingfield House
Reno, Nevada
89501

Innkeepers: David and Jana Ketchum
Address/Telephone: 219 Court Street; (702) 348–0766
Rooms: 4; 2 with private bath, 2 share 1 bath or, when both reserved as
   suite, with private bath.
Rates: $75 to $125, single or double, depending on day of week and
   room choice; $175, suite; EPB. No pets. No TV. No air condition-
   ing; fans available. No smoking inside. MasterCard, Visa, American
   Express accepted.
Open: All year.
Facilities and Activities: Dinner available for groups of 6 or more by
   prior arrangement. Catered weddings and receptions. Bar. Beautiful, sweeping backyard with lawn furniture. Nearby: University of
   Nevada—Reno, Fleischmann Planetarium, casinos, restaurants,
   museums. Hiking, fishing, downhill and cross-country skiing.

When George Wingfield came to Nevada during the nineteenth century, he was penniless but determined to strike it rich
in the silver mines. First he sought out a wealthy businessman,
who agreed to stake him for a try at mining. This is where old
George changed his direction. Instead of heading out with his
pick and shovel, he went directly to the gambling tables, where

216

Lady Luck came through with enough money to buy a good-sized mine. From there, George built a banking empire and dealt heavily in politics. Fortunately for us, along the way he built a beautiful mansion in the well-to-do section of Reno. Wingfield descendants lived in the house until 1978, after which it stood empty until David and Jana bought it in 1985 and began to love it back to life.

All the rooms are spacious and decorated to perfection From the huge entry hall, one enters the front parlor through an archway flanked by wooden pillars. This room has a bronze and Italian-marble fireplace and comfy furniture that encourages relaxed conversation. The back parlor has a similar fireplace, grand piano, and antique bagatelle table.

The guest rooms are elegantly appointed with lovely antiques and pleasant color schemes. The Prince George Room is done in gold, white, and soft yellow. It has a white marble fireplace, crystal chandelier, and heavy brass bed with lacy white skirt and vanilla taffeta quilt. Another room has its own enclosed sunporch, and still another contains the most elaborate, hand-painted, very French-looking antique armoire I have ever seen. Even if you don't book this room, ask if you can have a peek.

Chef Carol Stevens, mistress over the kitchen, whips up a whole wheat bread, from one of Jana's original recipes and including molasses and orange rind, that is outstanding. She also makes marvelous ham, turkey, chicken, mushroom, cheese, and fresh-vegetable quiches and magnificent omelets cooked in wine.

How to get there: Turn west onto Court Street from South Virginia (Reno's main street). Go 3½ blocks. Inn is on the right.

D: *This inn has a very special feature. It serves a tradi-tional High Tea in the formal dining room on Thursdays, Fridays, and Sundays from two to five. Open to the public, this is your chance to meet some of the locals and treat yourself to finger sandwiches, homemade scones, crumpets, and real Devonshire cream while listening to live, classical music.*

Mizpah Hotel
Tonopah, Nevada
89049

Innkeepers: Bill and Dolores Allison
Address/Telephone: 100 Main Street (mailing address: P.O. Box 952);
   (702) 482–6202
Rooms: 44, including 4 suites; all with private bath.
Rates: $21 to $58, single; $28 to $58, double; EP. Well-behaved pets
   permitted. MasterCard, Visa, American Express accepted.
Open: All year.
Facilities and Activities: Full-service dining room. Bar. Complimentary
   mine tours. Nearby: Central Nevada Museum; the Castle House,
   said to be haunted by a friendly ghost named George; the Old Dump
   Site, where generations of bottles and junk have accumulated. Exploring, hiking, fishing.

From 1908 to 1958, the Mizpah Hotel, all five stories of it,
was the tallest building in Nevada. Built for the wealthy, it was
first class all the way, with "suites, baths, lavatories, hot and cold
water, and electric and gas service." It boasted, "Nor does the
weary one have to climb stairs, for an electric elevator runs from
basement to garret."

And the ☞ Mizpah saw its share of celebrities. Jack
Dempsey tended bar and bounced the unruly from its doors;

Wyatt Earp frequented the hotel while employed by the Tonopah Mining Company in order to run claim jumpers out of the area; New York financier Bernard Baruch stayed at the hotel while investing heavily in the local mines; and Howard Hughes and Jean Peters were married by a justice of the peace at the Mizpah.

The old hotel still retains its grandeur with Italianate embellishments on the exterior, etched-glass windows, antique bar, and old-style registration desk. When I was there, the spacious lobby was being readied to include a casino. Although the excitement of slots and gaming tables may diminish some of the structure's dignity, one can easily escape upstairs where, on each floor, groupings of plush Victorian furniture allow quiet conversation over an afternoon cup of tea.

I was permitted to peek into many rooms and found all of them charming. Mine had a brass bed; handsome, oak-framed cheval mirror; armoire with hidden TV; brass and crystal hand-painted ceiling fixture with sparkling teardrops; claw-footed tub; and an oak, pull-chain water closet.

Dinner can be in the Dempsey Room for gourmet dining, but I chose the Deli with its amiable, café atmosphere and simple offerings such as Miners' Stew, homemade soups and chili, and very good pizza. Breakfast in the Deli was particularly enjoyable, with friendly, easy conversation between tables and the sharing of newspapers. My waitress had walked to work at five that morning but still managed to deliver a sizable portion of cheeriness along with my bacon, eggs, and potatoes Lyonnaise.

How to get there: Tonopah is at the intersection of highways 6 and 95, halfway between Reno and Las Vegas. The Mizpah is on Main Street, in the middle of town.

✸

D: *There is an old silver mine directly under the Mizpah Hotel, and* ☛ *free-of-charge mine tours are given to guests. This is a good way to learn some of Tonopah's history and gain respect for the gutsy miners.*

Old Pioneer Garden
Unionville, Nevada
89418

Innkeepers: Lew and Mitzi Jones
Address/Telephone: #79; (702) 538–7585
Rooms: 11; 4 with private bath.
Rates: $25 to $35, single; $30 to $40, double; EPB. Pets permitted. No
    TV reception but VCR and extensive library of older movies avail-
    able. No air conditioning (seldom needed). No smoking in guest
    rooms. Credit cards not accepted.
Open: All year.
Facilities and Activities: Breakfast, lunch, and dinner available. BYOB.
    Nearby: Rye Patch State Park and Reservoir, hot springs; hiking,
    fishing, boating, horse and mountain-bike trails. Peace and Quiet.

Snuggled under an antique, handmade quilt with the flickering fire as a night-light, I wondered about Thomas J. Hadley,
the blacksmith whose home this cottage had been back in the
1860s and who, besides shoeing the horses and repairing farm
and mining equipment, had raised the vegetables and fruit for
the community in his pioneer garden.

Unionville was a booming mining camp back then. Today it
has a population of twenty-two.

Lew and Mitzi live in the 1865 Talcott House, which has

four guest rooms. The Ross House is a rustic, two-bedroom, former-wagon-master's cabin, while The Hadley House, where I stayed, has six guest rooms, a library, a farm kitchen where breakfast is served at an eight-foot-long table, and a large sitting room.

Lew and Mitzi have done a commendable job of extending and refurbishing this last building, making it into ☛ one of the most inviting and attractive country inns I have visited. ☛ The emphasis is truly on "country" with all the right touches: baskets of dried flowers on window sills; brass, iron, and oak beds; fluffy quilts; old trunks; and a beautiful armoire handmade by Lew, who used screws and pegs but no nails. The upstairs ceilings slope over dormer windows; ceiling-to-floor book shelves line the walls; and heavy, perfect-condition, overstuffed furniture from the 1930s waits to envelop you with cozy security.

When I arrived, Lew had a warm fire going in my room. After settling in, ☛ I walked to dinner at the Talcott House under stars so bright they seemed to touch the ground. Mitzi had vegetable-beef stew, salad, and apricot-pudding cake waiting in the kitchen. Next morning's generous breakfast included apple-filled pancakes made with hand-ground cornmeal. Delicious! ☛ Meal conversation is so easy here that, long after you've oversatis-fied your appetite, you find you're still at the table chattering as though you've all been friends forever.

☛ This inn has it all—very special innkeepers; country-cottage accommodations; farm-style meals; clean air; an exten-sive orchard, grape arbor, and vegetable patch; a gazebo beside a rippling creek; and a fine assortment of friendly farm animals.

I can't wait to turn off onto the gravel road again and walk under the weathered "Old Pioneer Garden" sign and up the lane to a chorus of baa's from woolly white sheep and inquisitive brown goats. This is country at its best.

How to get there: From I–80 at Mill City (139 miles east of Reno), take Exit 149 south onto Highway 400 and proceed 16 miles to Unionville turnoff. Inn is only a short distance up the road, on the left.

Edith Palmer's Country Inn
Virginia City, Nevada
89440

Innkeepers: Norm and Erlene Brown
Address/Telephone: South B Street (mailing address: P.O. Box 756);
   (702) 847–0707
Rooms: 5; 1 with private bath, 4 share 2 baths.
Rates: $55 to $65 single, $60 to $70 double, May through October; $45
   to $55 single, $50 to $60 double, November through April; EPB. No
   pets. TV in common rooms. No air conditioning (not needed; elevation 6,200 feet). No smoking inside. Well-behaved children over
   age 12 only, please. MasterCard and Visa accepted.
Open: All year.
Facilities and Activities: Lunch and dinner by prior arrangement. BYOB.
   Catered garden or indoor weddings. Nearby: restaurants, saloons,
   museums, excursion train, mine tours. Hiking, fishing, exploring,
   downhill and cross-country skiing at Lake Tahoe, approximately 35
   miles away.

Built in 1862 for a senator from Connecticut who gave up
politicking to become a wine merchant during the local silver
boom, ☞ this prim and proper, picket-fenced Victorian provides a quiet escape from the glitz of Reno and the bustle of

Virginia City's main street. ☛ Beautiful gardens and brick-floored patios surround the building, and it is easy to see why ☛ many, many brides and grooms choose this inn for their weddings and honeymoons.

The large parlor has bay windows, fireplace, and a lovely antique writing desk that has been in Norm's family for years. The breakfast room looks out onto a stone-walled garden ablaze with columbine and golden alyssum in summer.

My guest-room choice was ☛ the Marilyn Monroe Room, so named because the movie great stayed in this particular chamber during the filming of *The Misfits*. Entered through a short hallway, it has a cherry-wood four-poster with blue-and-white quilted coverlet, two antique rockers, wood-shuttered windows, and a freestanding fireplace guarded by two replicas of Hessian soldiers. This is the sort of room in which you feel immediately "at home."

The back parlor, once the wine cellar, is cut into the mountainside and has walls made of stone and a fireplace constructed entirely of Nevada minerals and gem stones, including gold and amethyst.

During the 1960s, the inn was operated by Edith Palmer, who, with the help of a gifted four-star chef, catered to the gastronomical pleasures of many prominent world leaders and some of Hollywood's greatest stars. ☛ Norm and Erlene are carrying on the inn's reputation for fine dining, and ordinary meals are unheard of here. Breakfast, for instance, may begin with Erlene's special fruit compote, made of green apples, raisins, bananas, and cranberries and served warm with cream, if you like. Next it's sourdough biscuits, fresh-squeezed orange juice, and marvelous egg casseroles with sausage, cheeses, and, perhaps, fresh peaches. Lunch and dinner, served by prior arrangement, are always creative, unlike those that you are apt to prepare at home or find in restaurants. For instance, Erlene recently served pumpkin soup cooked in the pumpkin shell. Fun!

How to get there: From Reno, take Highway 395 south to Highway 341 turnoff to Virginia City. From the main street, turn west onto Mansions Street and proceed 1 block to B Street. Turn south on B. Inn is on the right.

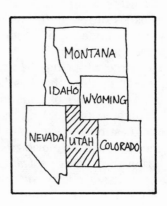

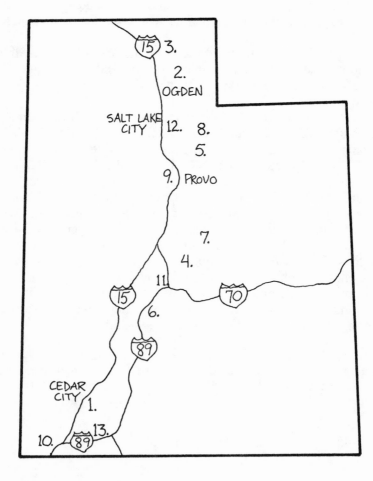

Utah

Numbers on map refer to towns numbered below.

1. Cedar City, Meadeau View Lodge..............................226
2. Huntsville, Trappers Inn......................................228
3. Logan,
    The Birch Trees Bed & Breakfast Inn.....................230
    Center Street Bed & Breakfast...........................232
4. Manti, Manti House Inn......................................234
5. Midway, The Homestead......................................236
6. Monroe, Peterson's Bed & Breakfast.........................238
7. Mt. Pleasant, Mansion House Inn............................240
8. Park City,
    The Blue Church Lodge..................................242
    The Imperial Hotel......................................244
    The Old Miners' Lodge..................................246
    Washington School Inn..................................248
9. Provo, The Pullman Inn......................................250
10. St. George,
    Greene Gate Village.....................................252
    Seven Wives Inn..254
11. Salina, The Burr House......................................256
12. Salt Lake City,
    Anselmo Inn..258
    Brigham Street Inn.....................................260
13. Springdale, Under The Eaves Guest House...................262

Meadeau View Lodge
Cedar City, Utah
84720

Innkeepers: Harry and Gaby Moyer
Address/Telephone: (P.O. Box 356); (801) 682–2495
Rooms: 9; all with private bath.
Rates: $28 to $38, single; $45 to $55, double. No charge for children
   aged 5 and under; $5 for those aged 6 through 13. EPB. No pets. No
   TV. No air conditioning (not needed; elevation 8,400 feet).
   MasterCard and Visa accepted.
Open: All year.
Facilities and Activities: Full breakfast served to inn guests only. Other
   meals upon request. BYOB. Nearby: Bryce and Zion national parks,
   Cedar Breaks National Monument; hiking, fishing, boating, rock
   hounding, photography, excellent cross-country skiing, snowmobil-
   ing.

   Meadeau View Lodge, 🖝 an oasis of cool air, grassy meadows, aspen groves, and mountain lakes, is 🖝 only an hour's
drive from spectacular Bryce and Zion national parks in southern
Utah.
   The lodge is made of peeled pine, both inside and out, and
features a circular fireplace in the center of the sitting room. This

is where guests gather before breakfast for that first cup of coffee.

Gaby and Harry are enthusiastic and knowledgeable about their area. Stay here for awhile, and you will feel the same way.

Early mornings are particularly special. Before breakfast, ☞ I sat for a time in a grove of trees where *My Friend Flicka* and *How the West Was Won* were filmed. I listened to the birds awaken and watched a marmot poke out of his underground home and scurry across the grass to disappear into the domicile of a friend. (Or was he entering his version of the local country inn?)

Breakfast that morning was cantaloupe; orange juice; eggs scrambled with ham, cheese, and mild green chilies; cornbread with real corn; and bran muffins made with whole wheat flour, pineapple, and raisins. Guests who were staying the week were still raving about the Grand Marnier French toast they'd had a few days before. Dinner included marinated roast beef and cheesy potatoes with sour cream and onions. Gaby is an excellent cook.

My room was entered via a private stairway leading from one corner of the sitting room. Large, with king-size bed, it was Western rustic, with a row of windows facing the meadow. The lodge was full to capacity during my stay, but, ☞ all cozy under my quilt with the windows open wide, I heard only the night calls of nocturnal birds and the faraway barking of a ranch dog. What a lovely way to fall asleep!

How to get there: From I–15, turn southeast onto Highway 14 at Cedar City. Go 30 miles. Inn is on the left.

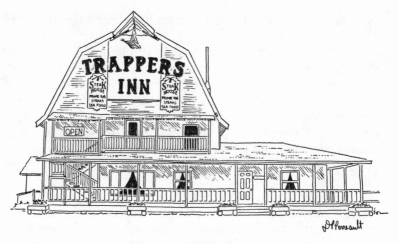

Trappers Inn
Huntsville, Utah
84317

Innkeepers: Bill and Michaeline Wangsgard
Address/Telephone: 7458 East 900 South (P.O. Box 165); (801) 745–2482
Rooms: 8; all with private bath.
Rates: $40 to $60, single or double; EPB. No pets. No air conditioning (usually not needed; elevation 4,920 feet). Cigarettes allowed but no cigars. MasterCard and Visa accepted.
Open: All year.
Facilities and Activities: Breakfast and dinner available every day; brunch and lunch served on Saturdays and Sundays; lunch available other days upon request. Lounge. Gift shop. Five rooms with Jaccuzi. Hayrides and sleigh rides. Snowmobile rentals. Nearby: Pineview Reservoir, Trappist monastery, museum, "Shootin' Star" Tavern (the oldest bar in Utah). Hiking, fishing, boating, water skiing, downhill and cross-country skiing, snowmobiling.

Set in a bucolic valley amid snow-peaked mountains, green meadows, and wildflowers, Trappers Inn is a family-run, down-home operation that offers ☞ unique accommodations and fantastic meals.

Bill and Michaeline, along with their seven children, do all the food preparation and innkeeping, and they take good care of their guests. ☛ Bill is chef, Michaeline does the baking, daughter Kecia waitresses, son Chris works the kitchen, David buses tables, and Joshua, Jeremiah, Barbara Anne, and Jacob are the backup crew.

The inn was ☛ built in 1941 as a dairy barn and operated in that capacity for thirty years. Bill has made a dedicated effort to retain the original structural shapes during his remodeling, and this adds a lot of charm to the inn. The second-floor walls follow the slope of the roof, providing slanted windows and a lovely cozy feeling. ☛ Some of the rooms have a sitting area, spiral staircase, sleeping loft, and a heart-shaped Jacuzzi built for two. Floors are nicely carpeted, window curtains and bedspreads are ruffled, beds are new and comfortable, and the general décor is country.

Plenty of behind-the-scenes care goes on in the kitchen. The ☛ wheat is ground by hand the very day the bread is baked. Bill grinds his own hamburger, cuts his own steaks, and makes the noodles for the soups.

Breakfast begins with a plate of fresh fruit and orange-raisin muffins, followed by either a perfectly executed omelet or, a favorite of guests, Bill's turkey Marco Polo: sliced turkey, ham, and cheese wrapped around a spear of broccoli, topped with hollandaise sauce, and served with home-fried potatoes. Dinner is just as enticing and the inn is becoming famous for its chicken fried steak, made from carefully trimmed and tenderized cuts and coated with a special homemade breading.

There's lots of outdoor activities in the area. In summer, Bill hitches his team of Clydesdales to the hay wagon for a trail ride and Dutch-oven dinner. And when the snow comes, it's sleigh-ride time.

How to get there: From Ogden, take Highway 39 (12th Street) through Ogden Canyon toward Huntsville. Inn is on the right just before Huntsville.

The Birch Trees
Bed & Breakfast Inn
Logan, Utah
84321

Innkeeper: Kristan Fjeldsted
Address/Telephone: 315 Boulevard; (801) 753–1331
Rooms: 4 share 1 bath.
Rates: $25, single; $30 to $35, double. Includes continental-plus breakfast. No pets. TV in living room only. No air conditioning (usually not needed; elevation 4,535 feet.) No smoking inside inn. Well-behaved children only. MasterCard and Visa accepted.
Open: All year.
Facilities and Activities: Sack lunches available. BYOB. Patio with porch swing, large yard centrally located. Nearby: Utah State University, Willow Park Zoo, Jensen Living Historical Farm, community recreation center and swimming pool, museums, parks. Hiking, fishing, tennis, downhill and cross-country skiing, snowmobiling, ice skating.

Looking remarkably like the old-fashioned, metal doll houses of the '30s and '40s, this Colonial Cape Cod stands on a wide corner lot in a fine residential neighborhood. White with green shutters, ☞ the two-story inn is truly beautiful inside. In the

230

entrance hall, a teddy bear in a wicker baby buggy waits to greet you while a crystal chandelier sparkles overhead. The raspberry-sherbet carpet, white walls, comfortable furniture, fireplace, arched doorways, and large ferns make the living room particularly attractive. In an upstairs sitting alcove, a small wooden sleigh adds a touch of nostalgia.

The ☞ guest rooms are meticulously decorated. I liked the Blue Room with its brass bed, reading corner, flower-bedecked straw hat and old-style doll dressed in blue. ☞ A basket of towels and soap sits in each room, along with a pitcher of ice water, fresh flowers, and a dish of candy.

Kristan and small daughter Jenilyn serve a generous continental breakfast of croissants, bran muffins made without sugar, grapes, strawberries or other fresh fruit in season, freshly ground Colombian Supreme coffee, and, if you like, hot oatmeal. Kristan will fix a sack lunch for you if you are off to enjoy the many activities in the area.

Logan sits in the middle of the lush, green Cache Valley, surrounded by snow-capped mountains. ☞ The Mormon Temple, built by church members who skillfully combined several nineteenth-century architectural styles, is directly across the street from the inn; a visitors center is only one block away; and downtown is closeby.

Come dinnertime, I know a great place to recommend. Within walking distance, at 19 North Main Street, The Blue Bird Restaurant features homemade candy, pies and ice cream, and great home cooking at moderate prices. On your right, as you enter, is an old-time soda fountain made from Mexican marble. All food is prepared on the premises, including sauces, gravies, salad dressings, pies, cakes, and rolls. I had a chicken salad and a strawberry soda, thick with berries and ice cream. Dinners come with a relish tray of crisp, fresh vegetables, sour cream, and chips; portions are ample; and service is excellent.

How to get there: From Main Street, turn east onto 100 North Street. After three blocks, you will find the inn on the left, across from the Mormon Temple.

Center Street
Bed & Breakfast
Logan, Utah
84321

Innkeepers: Clyne and Ann Long
Address/Telephone: 169 East Center Street; (801) 752–3443
Rooms: 10; 8 with private bath, 2 share 1 bath.
Rates: $20 to $60, single and double, during week; $20 to $65, single
   and double, on weekends. Includes continental-plus breakfast. No
   pets. Wheelchair accessible. Air conditioning in Blue Room and
   Garden Room only (usually not needed; elevation 4,535 feet). No
   smoking. Well-behaved children over age 8 are welcome.
   MasterCard and Visa accepted.
Open: All year.
Facilities and Activities: BYOB. Jacuzzis, VCRs, more than 50 movies.
   Off-street parking. Nearby: Utah State University, parks, recreation
   center, municipal swimming pool. Hiking, fishing, tennis, downhill
   and cross-country skiing, snowmobiling, ice skating.

This is an inn of surprises! Standing dignified and sedate,
the 1879, red-brick Victorian contains a fittingly appropriate
main-floor parlor with fireplace, polished hardwood floors,

Duncan Phyfe couch, and player piano. Upstairs, the guest rooms are Mormon proper with ☞ hand-stitched quilts, window seats, lace curtains, antique four-posters, and a brass bed dating from the 1840s.

Ah, but wait. The atmosphere begins to change as you climb the narrow, red-carpeted staircase to the third-floor Garden Room. Here we find a king-size water bed, covered with crimson spread and ivory ruffles, sharing space with a gray-marble Jacuzzi. A little sign on the door handle reads, "Do Not Disturb: Honeymoon in Progress." Okay. So what if, well hidden in the attic, there's one room a little out of character. It's always booked, I am told.

But this is only the beginning. In the carriage house, done with class and entirely in good taste, I must add, the Desert Oasis features a round scarlet bed set on a platform of lush beige carpet designed to simulate a sand dune. Draped in gold fabric to resemble a sultan's tent, the bed has a "star control" on the headboard. ☞ By pushing the little button, one gets instant stars on the ceiling! There's also a heart-shaped Jacuzzi and ☞ a special waterfall shower where water careens and crashes down a rock wall and ricochets onto one's sudsy self.

Ann ☞ dresses demurely in nineteenth-century costume when serving a continental-plus breakfast of fruit, yogurt, juice, and hot breads made from freshly ground wheat. There are many good restaurants nearby for lunch and dinner, some within walking distance. Ann suggests you try Chi Chi's for Mexican, Gia's for Italian, and, a few miles up Logan Canyon, Zanivoo's for excellent seafood, chicken, and steak. You will enjoy visiting with Ann. She is well versed in Utah lore and can also give you many suggestions concerning area activities.

How to get there: From Main Street (Highway 91), turn right onto Center Street, just before the Mormon Tabernacle. Go 1½ blocks. Inn is on the left.

Manti House Inn
Manti, Utah
84642

Innkeepers: Jim and Sonya Burnidge and Alan and T. K. Plant
Address/Telephone: 401 North Main Street; (801) 835–0161
Rooms: 6, including 2 suites; all with private bath.
Rates: $30 to $50, single; $35 to $55, double; $75, suite; EPB. No pets.
  No smoking allowed in the inn. Well-behaved children only please.
  MasterCard, Visa, American Express accepted.
Open: All year.
Facilities and Activities: Breakfast served to inn guests only. Lunch
  available daily except Sundays. Dinner served Thursday, Friday,
  and Saturday evenings; reservations required. BYOB. Homemade
  chocolates in guest rooms, turn-down service, evening refreshments, hot tub, horse-drawn carriage rides. Nearby: hiking, fishing,
  hot-air ballooning, golf, tennis, swimming, museum. Mormon Mir-
  acle Pageant, largest outdoor pageant in the U.S., performed each
  July.

  This inn is one of my favorites, and I can't decide if it's the
country charm of Sonya's hand-stitched quilts (two on every
bed!), Jim's hand-crafted furniture (his superbly executed pie
safe stands in the upstairs hallway), Alan's culinary creativity,

T.K.'s irresistible enthusiasm, or perhaps the warm way all four welcome you to their English Vernacular inn, built of limestone in 1868.

All the rooms are exquisitely done: tiny printed wallpapers, gigantic four-posters, and claw-footed bathtubs. ☛ A photograph of T. K. and Alan's baby daughter, Annalee (Jim and Sonya's granddaughter), splashing about in their 150-year-old English tin bathtub was featured in the book *A Day in the Life of America.*

My room was the bridal suite, and I heartily recommend that you ☛ reserve ahead for this masterpiece with its raspberry-sherbet carpet, white-railinged stairway leading down to the hot tub, private balcony, tiny window seat, and massive four-poster, so high it takes a two-step platform to climb into bed.

☛ Lace-covered French doors partition off the built-for-two, rose-colored tub and Jacuzzi with wraparound mirrors and ruffled burgundy drapes.

If it hadn't been for the aroma of bacon and oven pancakes, made with lemon and nutmeg from an old family recipe, I'd probably still be in that lovely room.

Breakfast here is wonderful, but dinner is even better because that is when Alan really has the opportunity to exhibit his expertise. ☛ A five-course affair, the meal may begin with an appetizer of crab-stuffed tomato, continue with either French onion or potato soup, fresh-fruit salad with pineapple topping, corn pudding, and country ham with raisin sauce, and conclude with a strawberry torte or Alan's raspberry mousse. Dinner is served on Thursday, Friday, and Saturday evenings, and reservations are a must. Lunch is available daily, except on Sunday, in the Ice Cream Parlor.

How to get there: From I–15 at Provo, take Highway 89 southeast to Manti. From I–70 at Salina, take Highway 89 north to Manti. Inn is on the main street of town.

⬎

D: *After breakfast, Jim and Sonya took me for* ☛ *a ride through the village in their Amish carriage pulled by faithful Tillie. A perfect way to see this pretty town, that ride has become one of my favorite memories.*

The Homestead
Midway, Utah
84032

Innkeepers: Jerry and Carole Sanders
Address/Telephone: 700 North Homestead Drive; (801) 654–1103 or (800) 327–7220
Rooms: 43; all with private bath.
Rates: $39 to $90, single and double; EP. No pets. No air conditioning. All major credit cards accepted.
Open: All year.
Facilities and Activities: Full-service restaurant. Sunday brunch. Liquor available at front desk, setups in dining room. Indoor swimming pool, outdoor swimming pool and hot tub, tennis, golf, horseback riding, hayrides, sleigh rides. Nearby: downhill skiing at Park City and Robert Redford Sundance ski areas, cross-country skiing, snowmobiling.

In 1886, Swiss-born Simon Schneitter may have cursed the mineral hot springs that made farming his land next to impossible. But as friends and neighbors arrived to bathe in the health-giving waters, he, a resourceful man, soon realized the potential of the warm water that bubbled from his "hot pots." He constructed a pool and bath houses, added a few guest rooms, and, when his wife, Fanny, began serving up country-fried chicken, built on a dining room. Simon decided that the resort business was much more lucrative than trying to grow alfalfa.

The Homestead is set on forty-three acres and comprises the main lodge plus seven distinctly different guest houses, including the Victorian Virginia House, the sprawling Ranch House, the rustic Barn, and the Milk House. My favorite is the Milk House with its provincial-print wallpaper and white woodwork. It's cool and clean, with a country feeling, just as a milk house should be. At one time, it was a cold storage for milk, and, during Prohibition, it housed liquor for a thriving gambling business.

This inn can be just about anything you want it to be: casual, elegant, social, or private. The spacious grounds and many amenities make it possible to be peacefully alone or deeply involved in country-club activities.

You can ☞ ride horseback through beautiful Heber Canyon, swim in either the indoor or outdoor pools, soak in a spring-fed mineral bath, or doze on a lawn chair under whispering pine and fluttering aspen.

The dining room is large, with an expanse of windows providing a view of rolling range lands. I can vouch for the chicken cordon bleu, stuffed to bursting with melted cheese and ham. But the clincher was the mousse cake, a ☞ French–Genoese delight made with butter, cream, and white chocolate and adorned with dark-chocolate mousse. The only item that can compete with this is The Homestead's praline cheesecake. You must try both, preferably at different meals.

How to get there: 3 miles north of Heber City on Highway 40, turn west onto River Road, right onto Burgi Lane, and then left onto Cari Lane. The way is well marked with signs.

Peterson's Bed & Breakfast
Monroe, Utah
84754

Innkeepers: Howard and Mary Ann Peterson
Address/Telephone: 95 North 300 West (mailing address: P.O. Box 142);
    (801) 527–4830
Rooms: 3; all with private bath.
Rates: $25, single; $35, double; EPB. No pets. No smoking in inn. No
    liquor allowed on premises. Well-behaved children only, please.
    Credit cards not accepted.
Open: All year.
Facilities and Activities: Breakfast only meal served. Complimentary
    coffee, cocoa, tea, cookies, and candy available at all times. Private
    yard with lawn chairs under ancient apple tree. Free maps and
    brochures. Nearby: restaurants. Nonsulphurous–hot-springs pool.
    Within easy driving range of 5 national parks and 4 national forests,
    including Fish Lake National Forest, where Mackinaw trout weigh-
    ing from 25 to 30 pounds are caught. Hiking, fishing, golf, tennis,
    photography.

    This inn may be on the small side; but if you are looking for
a homey atmosphere, a base camp from which to see the many
wonders of southern Utah, or someone who really knows the
state, then this just may be the perfect place for you to settle into.

Mary Ann is an administrative assistant to the Utah Travel Council, and if she doesn't know the answers to your questions, she will search them out for you. ☞ She has an extensive selection of maps, pamphlets, and brochures that she gladly shares with guests.

And, ☞ if you are a Disney fan, you will definitely enjoy chatting with Howard, who, up until a few years ago, spent his days at Disneyland trying to keep Mickey, Donald, and Goofy in line. Actually, he was maintenance director, and he has many fascinating Disney mementos around the house.

From the front, this inn appears to be a family bungalow, but the appearance is misleading because the guest rooms are in their own extended wing with private yard, baths, and entrances. They are nicely furnished with lots of little comfort and convenience touches. Soft drinks are available on the honor system, and fruit juice, cookies, and candy snacks are always handy.

☞ Breakfast at the Petersons' was the highlight of my day. In the cozy dining room, I was served fresh orange juice, milk, and a unique Mexican quiche. Seasoned exactly right with a hint of hot spices, it was accented perfectly by the cool melon slices that came with it.

If you want to be pampered, add this inn to your itinerary. ☞ I have never felt more welcome anywhere than I did here.

How to get there: From I–15, north of Cedar City, take I–70 east to Joseph. At Joseph, take Monroe turnoff to Monroe. From main street, turn west at City Park and go 3 blocks to 300 West.

D: *Mary Ann has published a Mormon cookbook and has a* ☞ *private collection of more than 2,000 recipe books that she generously lets guests browse through.*

Mansion House Inn
Mt. Pleasant, Utah
84647

Innkeepers: Denis and Terri Andelin
Address/Telephone: 298 South State Street (mailing address: P.O. Box 13); (801) 462–3031 or (801) 462–3034
Rooms: 4; all with private bath.
Rates: $39, single; $49, double; EPB. No pets. No smoking inside inn. Children over age 12 are welcome. MasterCard and Visa accepted.
Open: All year.
Facilities and Activities: Dinners available with prior arrangements. BYOB. Nearby: Manti–La Sal National Forest. Hiking, fishing, cross-country skiing.

This one's a beauty and bears a well-chosen name. The stately 1897 red-brick Victorian sits on a shady lawn skirted by a white picket fence. A ☞ handsomely carved bannister, winding staircase, and massive stained-glass window dominate the entrance hall. At the top of the stairs you find a small sitting area and four fetching guest rooms. Quilted bedspreads, dust ruffles, and lots of eyelet and lace enhance the immaculate bed chambers. The room facing front is perfectly charming, with etched and stained-glass window, tiny white dots on blue wallpaper, white shutters, and a quilted, ruffled bed with six pillows to match. Another room is done in shades of peach and brown, with ivory eyelet-trimmed bed cover and ☛ a tiny balcony all its own.

Breakfast here is a most pleasant occasion. Denis, a professional photographer, and Terri have seven children; and, as you can well imagine, Terri has spent plenty of time in the kitchen perfecting her cooking skills. At a prearranged time, she brings a tray laden with either fruit-filled muffins, omelet with bacon and sausage, or Belgian waffles with fruit and whipped-cream topping to your room. ☛ And you can have breakfast either in bed, at a small table in your room, or, my choice, on the shared balcony just off the upstairs mini-parlor. If you make arrangements ahead of time, and I highly recommend that you do, Terri will serve you a hefty portion of whatever she has planned for her family's dinner. There's a plaque in the front hall that proclaims "Happiness is Homemade," and this motto definitely carries over into mealtime.

The inn is only a few blocks from Main Street, where one finds a few shops and typical small-town cafés.

How to get there: Mt. Pleasant is south of Provo on Highway 89. From Main Street, turn south onto State Street and drive for 3 blocks. Inn is on the right.

᪥

D: *You won't want to leave this inn without first stepping into Denis's downstairs studio for a chance to admire some outstanding photography. His portraiture, with its excellent use of lighting, is exceptional.*

The Blue Church Lodge
Park City, Utah
84060

Innkeeper: Nancy Schmidt
Address/Telephone: 424 Park Avenue (mailing address: P.O. Box 1720); (801) 649–8009
Rooms: 12, including 7 in church and 5 in annex; all with private bath.
Rates: $50 to $170, for units ranging from 1 bedroom with bath to 4 bedrooms with 3 baths and accommodating from 1 to 10 persons, during off-season. Same units are $75 to $265 in season. Includes continental breakfast. Small pets allowed with prior approval. No air conditioning (not needed; elevation 7,000 feet). MasterCard and Visa accepted.
Open: November 1 to May 1; other times by special arrangement.
Facilities and Activities: BYOB, dry bar. 2 hot tubs, 2 Jacuzzis, ski lockers, covered parking area, laundry facilities, kitchens. Nearby: Deer Valley Ski Resort, restaurants, shopping. Championship golf courses, indoor and outdoor tennis, hiking, fishing, alpine slide, gondola rides, swimming, horseback riding, hot-air-balloon rides, excellent downhill and cross-country skiing, helicopter skiing, snowmobiling.

If I were the proverbial church mouse looking for a home, I'd give myself a big pat on the back for finding The Blue Church. Built in 1890, it was ☞ Park City's first Mormon Church and served in that capacity until 1962. ☞ Its Victorian exterior has been left intact, earning it a placement on the National Register of Historic Places. Inside, it has become an exceptionally attractive inn. The former congregation area is now a comfy parlor with raised hearth fireplace, oriental rugs, oval dining-room table, and wet bar. A continental breakfast of sweet rolls, juice, coffee, chocolate, and tea is served here each morning.

The décor is soft blue, beige, and off-white throughout, with oak and pine antique replicas and all sorts of modern conveniences.

The accommodations are luxurious, with one of the nicest guest rooms being a two level unit facing front. It has a cozy living room, fireplace, and complete kitchen, including a blender and crockpot. A narrow staircase leads to an upstairs bedroom with steep-gabled sitting nook and circle window. Above the bed, ☞ a large skylight lets in the morning sun and the midnight stars or provides the ☞ memorable experience of lying in bed and watching snowflakes fall overhead.

Hidden away in the church cellar, and large enough for fifteen to twenty people, is a luxurious spa with rock walls, patio furniture, many plants, and an exquisite stained-glass window. There is a smaller, outdoor spa as well.

Wooden steps beside the church take you down to Main Street and many shops and restaurants. Nancy recommends The Claim Jumper for an oversized steak and giant baked potato or Shannon's for excellent French cuisine.

How to get there: From I–80, take Highway 224 south to Park City. 224 turns into Park Avenue at Park City. Inn is on left side of street.

The Imperial Hotel
Park City, Utah
84060

Innkeeper: Peggie Varney Collins

Address/Telephone: 221 Main Street (mailing address: P.O. Box 1628);
(801) 649–1904

Rooms: 12, including 2 suites; all with private bath.

Rates: $75 to $135, winter ($85 to $150, December 21 to January 4); 40
percent off, summer; 3-day-minimum stay during ski season; EPB.
No pets. No air conditioning (not needed; elevation over 6,000 feet).
No smoking. Well-behaved children only. All major credit cards
accepted.

Open: All year.

Facilities and Activities: Dinner served 3 to 4 nights a week by reservation. No lunch. BYOB. Complimentary afternoon refreshments.
Ski lockers, sauna and hot tub, staff assistance with ski arrangements, transportation, theater and dinner reservations. Nearby:
many restaurants, shops, art galleries, theater; hiking, tennis, golf,
biking, downhill and cross-country skiing.

When it was first built in 1904, the Bogan Boarding House
was a haven for silver miners as they emerged each evening after
twelve long hours in the mines. Its reputation for outstanding
hospitality soon spread, and, when the "boarding house" label no
longer seemed to fit, it was renamed The Imperial Hotel.

I can't help but wonder what those same miners would think if they could return to their Imperial and sit down to breakfast served on heart-shaped place mats, drink fresh-ground Viennese coffee, relax in the sauna and hot tub, savors hors d'oeuvres in the afternoon, and catch the scent of fresh flowers in nearly every room.

Romantic with subtle hints of hearts and flowers, this inn features fine antiques, a stone fireplace in the parlor, and French doors and Roman bathtubs in some of the guest rooms. The exquisitely decorated and furnished rooms are the work of inn-keeper Peggie Varney Collins, a former interior designer and author of the book *Beyond Interior Design.* She is a friendly, outgoing hostess, the kind who comes to the front door in her stocking feet. When you leave, you may not be able to resist giving her a hug. And when was the last time you hugged your hotel concierge?

At breakfast, Peggie served the first course—coffee, melon chunks, and gigantic fresh strawberries, along with sour cream and raw sugar for dipping—in the parlor. Next she brought made-to-order omelets to the dining room, where baskets of hot muffins and breads awaited our discovery.

Dinner here is on a request-ahead basis, and I definitely advise you to "request ahead." The evening meal consists of hearty homemade soups, French or German stew or perhaps a Spanish casserole, hot breads, salad, and a light dessert. Perfect after a summertime hike or a winter's day on the slopes.

How to get there: At the intersection of I–80 and Highway 224, 26 miles east of Salt Lake City, go south on 224 for 6 miles to Park City. Turn left onto Heber Ave. and right onto Main St. Hotel is on the right.

The Old Miners' Lodge
Park City, Utah
84060

Innkeepers: Susan Wynne, Hugh Daniels, and Jeff Sadowsky
Address/Telephone: 615 Woodside Avenue (mailing address: P.O. Box
    2639); (801) 645–8068
Rooms: 7; 4 with private bath, 3 share 2 baths.
Rates: $40 to $80, summer; $70 to $135, November through April; $90
    to $155, December 19 to January 4; EPB. No pets. No TV. No air
    conditioning (not needed; elevation 7,000 feet). Smoking in living
    room only. MasterCard, Visa, American Express accepted.
Open: All year.
Facilities and Activities: Dinner for groups upon request. BYOB. Com-
    plimentary wine. Kitchen and laundry privileges. Nearby: Deer Val-
    ley Ski Resort, championship golf courses, indoor and outdoor tennis,
    hiking, fishing, alpine slide, gondola rides, swimming, horseback
    riding, hot-air-balloon rides, excellent downhill and cross-country
    skiing, helicopter skiing, snowmobiling.

    Built in 1893 as a boarding house for miners, this Western
Victorian has been standing above this old mining town for generations.
    Whereas the miners probably stayed in dorm-style rooms

with a minimum of comforts, today's guests enjoy down quilts, feather pillows, electric mattress covers, turn-down service, and complimentary wine, cider, cheese, and popcorn in the evenings. Such amenities would have been wishful thinking only on the part of even the most imaginative of miners.

During winter, you can ☞ ski out the back door or ☞ sit in the hot tub and watch fellow skiers glide by on the ski lift within a few feet of your steamy domain. In summer, the hot tub is just as special after a long hike.

The guest rooms are named after colorful characters from the town's past. The Jedidiah Grant has a king-size bed, enclosed sun porch, ruffled curtains, claw-footed tub, and corner sink. It shares the best view in the house with the Flip Wing Suite. Both look down into the valley and up to Old Town.

The most interesting guest room is the Black Jack Murphy. ☞ One enters via a narrow, timbered passageway constructed to resemble a mine shaft. The room itself, reminiscent of a miner's cabin, has log walls, bare light bulb hanging from the ceiling, and curtained closet; but I noticed that even bad Jack had a mint on his pillow and a terry-cloth robe for walking to the hot tub. Black Jack Murphy's claim to fame (or infamy) comes from his being the only person in Park City's history to have been lynched. He is said to have jumped a claim and murdered the owner. As the sheriff took him to jail, he was seized by a mob of outraged miners and hanged.

Breakfast is miner size and might be German pancakes with bacon, egg burritos, or whole wheat waffles from an old-time recipe. Hugh, the main chef, will prepare a seven-course dinner for groups of six to eight people with prior arrangement. Or it's only a couple blocks down the hill to numerous restaurants.

How to get there: Highway 224 south turns into Park Avenue at Park City. Turn right onto 8th Street and proceed 1 block to Woodside Avenue. Turn left onto Woodside. The inn is on the right.

❀

D: *Children are especially welcome here, and there are toys and games provided.*

Washington School Inn
Park City, Utah
84060

Innkeeper: Richard Scott
Address/Telephone: 543 Park Avenue (mailing address: P.O. Box 536);
(800) 824–1672 outside Utah, (800) 824–4761 inside Utah
Rooms: 15, including 3 suites; all with private bath.
Rates: $60 to $100, spring and summer; $125 to $200, ski season; EPB.
No pets. Wheelchair accessible. No air conditioning (not needed;
elevation 7,000 feet). Smoking on mezzanine only. Well-behaved
children over 12 years old only, please. MasterCard, Visa, American
Express accepted.
Open: All year except for 2 weeks following ski season.
Facilities and Activities: Lunch for groups of 10 or more. Occasional
dinners by reservation. BYOB. Hot tub, Jacuzzi, sauna, steam
showers, concierge services. Nearby: restaurants; golf, tennis, hiking, fishing, horseback riding, downhill and cross-country skiing.

There's no more "readin', 'ritin', and 'rithmetic" at the old
Washington School. The 3 Rs now more accurately stand for
"regal," "refined," and "resplendent." Built in 1889, the structure
☛ served as a public school for forty-two years, became a social
hall during the '30s, and lay vacant from the '50s until 1984. The

hammered-limestone exterior, bell tower, dormer and classroom windows, and curved entry porticos have been retained, thus qualifying the inn for the National Register of Historic Places.

The entry hall still has the feeling of an old-fashioned school house, with exposed original timbers supporting the ☞ three-story bell tower. A library/mezzanine overlooks the elegant living room, where complimentary beverages await your arrival and refreshments are served during the afternoons.

Each morning, an antique side board in the formal dining room is ☞ lavishly spread with breakfast items such as eggs Florentine or cheese Strada served with bacon, ham, or sausage; fresh fruit and lemon-nut bread; homestead pumpkin bread; Grandma Anderson's brown bread; or, perhaps, Utah beer bread.

The occasional ☞ candlelight dinners are a gourmand's delight. They are *prix fixe* and table d'hôte, and a sample menu might include roasted-red-pepper soup, watercress-oyster-mushroom salad, and beef tenderloin wrapped in phyllo with cabernet sauce. Inquire ahead for dates. Reservations are a must.

All guest rooms are ☞ elaborately custom-decorated and bear the names of former school teachers. "Miss Thatcher" has a brick fireplace, king-size bed, rose carpet, and, heavens to mercy!, a pink-flowered love seat and a wet bar. "Miss Thompson" has a green iron-and-brass bed, fireplace with round windows on either side, and, also, a love seat and wet bar. My favorite room was "Miss Urie." Bright and sunny, it has pink and blue flowers sprinkled on yellow wallpaper, a chatting corner, and a writing alcove. A pine chest sits at the foot of a pine four-poster with burgundy pillows plumped on the lemon yellow bedspread. An antique book acts as doorstep.

The lower level of the inn features a wine cellar and a ☞ luxurious whirlpool spa with stone floor, bent-willow furniture, dry sauna, and steam showers. Wouldn't the Misses Thatcher, Thompson, and Urie have loved this as their "Teacher's Room"?

How to get there: From I–80, take Highway 224 south to Park City. 224 turns into Park Avenue at Park City. Inn is on the right side of street.

The Pullman Inn
Provo, Utah
84601

Innkeepers: Tim, Dennis, and Kelly Morganson
Address/Telephone: 415 South University Avenue; (801) 374–8141
Rooms: 6; 4 with private bath, 2 share 1 bath.
Rates: $28 to $42, single; $35.50 to $49.50, double; EPB. No pets. TV in
    sitting room only. No smoking. Well-behaved children only, please.
    MasterCard, Visa, American Express accepted.
Open: All year.
Facilities and Activities: Dinner served on Friday and Saturday eve-
    nings, reservations a must; dinner available other times for groups
    of 10 or more. BYOB. Hand-dipped chocolates on bedside tables.
    Nearby: Brigham Young University, Utah Lake State Park, Osmond
    Entertainment Center and Studios, Bridal Veil Falls, Sundance
    Summer Theatre. Hiking, fishing, water skiing, sailing, downhill
    and cross-country skiing.

There's something about climbing a ☞ red-carpeted turret
staircase up to your bedroom that is hopelessly romantic. And
when that room itself turns out to be a masterpiece, you congrat-
ulate yourself for being so wise as to have reserved a room in such
an outstanding inn.

Actually, I knew I had made the right choice the moment I walked up to this Romanesque–Revival Victorian and met innkeeper Tim waiting on the front steps. His greeting and warm handshake were the types that make you feel good all over.

Three congenial brothers operate this inn, and their mother has hand-stitched extraordinarily exquisite quilts for all the beds. Some of her work is for sale in the small gift shop to the right of the stairs. I am saving my pennies for my next visit.

The guest rooms are furnished with quality antiques. In the Master Bedroom on the second floor, I found a circa-1870 inlaid-mahogany wardrobe from England, stained-glass window original to the inn, peach-and-burgundy quilt with matching pillows, and curved-glass side windows that overlook the front yard and garden.

The Morganson brothers do all the cooking, and a full breakfast of egg dishes, meat, fresh fruit, and Dennis's wonderful cinnamon rolls or pumpkin bread is served on their grandmother's dining-room table beneath a crystal chandelier. Dinners are available on Friday and Saturday evenings and are much in demand, so be sure to make a reservation. The house specialty is trois fillet de Lacieux: fillets of ham, beef, and turkey layered with pecan dressing and Monterey Jack cheese, wrapped in puff pastry, and topped with mushroom gravy. Just the sort of meal this grand old mansion demands.

For those evenings when you choose to eat out, I recommend a special place only six blocks away called Sil's Ivy Tower, where three separate restaurants are housed in a gorgeous stone building that was Provo's first Latter Day Saints' church.

How to get there: Inn is on the east side of University Avenue, which is Provo's main street.

D: *Those luscious* *hand-dipped chocolates you find on your bedside table were made by the Morgansons' mother. There are usually some freshly made and packaged ones for sale in the gift corner.*

Greene Gate Village
St. George, Utah
84770

Innkeepers: Mark and Barbara Greene
Address/Telephone: 76 West Tabernacle Street; (801) 628–6999
Rooms: 6; 5 share 4 baths, 1 suite with private bath.
Rates: $25 per person, $10 each for children 18 years and younger;
　　EPB. No pets. No smoking allowed. MasterCard and Visa accepted.
Open: All year.
Facilities and Activities: BYOB (no hard liquor permitted; wine only).
　　Heated outdoor pool. Hot tub. Nearby: Zion National Park, Snow
　　Canyon, many historical sites. Restaurants, shopping; hiking, fish-
　　ing, tennis, photography.

　　Greene Gate Village comprises three separate, 🖛 meticulously restored, Mormon pioneer homes, operated collectively as
an inn. Sitting side by side on one city block and surrounded by
wide lawns, flower beds, fountain, swimming pool, and hot tub,
they are furnished with mint-condition antiques.

　　Although there were other guests present during my stay
(even an outdoor wedding taking place in an old cupola), I had
the feeling I was the very first person to spend the night here.
Everything was perfect.

　　I stayed in the Orpha Morris Home, a two-story stone cottage with wide front porch, fireplace, and sloped-ceilinged bedrooms. In the morning, I sat in the elaborate, red velvet–bedecked parlor of The Bentley House while waiting for the homemade cinnamon rolls to come out of the oven. Breakfast began with huge red strawberries, succulent green grapes, and bananas so perfectly yellowed, they looked as though they were made of wax. Next came a pitcher of orange juice and one of milk, crisp bacon, and those eagerly awaited cinnamon rolls. All this served on a golden oak table embellished with china and silver. Breakfast should always be like this!

Mark is an orthopedic surgeon, and Barbara is deeply involved with the preservation of Mormon history.

On the corner sits Judds Store, operated by third-generation Judds. It is the oldest, continually operating, family-run mercantile establishment in Utah. Mr. Judd sells all sorts of goodies, including home-baked pastries and breads and a large selection of candies. It is said that children have been coming to Judds from the elementary school across the street since the days when they would bring a still-warm egg snatched from a nesting hen to exchange for a sweet treat.

For dinner, I walked the couple blocks to The Homespun Restaurant, a lovely old 1892 homestead, where I had some of the best chicken kiev and cheese cauliflower soup to be found anywhere.

How to get there: From St. George Blvd., turn south onto Main Street, then right onto Tabernacle. Inn is on the right.

❀

D: *In 1877, Brigham Young ordered green paint for the fences and gates surrounding the newly constructed St. George Temple. Being a prudent man, he offered the excess paint free-of-charge to the Mormon pioneers if they would use it on their gates and fences. Soon yard after yard was edged in bright green. Two of the original "green gates" remain, and one of those belongs to Greene Gate Village.*

Seven Wives Inn
St. George, Utah
84770

Innkeepers: Jay and Donna Curtis, Jon and Alison Bowcutt
Address/Telephone: 217 North 100 West; (801) 628–3737
Rooms: 9; all with private bath.
Rates: $25 to $65, single or double; EPB. Well-mannered pets allowed.
Wheelchair accessible. No smoking inside inn. Well-behaved children only, please. MasterCard and Visa accepted.
Open: All year.
Facilities and Activities: Picnic lunches available if requested ahead.
Honeymoon breakfast brought to room. BYOB. Swimming pool, hot tub, Jacuzzi. Nearby: Zion National Park, Snow Canyon (where many movies have been filmed), Brigham Young's winter home, Mormon scout Jacob Hamblin's home, LDS Temple and Tabernacle, restaurants, shopping, museums, art galleries. Five golf courses, hiking, fishing, tennis, horseback riding, great scenic photography.

This inn is steeped in Mormon history. When Donna and Jay were remodeling the 1873 structure, ☛ they found a concealed door leading to the attic, hooks that could have been used to suspend hammocks from the rafters, and a small section of the chimney where a stove may have been vented. All these finds led them to believe that, ☞ long ago, persecuted polygamists may have used the attic area as a hideaway.

Brigham Young is thought to have stayed here while building his own house across the street. Donna's great-grandfather Benjamin Johnson, private secretary to Mormon church founder Joseph Smith, wrote his memoirs in Brigham Young's nearby home; having taken seven wives, he is believed to have been one of those who hid in the attic. ☞ Donna and Jay named their inn and its guest rooms in honor of her great-grandfather and his many wives.

The room called Melissa, after Johnson's first wife, has a fireplace, lace-draped oak bed, and a tin bathtub rimmed in oak. Clarinda has an antique pine bed and caned-back rocker; Harriet, a peachy-pink comforter, mahogany bed, and private balcony; Sarah, a pair of church pews in front of the fireplace; Mary Ann, two iron beds and an oak dresser; and Susan, named for wife number six and sister to Harriet and Sarah, a Franklin stove, primitive wood furnishings, and its own outside entrance.

The most intriguing room of all, I think, is the one called Jane (for wife number seven). Located in the third-floor attic, where the polygamists are purported to have hidden, it has a braided rag rug, green stenciling on off-white walls, skylight, a bathroom sink fashioned from an old treadle sewing machine, and a claw-footed bathtub.

Breakfast is extensive and delicious. Served in the formal dining room, it might be German apple pancakes or a cheesy egg dish, homemade granola, hot breads, and ham or sausage. For dinner, Donna recommends Andelin's Gable House for five-course meals served in an English atmosphere. Several other restaurants are within walking distance.

How to get there: Take I–15 south to St. George turnoff (St. George Blvd.). Turn north onto 100 West and proceed 1 block. Inn is on the northwest corner.

The Burr House
Salina, Utah
84654

Innkeepers: Wayne, Tammy, and Shonnie Sittre
Address/Telephone: 190 West Main Street; (801) 529–7320
Rooms: 6; all with private bath.
Rates: $30 single, $35 double, summer; $25 single, $30 double, winter.
 Includes continental-plus breakfast. Well-mannered pets allowed.
 All major credit cards accepted.
Open: All year.
Facilities and Activities: Inn-operated full-service restaurant a few doors
 away. Breakfast in bed for honeymooners. Wake up calls. BYOB.
 Nearby: Fish Lake; golf, swimming, fishing, downhill skiing.

This is an intriguing old place with gabled and domed roof, upstairs porch, downstairs veranda, and a peek-a-boo cupola jutting out of the attic. I was met at the door by Tammy and Shonnie, two up-and-coming innkeepers, who were minding the inn while Dad was out. Dad Wayne, by the way, is a very busy innkeeper. Besides running a tight ship and making sure all guests' needs are met, he owns and manages the Branding Iron Inn, a full-service dining facility just down the street. He is also a city councilman and volunteer fireman.

The guest rooms are done in antiques that include several

claw-footed tubs, one with a polished oak ring skirting the top. Papa's Room has a white iron bed, chandelier, and redwood-paneled bath. Mama's Room boasts Wayne's mother's blue-and-white quilt, three large windows with stained glass, white iron bed, and blue-and-peach wallpaper set off by white woodwork.

If you don't stay in the Wood Room, make friends with its occupant so that you can get a glimpse of its bathroom. Fashioned after an outhouse, it has wood walls, slanted ceiling, skylight, and privy-style commode with modern, but hidden, fixture. Wayne obviously has quite a sense of humor. I'm sure he got many a chuckle out of designing this room!

A continental-plus breakfast of cereal, hot sweet rolls, fresh fruit, milk, orange juice, and coffee is served in the cheery dining room. Honeymooners are treated to a full breakfast in bed. Or you might want to walk the couple of blocks to the Branding Iron, where they serve a dandy crab omelet. If you choose to have dinner here, I suggest you try the rib-eye steak, marinated in Wayne's own special sauce and served with savory rice.

Salina is a small town with about 2,200 residents. It was first settled in 1863, abandoned because of Indian problems, and re-settled in 1871. Shopkeepers are friendly and knowledgeable of their area. A walk up and down Main Street and a chat or two can be very rewarding.

How to get there: From I–70, take Highway 89 exit north to Salina. From I–15, south of Nephi, take Highway 28 south to Gunnison. At Gunnison, take Highway 89 south to Salina. Inn is on main street of town.

Anselmo Inn
Salt Lake City, Utah
84102

Innkeepers: Chris and Julie Davies
Address/Telephone: 164 South 900 East; (801) 533–8184
Rooms: 5 rooms share 1 bath with separate shower and tub.
Rates: $29 to $39, single; $39 to $49, double; EPB. No pets. TV in TV
    room only. Evaporative coolers and fans. No smoking inside inn.
    Credit cards not accepted.
Open: All year.
Facilities and Activities: Dinners for five or more on request. BYOB.
    Sauna. Nearby: Temple Square, Great Salt Lake State Park, state
    capitol, University of Utah, LDS Genealogical Library, museums;
    restaurants, shopping. Hiking, fishing, swimming, downhill and
    cross-country skiing.

As neat as a pin both inside and out, this white brick with blue shutters has several claims to fame. First, Fortunato Anselmo, the Italian vice consul to the states of Utah and Wyoming from 1915 to 1965, lived here with his family for thirty years, thus giving it the necessary ☞ historical significance to qualify it for inclusion in the National Register of Historic Places. It is also the first bed and breakfast establishment in Salt Lake City and the longest-operating one in the state.

The inn still carries the name of the vice consul, and the Italian influence lingers. And no wonder. During the Anselmos' occupancy, ☛ many notables came to visit, including Cardinal Eugenio Pacelli (who later became Pope Pius XII), members of the 1932 Italian Olympic Team, and Mussolini's mistress.

The upstairs front guest room is called Nonno (Italian for grandpa) and has ruffled curtains, blue print wallpaper, and a rose, hand-crocheted bedspread that belonged to Julie's grandmother. The room next door, Nonna (for grandma), is made special by a wood-burning stove and a white iron-and-brass bed. The room named Ospite (guest) is where the cardinal stayed.

☛ You become part of the family here, and your "little angels" are welcome, too. Small daughter Alees shares her toys willingly, and there is a bassinet, crib, and playpen to borrow. A silver-trimmed, jet-black Great Majestic wood stove dominates the kitchen, where taffy pulls and divinity and fudge-making parties take place. Guests are invited to participate in the candy making and to join in with Chris, Julie, and their friends when they host socials.

Julie serves a generous breakfast of perhaps homemade *abelskievers,* cinnamon monkey bread, or Mormon pioneer doughnuts from an old family recipe. Along with this comes fresh fruit, milk, juice, and coffee. Dinner is available for groups of five or more if requested ahead. Italian, of course, it may be pasta salads and lasagna or spaghetti and sausage.

There's lots of extras here, like turn-down service, homemade candies at your bedside, carefully pressed sheets, and the use of parlors and dining room by guests. And a front porch swing for conversation and contemplation.

How to get there: Take North Temple east to State Street (Salt Lake City's main street), then east to 900 East and just past First South. Inn is on the right.

Brigham Street Inn
Salt Lake City, Utah
84102

Innkeepers: John and Nancy Pace
Address/Telephone: 1135 East South Temple; (801) 364–4461
Rooms: 9; all with private bath.
Rates: $65 to $140, single; $75 to $150, double. Includes continental-plus breakfast. No pets. Well-behaved children over age eight are welcome. MasterCard, Visa, American Express accepted.
Open: All year.
Facilities and Activities: BYOB. Lots of personal service. Nearby: Temple Square, Great Salt Lake State Park, state capitol, University of Utah, LDS Genealogical Library, museums; restaurants, shopping. Hiking, fishing, swimming, downhill and cross-country skiing.

This is a designers' showcase. Literally.

Owners John Pace, an architect, and his wife, Nancy, a patron of the arts dedicated to saving this magnificent structure from a certain demise, ☛ worked with twelve prominent designers to restore the two-and-one-half-story red-brick Victorian to its former dignity and grace.

It was built in 1898 for Walter Cogswell Lyne. Abandoned by his parents on the streets of Salt Lake City at the age of twelve, he supported himself as an errand boy for a local drug store, later

260

bought the company, and went on to become a successful wool broker and philanthropist.

As I entered the foyer, ☞ I was met by the glow of coffered oak wainscoting and a golden oak staircase. The sun shining through the beveled glass window spread a rainbow on the soft gray carpet.

In the parlor to the left, off-white and muted green couches face the delicately carved bird's-eye–maple fireplace, while on the right, the living room, with its striking black walls, white ceiling, and oyster carpet, is dominated by a massive black piano.

The guest rooms are every bit as grand, each designed and furnished by an individual specialist. A favorite was difficult to come by; but if I had to choose only one, it would be Number Seven in the third-floor attic. Done in navy blue accented with beige, it is enhanced with a maple fireplace, dormer windows, custom-designed bed, and an antique cherry-wood–covered support pillar.

A continental-plus breakfast of fresh strawberries, melon and other fruits in season, just-baked croissants and apple Danish, juice, and fresh-ground, French-roast coffee is brought to the blue-and-white, formal, and very English dining room by ☞ prim and proper maids in black dresses with white half-aprons. No other meals are served, but there are several four-star dining establishments within a ten-block radius. Your hosts, besides laying your evening fire, bringing ice for your champagne, and catering to your every whim, will help you select a restaurant.

☞ If you like feeling very elegant, very wealthy, and very special, you'll like it here. It's the kind of place you drive by and wish you could see on the inside. Now you can.

How to get there: Take North Temple (Salt Lake City's main street) east to State Street, turn right onto State, and proceed to South Temple. Turn left onto South Temple. Inn is on the left.

Under The Eaves Guest House
Springdale, Utah
84767

Innkeeper: Marcus R. T. Thomson
Address/Telephone: 980 Zion Park Boulevard (mailing address: P.O. Box 29); (801) 772–3457
Rooms: 4; 1 suite with bath, 1 cottage with bath, 2 rooms share 1 bath.
Rates: $25 to $55, single; $35 to $65, double; $65, cottage (sleeps 4); EPB. Breakfast not included. Pets allowed in suite only. Smoking in sitting room only. Well-behaved children only. MasterCard, Visa, American Express accepted.
Open: All year.
Facilities and Activities: Dinner available if requested in advance. BYOB. Nearby: Zion National Park, Grafton Ghost Town and Movie Location, museums, art galleries. Hiking, biking, swimming, tubing, outstanding photography possibilities.

Designed by Gilbert Underwood, famous architect for many national park lodges, this inn resembles a ☞ cozy English Tudor cottage. It is certainly environmental, for its timbers were brought down from nearby Cable Mountain, and its sandstone blocks were cut from the walls of Zion Canyon.

Two guest rooms, each with its own sink, share a common bath on the first floor. An expansive suite with raised sitting area,

262

dining corner, and large sleeping quarters takes up the entire second floor. With sloped ceiling, it is truly tucked "under the eaves." One of the three windows, each facing a different direction and offering outstanding views of the canyons, is a full-length beauty salvaged from an old church that was being demolished. The bed was hand-crafted in the Adirondacks and is covered with a hand-stitched quilt in the Dresden-plate pattern. A tole-painted, claw-footed bathtub sits in one corner.

Breakfast is a delight and, as with everything else in this inn, is presented with much attention given to detail. Marcus arises early to stir up the biscuits and grind the coffee. His specialty is 🖝 huevos rancheros, topped with his homemade salsa. Dinner might be barbecued chicken or lamb grilled on a bed of rosemary—or perhaps grilled halibut teriyaki served with vegetables fresh from the garden. Marcus has several other equally enticing selections, and I suggest you reserve ahead for the occasion.

This inn is 🖝 only steps from the west entrance to Zion National Park and makes a perfect base camp for activities in the area. Marcus is an avid hiker and knows the best trails through Zion. When his innkeeping duties permit, he will act as guide for guests. The day before I arrived, he had led six of his guests on a nine-mile trek around the north rim of the canyon.

A highlight of staying at Under The Eaves is 🖝 sitting on the front porch as dusk approaches and watching the colors change and intensify on the canyon's sheer rock walls and unique outcroppings.

How to get there: From I–15, north of St. George, take Highway 9 east to Springdale. Inn is on northwest side of Zion Park Blvd., Springdale's main street.

⁓

D: *For those evenings you choose to dine out, I recommend Flanigan's Inn for well-prepared, distinctively presented, and moderately priced meals.*

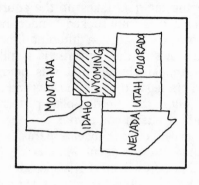

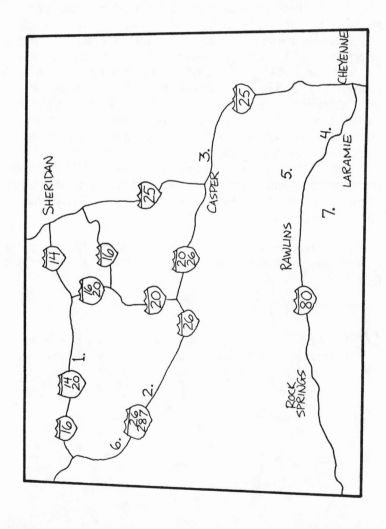

Wyoming

Numbers on map refer to towns numbered below.

1. Cody,
   Bill Cody's Ranch Inn...................................266
   The Irma...268
   The Lockhart Inn..270
   Rimrock Dude Ranch......................................272
   Siggins Triangle X Ranch................................274
2. DuBois, Lazy L & B Ranch..................................276
3. Glenrock, Hotel Higgins...................................278
4. Laramie, Annie Moore's Guest House........................280
5. Medicine Bow, The Historic Virginian Hotel...............282
6. Moran, Jenny Lake Lodge..................................284
7. Saratoga, Saratoga Inn...................................286

Bill Cody's Ranch Inn
Cody, Wyoming
82414

Innkeepers: Bill and Barbara Cody
Address/Telephone: 2604 Yellowstone Highway (mailing address: P.O. Box 1390); (307) 587–2097
Rooms: 16; all with private bath.
Rates: $52 to $62 double, June 20 through August 20; $42 to $52 double, August 21 through June 19; EP. Packages available, including all meals and limited or unlimited horseback riding, ranging from $175 to $200 per day for two people. No pets. No TV. No air conditioning (not needed; elevation 6,200 feet). All major credit cards accepted.
Open: All year.
Facilities and Activities: Full-service restaurant, Sunday brunch. Lounge. Horseback riding, heated outdoor Jacuzzi, volleyball court. Nearby: fishing, hiking, downhill and cross-country skiing.

No, it's not your imagination playing tricks on you. The gentleman at the desk *is* Bill Cody, and, you're right, he does look like Buffalo Bill. And for good reason. ☞ Innkeeper Bill Cody, with mustache, goatee, blue jeans, and cowboy boots, is the grandson of Col. William F. "Buffalo Bill" Cody.

The accommodations at Bill's ranch are first class. Guests stay in western, not rustic, log cabins with polished, knotty-pine walls, hand-crafted queen-size beds, and full baths. A wine-and-fruit basket waits on the bedside table, and original western art decorates each room.

Eighty percent of the guests who come here have never ridden a horse before, but there is no cause for the novice to worry. ☛ Horseback riding is taken seriously by the staff, and before each participant hits the trail, the wrangler makes sure the saddle fits perfectly, the stirrups are adjusted properly, and the rider is comfortable and at ease with his or her horse. All this preparation ensures a more enjoyable ride and fewer stiff muscles later.

Meals are served in the main ranch building, and guests choose from a varied menu ranging from New York strip sirloin to ☛ Grandma Cody's chili. I had pork chops with cornbread stuffing, a salad plate, and juicy apple pie. Countrified and delicious.

The town of Cody, only twenty-five miles away, offers an abundance of attractions. The Buffalo Bill Historical Center, a multi-million-dollar complex housing the Whitney Gallery of Western Art, the Buffalo Bill Museum, the Plains Indian Museum, and the Winchester Gun Collection, is a must. The Cody Night Rodeo performs nightly, June through August; and you won't want to miss a stroll through the Old Trail Town, a collection of authentic pioneer buildings reconstructed on the original town site.

How to get there: Inn is located on U.S. Highway 14–16–20, 25 miles east of east entrance to Yellowstone National Park and 25 miles west of Cody, Wyoming.

The Irma
Cody, Wyoming
82414

Innkeeper: Stan Wolz
Address/Telephone: 1192 Sheridan Avenue; (307) 587–4221
Rooms: 40, including 15 Victorian suites; all with private bath.
Rates: $40 to $55 single, $44 to $55 double during summer; $30 single, $33 double during winter; EP. Pre-approved, well-mannered pets allowed. All major credit cards accepted.
Open: All year.
Facilities and Activities: Full-service dining rooms. Bar. Swimming pool. Nearby: Buffalo Bill Historical Center housing the Whitney Gallery of Western Art, Buffalo Bill Museum, Plains Indian Museum, and Winchester Gun Collection. Cody Night Rodeo. Old Trail Town. Shopping, fishing, hiking, horseback riding, downhill and cross-country skiing.

The boardwalks and dirt streets have been replaced with cement, and T-shirt boutiques and art galleries stand where the blacksmith shop and general store once stood. But The Irma is much the same as it was when Buffalo Bill had it built in 1902, naming it for his youngest daughter.

☛ Local stockmen, woolgrowers, and oilmen still meet in the dining room, make deals involving tens of thousands of dollars, and seal them with nothing more than a handshake, proving that there is still honor among men (and women!).

I know the phrase "going back in time" is overworked, but that is truly how it felt to have dinner here and listen to talk of livestock and the price of wool coming from the next table. And sure there are tourists, lots of tourists; but it's easy to identify the locals because their jeans aren't of the designer species, their cowboy hats are weathered, and their boots are scuffed.

You can even get a feel for the territory from the menu. No escargot and petits fours served from this chuckwagon. If you want an appetizer, it's apt to be Rocky Mountain oysters, and the entrées include 28-ounce Porterhouse steaks and 22-ounce T-bones. And how many breakfast menus have you seen that, besides hot cakes and steak and eggs, include sliced bananas and cream, stewed prunes and figs, and *milk toast!* And this is not for show. These items stay on the bill of fare because folks still order them.

Most of the rooms are done in Victorian style, the finest being the Buffalo Bill Suite. My room was the Ned Frost Suite, named for a renowned mountain man and nature photographer. It had a twelve-foot ceiling, antique bed and dresser, and a rocker with just the right squeak.

Stan came to work here when he was only thirteen years old and began his hotelier career as a pot washer in the kitchen. Later he studied hotel management and returned to become The Irma's innkeeper.

How to get there: From I–25 north of Sheridan at Ranchester, take Highway 14 west to Cody. Hotel is on the main street.

✳

D: *The* *massive cherry-wood backbar was a gift to Buffalo Bill from Queen Victoria in appreciation for a command performance at the palace. It was made in France and arrived in Cody via steamship, rail, and horse-drawn wagon. It is a beauty!*

The Lockhart Inn
Cody, Wyoming
82414

Innkeepers: Mark and Cindy Baldwin
Address/Telephone: 109 West Yellowstone Avenue; (307) 587–6074
Rooms: 6; all with private bath.
Rates: $50 to $55 single or double, summer; $35 to $40 single or double, winter; EPB. No pets. No smoking in dining room. Well-behaved children over 4 years old are welcome. MasterCard and Visa accepted.
Open: All year.
Facilities and Activities: Box lunches available. BYOB. Complimentary fresh fruit and champagne for special occasions. Nearby: Big Horn Sheep Preserve, Buffalo Bill Historical Center, Yellowstone Park, hot springs; hiking, fishing, golf, horseback riding, tennis, windsurfing. Downhill and cross-country skiing and snowmobiling 50 miles away.

During my visit to The Lockhart Inn, I kept hoping that some of the spirit, talent, and fortitude of its namesake and former owner was rubbing off on me. Caroline Lockhart was quite a gal! The *Boston Post*'s first newspaperwoman, she did all sorts of outlandish things to get her stories. One of her biggest successes resulted from moving in with the Osage Indians and becoming

Chief Bacon Rind's cook, thus obtaining an inside story of the tribe's status after it became rich overnight from oil-land royalties. This article appeared in the *Denver Post*, and the paper sold out in less than a half hour. Writer, actress, cattle woman, entrepreneur—Caroline was all of these. Not surprisingly, her spirit and memory are everywhere in this wayside inn.

The rooms are partially furnished with antiques, including ☞ Caroline's wind-up phonograph, rocking chair, and saddle. White iron beds with carefully pressed linens, fresh mints on tiny cloisonné trays, claw-footed bathtubs, dainty wallpapers, ceiling fans, and writing desks make every room inviting.

The dining room is bright and cheery with small blue tables set amongst antiques and Lockhart memorabilia. Mark grinds and blends his own sausage; the French toast, an inch thick, is made with farm-fresh eggs; the currants for Cindy's preserves are hand-picked; and there's real cream, real butter, and fresh-ground espresso.

Before exploring the many attractions around Cody, request ahead ☞ a box lunch of meaty pita-bread sandwiches, home-made trail mix, and other goodies. When you return, you'll be treated to the unbeatable aroma of tomorrow morning's bread rising on the warming racks of the blue enamel wood stove in the parlor.

For dinner, it's across the street to Cassie's. A former "house of ill fame" where bootleg liquor was brewed and bottled in the cellar, this restaurant serves, among other specialties, a 20-ounce prime rib that is hard to beat. The dining areas are set up in former bedrooms, and the place is full of genuine cowboys. Don't pass this one by.

If you are unable to stay at The Lockhart, try to stop by between noon and 2:00, and Cindy and Mark will give you a tour and answer any questions you might have. If you do, I'll bet the next time you are in Cody, your nesting place will be The Lockhart Inn.

How to get there: Inn is on Yellowstone Avenue (Highway 14, 16, and 20), just a few blocks west of downtown Cody.

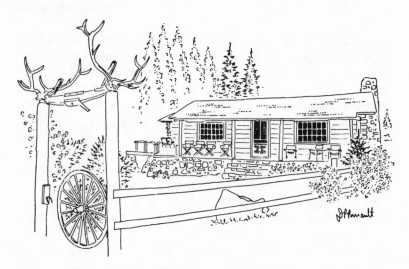

Rimrock Dude Ranch
Cody, Wyoming
82414

Innkeepers: Glenn and Alice Fales
Address/Telephone: 2728 North Fork Road; (307) 587–3970
Rooms: 9; all with private bath.
Rates: $90, single; $69 per person, double. Reduced rates for additional guests sharing same cabin. Rates are for 7-day minimum stay, AP, and include horse and all ranch activities. No pets. No TV. No air conditioning (not needed; elevation 6,500 feet). Credit cards not accepted.
Open: June 1 through August 31.
Facilities and Activities: BYOB bar with locked cubbyhole for your bottle; ranch furnishes ice and mixes. Recreation room. Riding instruction, breakfast rides, wine-and-cheese rides, float trips, western dancing; rodeo tickets, tour of Yellowstone Park; stocked trout pond. Nearby: Big Horn Sheep Preserve, Buffalo Bill Historical Center, Yellowstone Park, hot springs; hiking, great fishing, golf, tennis.

I've had an occasional innkeeper tell me that former guests sometimes send letters or small gifts of appreciation and invitations to come visit *them*. Well, Alice and Glenn have received all three, but they can go one more. Their ranch dog, Badger, who has learned his share of social skills, was recently the recipient of a box of new toys, sent by one of many human pals he has made over the years. It looks to me as though ☞ folks depart the Rimrock feeling more like they are *leaving* home rather than *returning* home.

And it's no wonder. Alice is ☞ one of the warmest inn-keepers I've met, the sort who makes you feel like family. And Glenn, former rodeo contestant, range cowboy, and horse trader, will do anything possible to make your stay exactly as you hoped it would be.

Rocky steps and dirt paths lead through natural grass to log cabins, perfectly placed along a bubbling brook that flows through the property. Furnished in western fashion with log walls and braided rugs, some cabins have stone fireplaces and sitting rooms, and all have baths, heat control, and maid service. Sitting on ☞ your own private porch among shade trees and bright flowers, while listening to the water tumble past your front door, is one of the most peaceful experiences possible.

The meals here are outstanding. Guests and ranch hands eat together, and this results in a hearty helping of laughter and camaraderie served up with ranch cooking at its best. Once a week there is a full Thanksgiving-type dinner with roast turkey and all the trimmings. Other days it's prime rib, steak cook-outs, and fried chicken, the likes of which would make the Colonel take to grilling hot dogs.

Some families have been returning to Rimrock for as many as twenty-two years, and young adults who began coming here as children are now bringing their own youngsters. According to Alice, "All activities are geared around children, and we let the adults join in." Now, that should make it a perfect place for all us "grown-up kids," right?

How to get there: Ranch is located on Highway 14–16–20, 26 miles west of Cody and halfway between Cody and Yellowstone National Park. Watch for sign, turn south on gravel road, and proceed for 1 mile.

Siggins Triangle X Ranch
Cody, Wyoming
82414

Innkeepers: Stan and Lila Siggins
Address/Telephone: 3453 Southfork Road; (307) 587–2031
Rooms: 4 rooms in bunkhouse, 5 cottages; all with private bath.
Rates: Upon request. Accommodations are for 7-day periods, from Sunday to Sunday. AP. No pets. Wheelchair accessible. TV in sitting room only. No air conditioning (not needed; elevation 6,500 feet). Credit cards not accepted.
Open: June 1 through August 30.
Facilities and Activities: Set-ups for pre-dinner cocktails. BYOB. Indoor swimming pool, recreation lodge, tennis court, hot tub, hayrides, horseback riding, wilderness trips, hiking, excellent fishing. Extensive, well-supervised, month-long ranch camp for youngsters aged 9 through 17. Nearby: Yellowstone Park, Buffalo Bill Historical Center.

The road from Cody, Wyoming, to the Triangle X Ranch winds through rolling ranchlands banked by majestic rock cliffs. On the day I arrived, a light rain had fallen, and 🖝 the sweet scent of sagebrush was heavy on the air.

Innkeepers Stan and Lila have deep roots in Wyoming. 🖝

274

Lila's grandfather, Henry Dahlem, was the first sheriff of Cody, and 👉 Stan's grandparents homesteaded the Triangle X in 1914. In 1928, the ranch was opened to guests and has operated as a guest ranch ever since.

Sweeping green lawns, shade trees, rock gardens, and weedless flower beds surround the main lodge, bunk house, and cottages. The guest accommodations are furnished with antique dressers and peeled-log beds, the latter handcrafted by Stan's brother.

My favorite place to stay was in the bunkhouse. Not the sort that the cowhands of the Old West lived in, these have comfy sitting rooms, pretty bedrooms, complete baths, and private entrances.

When the dinner bell clangs, there is no loitering. Meals are served family style on long tables that look out on an expansive view of lawn, flatlands, rounded hills, and mountain peaks. Breakfast brought sourdough pancakes, bacon, scrambled eggs, juice, milk, and coffee. Dinners are hearty, and there's 👉 a supper trail ride with steak and wine that isn't soon forgotten.

Horseback riding is the center of activity at the ranch, but that is not to say that one must ride horses to have a good time here. 👉 The 22′ × 35′ indoor pool is a great alternative to bouncing in the saddle, and, just in case you *do* take to the trail and come back a bit stiff and sore, there's the "Magic Spa" with its vigorously churning 98-degree water to refresh and restore. The tennis court and Wickiup Recreation Lodge with its pool table, ping-pong, foosball, and player piano are welcome additions, too. The wildlife, mountain scenery, and wildflowers make fascinating subjects for photo enthusiasts, and the Siggins know of some great spots to shoot from.

This region is known as "The Valley of the Blue Giants" in reference to the towering, 13,000-foot Blue Giant Mountains of the Absorka Range, part of the Rocky Mountains. Stan's grandparents sure knew what they were doing when they picked this spot to homestead!

How to get there: From Cody, Wyoming, take Highway 291 southwest for 38 miles. Watch for ranch sign on right.

Lazy L & B Ranch
DuBois, Wyoming
82513

Innkeepers: Bernard and Leota Didier

Address/Telephone: East Fork Road; (307) 455–2839 in summer, (312) 945–0107 in winter

Rooms: 21 cabin units; 16 with private bath.

Rates: $395 a week per person, AP, horses and all activities included. Pets allowed. No TV reception but large selection of video tapes. No air conditioning (not needed; elevation 7,000 feet). MasterCard and Visa accepted.

Open: June 1 through September 10.

Facilities and Activities: Nightly "Happy Hour" in Ranch House; setups; BYOB. Horseback riding, square dancing, hayrides, breakfast rides, steak frys, outdoor swimming pool, supervised riding and planned activities for children. Nearby: fishing, hiking, visits to cowboy town of DuBois and to ghost town.

Settled in the late 1800s by Scottish sheepherders, Scots Valley is ☞ a lush, green carpet of land flanked by flaming red rock, sagebrush-dotted hills, and three mountain ranges.

Tucked away in the midst of all this splendor is the Lazy L & B Ranch. The accommodations are rustic but comfortable log cabins. The dining room and library are located in the original farmhouse.

The daily trail rides are special because of the ☞ primitive, unspoiled area they traverse. A short venture through the valley took us to the old Duncan homestead, now owned by Bernard's brother and sister-in-law. A tiny regional post office, operational until only a few years ago, sits on the front porch. Only about four by five feet, it still has the original cubbyholes used for the ranchers' mail.

Another trail takes riders to the scenic East Fork Gorge, where one views a spectacular panorama of mountains, valley, badlands, and prairie.

My favorite outing was to ☞ an abandoned Scottish homestead. The log house stands alone on the prairie, its sod-roofed outbuildings, corral, and root-cellar still intact. I pondered the fate of the people who had brought their hopes here, labored here, and, perhaps, died here. Did their dreams come true? I wonder.

Meals are served family style, and no one is allowed to leave hungry. I was treated to ☞ a garden salad so fresh it actually had been part of the garden an hour before. Your entrée might be steak, chops, or trout; but whatever the cook's choice happens to be, it is always hearty, tasty, and filling.

The children are served first and then entertained by the wranglers while the adults dine. A nice feature, I think.

Breads are homemade, a specialty being "bucket bread." This is a whole wheat bread baked in cans and often served on trail cookouts because it doesn't smash when it is carried in the cans.

If you are looking for an authentic Old West experience, you are sure to like this place.

How to get there: 11 miles east of DuBois on Highway 26–287, watch for sign, "Elk Winter Feeding Refuge." Take gravel road north for 12 miles. Ranch is on right.

D.Perreault

Hotel Higgins
Glenrock, Wyoming
82637

Innkeepers: Jack and Margaret Doll
Address/Telephone: 416 West Birch Street (mailing address: P.O. Box
    741); (307) 436–9212
Rooms: 11; 8 with private bath, 3 share 1 bath.
Rates: $29 to $34 single, $36 to $46 double in summer; $24 to $29
    single, $31 to $41 double in winter; EPB. No pets. Wheelchair
    accessible. TV in sitting room only. MasterCard, Visa, American
    Express accepted.
Open: All year.
Facilities and Activities: Full-service restaurant. The Highlander Bar.
    Gourmet breakfast included in price of room. Nearby: Oregon Trail,
    Mormon Trail, Pony Express Route. Excellent fishing, tennis, mu-
    nicipal swimming pool, golf, city park, downhill and cross-country
    skiing.

    Thousands of people hurry by Glenrock, Wyoming, on busy
Interstate 25, never realizing that hidden away in the historic
Hotel Higgins is ☛ one of the finest, if not *the* finest, gourmet
restaurants in the entire state.
    Now ☛ listed on the National Register of Historic Places,

the hotel was built in 1916 and was proclaimed to be "the finest hotel north of Denver." It may no longer live up to that presumptuous claim, but it is a jewel, particularly its interior. The original mahogany and dark-stained oak woodwork, beveled glass doors, and light fixtures still enrich the post-Victorian structure; some of the original furnishings remain as well: a stately Seth Thomas pendulum clock in the lobby, brass and iron beds, and oak and walnut dressers. To these, the Dolls have added many good pieces, including the magificent wooden bed in room 208, a treasure from Jack's family.

And the bed isn't the only family heirloom in the hotel. On the dining-room wall hangs ☞ a framed and priceless hand-loomed shawl, made in Paisley, Scotland, sometime before 1870 and brought to America in 1903 by Margaret's grandfather as a gift for her grandmother. Hence, the name of the dining room: The Paisley Shawl.

Jack and Margaret's daughter, Beverly McMillin, is the chef, and I seriously believe she could teach the best of chefs a few tricks.

On Friday nights, the special is international cuisine, different each week. Enhanced by linen, crystal, and impeccable service, my West Indies dinner began with a fruit-flavored Trade Winds cocktail followed by: pepperpot soup with a trace of ginger; hot bread; sweet-and-sour shrimp served in a pineapple boat with stir-fried scallions, green pepper, and pineapple chunks; steamed rice; and coconut-banana Bake.

One might expect breakfast to be a letdown after an evening meal like that. Not so. In one of two private dining areas that flank the front entrance to the hotel, I found a ☞ tall goblet of champagne, a fruit plate, and the morning paper. Then came an absolutely delicious broccoli quiche, grilled ham, and coffee. You can substitute juice for the champagne. Did I? Of course not. How often do you have bubbly for breakfast at home?

How to get there: From I–25, take Exit 165 north to main street of Glenrock. Turn right onto West Birch. Hotel is on the right.

Annie Moore's Guest House
Laramie, Wyoming
82070

Innkeeper: Diana Kopulos
Address/Telephone: 819 University Avenue; (307) 721–4177
Rooms: 6 share 4 baths; 4 rooms have own sink.
Rates: $33 to $43, single; $40 to $50, double; includes continental-plus
breakfast. No pets. TV on sun porch only. Smoking on sun porch
only. Not suitable for very young children. MasterCard, Visa, American Express accepted.
Open: All year.
Facilities and Activities: BYOB. Use of several common rooms. Nearby:
University of Wyoming directly across the street. Only 6 blocks
from downtown restaurants and shopping. Hiking, fishing, boating,
downhill and cross-country skiing.

Annie Moore's hospitality lives on. In 1935, recently widowed and on her own, she opened Mrs. Moore's Boarding House, renting out the rooms on the upper level; serving meals to as many as fifty diners at a seating, six times a day, on the main floor; and living in a small basement room nicknamed "Annie's Cave."

She employed male university students as waiters and dishwashers and, in turn, gave them free meals for their services.

Even today, after forty to fifty years, former employees occasionally drop by to share their fond memories of goodhearted "Aunt Annie" with present-day innkeeper Diana Kopulos.

☛ Diana is a professional photographer whose work enhances several walls in this lovely, post-Victorian Queen Anne.

The Purple Room, on the second floor, is the fanciest room in the house, with heavy antique brass bed and lavender and orchid stained glass. But my favorite is the one I stayed in on the garden level facing east and aptly called the Sunrise Room. Five windows line two walls and ☛ open onto a terraced flower garden. A hand-tied, green-checked quilt covers the pine four-poster, and a varied-green afghan drapes a rocking chair in one corner. This room reached perfection when Diana's pure white cat spread herself peacefully across my bed. Named Sage for her exceptionally green eyes, she comes with the room only if invited. I welcomed her gladly because I so miss my Cream Persian, Murphy, and my black shorthair, Tuffy, when I travel.

☛ Guests at Annie's have full use of the dining room, parlor, glassed-in sun porch, and huge, outdoor deck on the second floor.

Breakfast was blueberry-walnut muffins, homemade maple-nut granola, orange juice, and imported mocha-Java coffee.

At dinner time, I walked the six blocks to Jeffrey's Bistro and had linguine Carbonara, an outstanding pasta dish with sautéed bacon, garlic, Romano cheese, and heavy cream. Desserts include such fantasies as chocolate Bavarian mint and brandy Alexander cheesecakes.

The university campus, just across the street from Annie's, proved to be the perfect place for an after-dinner stroll.

How to get there: From I–80, take Exit 313 north on 3rd to University Avenue. Turn right onto University. Annie Moore's is on the left.

The Historic Virginian Hotel
Medicine Bow, Wyoming
82329

Innkeepers: Vernon and Vickie Scott
Address/Telephone: P.O. Box 127; (307) 379–2377
Rooms: 21; 4 suites with private bath, 17 rooms share baths.
Rates: $17.50 to $65, single; $19.50 to $70, double; EP. Well-behaved
  pets allowed. TV in 3rd-floor parlor only. Air conditioning in dining
  room and saloon only (not needed for sleeping; elevation 6,563 feet).
  ▪MasterCard and Visa accepted.
Open: All year.
Facilities and Activities: Full-service restaurant. Saloon. Sink in every
  room. Ice water brought to rooms in antique pitchers. Comforters
  on all beds. Nearby: museum. Tours of world's largest wind gener-
  ator. World's largest dinosaur find. Fossil Cabin, said to be the oldest building on earth. Ghost town. Hiking, fishing, downhill and
  cross-country skiing.

  If Medicine Bow, Wyoming, is not on your route, you might
consider adding it to your itinerary, because you may never have
a better chance to experience a truer example of an elegant Old
West hotel.
  As I sat on a red velvet settee in the Virginian's upstairs

parlor, wishing for a long skirt, ruffled blouse, and high-top shoes to replace my jeans and Nikes, a gentleman asked me incredulously, "Can you really *stay* here? Do they actually take in *guests*?" That's how authentic the furnishings and décor are in this 1911, ☞ National Historic Landmark hotel. It's ☞ like a "hands-on" museum where you can not only touch but actually sleep in the beautiful, many-pillowed beds, bathe in one of the oversized claw-footed tubs, sip a cup of tea in a plush parlor, and feel like a rich turn-of-the-century banker.

The three-story building is named after Owen Wister's 1902 novel *The Virginian*, of "When you call me that—smile" fame. The walls of the Shiloh Saloon are covered with memorabilia from the novel and the movie of the same name; and signed photographs of Wister and his best friend, Theodore Roosevelt, who encouraged the author to write such a story, are in several rooms.

The Owen Wister Suite features two bedrooms, one with lace-canopied bed and the other with a one-hundred-year-old heavy brass bed. The sitting room is enhanced by a matching, ornately carved, red velvet settee, rocker, and chair set, all in mint condition.

An abundance of doilies, pillows, quilts, and comforters contribute to the cozy feeling, and an original sign in Room 30 advertises "Oats for horse 1¢ a gallon. Horses stabled free. Liquor 6¼¢ a glass, wine 25¢ a gallon."

The Eating House serves light lunches, and The Owen Wister Dining Room offers plentiful fare, such as 10-ounce lobsters and 16-ounce steaks. Less hearty meals of chops and seafood are also available.

This hotel ☞ sits out on the "lone prairie" where, indeed, the antelope still roam, and it is a must for anyone wanting a true glimpse of Old West elegance.

How to get there: From I–80 at Laramie, take Highway 30 north. Or, from I–25 at Casper, take Highway 220 south to 487, then drive south on Highway 487 to Medicine Bow. Hotel is on the main street.

Jenny Lake Lodge
Grand Teton National Park,
Moran, Wyoming
83013

Innkeeper: Clay James
Address/Telephone: (P.O. Box 250); (307) 733–4647
Rooms: 30; all with private bath.
Rates: $190, single; $220 to $320, double; MAP. No pets. Wheelchair
   accessible. No TV. No air conditioning (not needed; elevation more
   than 6,000 feet). MasterCard, Visa, American Express accepted.
Open: June 1 through 3rd week in September.
Facilities and Activities: Full-service restaurant, reservations a must.
   Sunday brunch with reservations. Lounge. Horse stables. Swim-
   ming pool available to Jenny Lake guests at Jackson Lake Lodge.
   Nearby: hiking, fishing, trail rides, river rafting, championship golf
   course, tennis, tram ride.

According to legend, several Indian tribes frequented this
part of Wyoming long *before* the mountains were formed. That
would be quite some time ago, indeed, because the 13,766-foot
Grand Teton Range looks as though it has been here forever.
White trappers were the first to publicize the beauty of the area,
and Jenny Lake is named for the Indian wife of one of them.

If you're into nature, wilderness, and breathtaking mountain vistas, but you don't really care for "roughing it," you're going to like it here.

All accommodations are in spiffy cabins tucked in amongst tall evergreens and aspen. ☛ Log walls, beautiful handmade quilts, electric blankets, braided rugs, small dressing rooms, private baths, ice and national newspapers delivered daily to your door, and gourmet dining all contribute to a pampered, woodland experience.

☛ The dining room earned the *Travel-Holiday* award for excellence, and one look at the menu may make you wonder if you're not really in the Edwardian Room in New York City's Plaza Hotel. Escargots duxelle; chateaubriand aux deux sauces; broccoli Mornay; profiteroles au chocolate and fresh raspberries with chantilly cream—all this is possible at one meal! And breakfast isn't exactly a letdown, either. Ah, yes, we've all had Belgian waffles. But with cherries jubilee? And there's calves' liver and bacon, Rocky Mountain trout, and eggs either poached, boiled, scrambled, fried, or shirred. ☛ What a contrast it is to step from your log cabin, see the Grand Tetons so close that you are sure you could reach out and touch them, walk along a path bordered with wildflowers, and then enter a dining room capable of such gourmet magic as this!

The horse stables are but a short walk from the main lodge building; off to the left is a sprawling meadow where an elk herd lives; and, around any tree, you might see the ☛ resident moose. She likes living here so much that she convinced her bull moose friend to spend the summers at the lodge with her. Marmots are everywhere; a buffalo herd is closeby; and from far off in the hills, one can hear the presence of coyotes.

Yes, indeed, man and nature have worked out a memorable meld at Jenny Lake Lodge.

How to get there: Lodge is in Grand Teton National Park on the Jenny Lake Loop Road, just 18 miles southwest of Moran Junction.

Saratoga Inn
Saratoga, Wyoming
82331

Innkeeper: Dave Johnson
Address/Telephone: East Pic Pike Road (P.O. Box 869); (307) 326–5261
Rooms: 58; all with private bath.
Rates: $35 to $92, single; $42 to $92, double; EP. Pets allowed. Wheelchair accessible. No air conditioning (not needed; elevation 6,972
feet). MasterCard and Visa accepted.
Open: All year.
Facilities and Activities: Full-service dining room; fireside lounge, live
entertainment 6 nights a week. Original art work and quality items
in Cedar Chest Gallery. Hot mineral springs feed Olympic-size pool,
9-hole golf course, 2 tennis courts, volleyball field, stocked lake for
children, snowmobiles, guides and clothing for rent, planned events
and activities. Nearby: excellent trout fishing, ice fishing, hiking,
150 miles of groomed cross-country ski trails.

I have discovered a very special place and, although the
regular guests would probably prefer that I keep it a secret, I am
going to share it with you.

The Saratoga Inn is a green and shady, quiet and restful
oasis ☞ often visited by professional athletes, artists, perform-
ers, the well known, and the unknown. The rooms are nicely

furnished and comfortable, but it is difficult to stay inside because the grounds are beautiful and there is so much to do outdoors.

The nearby mineral hot springs feed the ☞ Olympic-size swimming pool as well as a soaking pool. The 9-hole golf course is said to be the finest in Wyoming. Many guests try their hand at ☞ gold panning, and others glide leisurely down the North Platte River on a guided float trip. The kids have a great time at the trout pond stocked just for them.

Dave seems to know every guest by his or her first name, and what I particularly noticed was how each and every one of them always seemed so pleased to see him. ☞ His chuckle is contagious and his caring is sincere. The entire staff is especially courteous and helpful.

The Cedar Chest Gallery and Gift Shop has a fine selection of original artwork, including that of internationally known painter Vivi Crandall.

Dinner was a special delight. It began with homemade chicken-rice soup and ended with a favorite of mine, mud pie, an ice cream, chocolate cookie, whipped cream, cherry-topped concoction that has to be sinful, it is so good. In between, I had fresh, pan-fried Rocky Mountain trout, prepared with white wine, garlic, paprika, and toasted almonds. Sensational! White linen tablecloths, red linen napkins, and excellent service made this a meal to remember.

How to get there: From I–80, take Exit 235 south and proceed 21 miles to Saratoga. Turn left at East Bridge Street, cross the bridge, take first available right (River Street), then turn left at Pic Pike Road. Inn is on the right.

Indexes

Alphabetical Index to Inns

Allenspark Lodge (CO) . . . 2
Alpine Lodge (CO) 70
Annie Moore's Guest House
  (WY) 280
Anselmo Inn (UT) 258
Aspen Lodge at Estes Park,
  The (CO) 30
Averill's Flathead Lake
  Lodge and Dude Ranch
  (MT) 174
Back Narrows Inn (CO). . . 108
Baker's Manor Guest
  House (CO) 112
Bigfork Inn (MT) 176
Bill Cody's Ranch Inn
  (WY) 266
Birch Trees Bed &
  Breakfast Inn, The (UT). 230
Black Canyon Inn (CO). . . 32
Blackwell House, The (ID). 150
Blue Church Lodge, The
  (UT) 242
Briar Rose, The (CO). 8
Brigham Street Inn (UT). . 260
Burr House, The (UT). . . . 256
Cambridge Club (CO) 22
Center Street Bed &
  Breakfast (UT) 232
Chico Hot Springs Lodge
  (MT) 192
Cricket on the Hearth (ID). 152
Crosscut Ranch (MT) 180
Crystal Lodge, The (CO) . . 106
Davidson's Country Inn
  (CO) 120
Dove Inn, The (CO) 46
Duck Inn (MT) 196
Edith Palmer's Country Inn
  (NV) 222

Ellsworth Inn, The (ID). . . 158
Fairweather Inn (MT) 194
Fireside Inn (CO) 82
Fools Fe S2 Gold Inn (CO). 124
Foxwood Inn, The (MT) . . 198
Gables, The (ID) 154
General Palmer House, The
  (CO) 86
Genoa House Inn, The
  (NV) 206
Glen-Isle on the Platte
  (CO) 6
Gold Creek Inn (CO). 110
Gold Hill Inn and Bluebird
  Lodge, The (CO) 10
Golden Rose Hotel, The
  (CO) 16
Grand Imperial Hotel, The
  (CO) 126
Gray's Avenue Hotel (CO) . 58
Greenbriar Inn (ID) 156
Greene Gate Village (UT). . 252
Harbor Hotel (CO) 132
Hardy House, The (CO). . . 42
Haus Bavaria (NV) 214
Hearthstone Inn, The
  (CO) 18
Helmshire Inn (CO) 40
Heritage Inn (ID) 166
Historic Delaware Hotel
  (CO) 52
Historic Dorsett House
  (ID). 162
Historic Jameson, The
  (ID). 170
Historic Riverside Hotel
  (CO) 100
Historic Virginian Hotel,
  The (WY) 282

Holland Lake Lodge (MT) . 184
Home Ranch, The (CO). . . 84
Homestead, The (UT) 236
Hotel Boulderado (CO) . . . 12
Hotel Colorado, The (CO). . 94
Hotel Higgins (WY) 278
Hotel Jerome (CO) 72
Hotel Lenado (CO) 74
House of Yesteryear (CO). . 114
Idaho City Hotel (ID) 160
Idaho Rocky Mountain
    Ranch (ID). 168
Idanha, The (ID) 148
Imperial Hotel, The (CO). . 20
Imperial Hotel, The (UT). . 244
Inn of Glen Haven, The
    (CO) 44
Inn of the Black Wolf
    (CO) 66
Irma, The (WY) 268
Izaak Walton Inn (MT) . . . 186
Jenny Lake Lodge (WY) . . 284
Johnstone Inn (CO) 134
Lake McDonald Lodge
    (MT) 188
Lazy L & B Ranch (WY) . . 276
Little Red Ski Haus (CO). . 76
Lockhart Inn, The (WY) . . 270
Mansion House Inn (UT). . 240
Manti House Inn (UT) . . . 234
Mar Dei's Mountain
    Retreat (CO). 92
Meadeau View Lodge (UT). 226
Millers Inn (CO). 142
Mizpah Hotel (NV) 218
Molly Gibson Lodge (CO). . 78
Nevada City Hotel (MT). . . 190
New Sheridan Hotel, The
    (CO) 136
O'Duach'ain Country Inn
    (MT) 178
Old Miners' Lodge, The
    (UT) 246
Old Pioneer Garden (NV). . 220
Orchard House (NV). 208
Outlook Lodge (CO) 50
Oxford, The (CO) 24
Peaceful Valley Lodge and
    Guest Ranch (CO). 56
Pearl Street Inn (CO) 14

Peck House, The (CO). . . . 28
Peterson's Bed & Breakfast
    (UT) 238
Ponderosa Lodge (CO). . . . 60
Poor Farm Country Inn,
    The (CO) 62
Pullman Inn, The (UT) . . . 250
Redstone Inn, The (CO) . . 122
Rimrock Dude Ranch
    (WY). 272
River Birch Farm (ID). . . . 164
River Song Inn (CO). 34
St. Elmo Hotel (CO) 116
Saratoga Inn (WY) 286
Sardy House (CO). 80
Seven Wives Inn (UT). . . . 254
Siggins Triangle X Ranch
    (WY). 274
Silverheels Country Inn
    (CO) 140
Ski Tip Ranch (CO) 104
Skyline Guest Ranch (CO). 138
Smedley's (CO) 128
Stagecoach Stop (CO) 102
Stanley Hotel, The (CO) . . 36
Strater Hotel, The (CO). . . 88
Sundance Lodge Montana
    (MT). 200
Sweet Adeline's (CO). 64
Sylvan Dale Ranch (CO) . . 54
Talbott House (CO). 96
Taylor House, The (NV). . . 210
Trappers Inn (UT) 228
Tumbling River Ranch
    (CO) 48
Under The Eaves Guest
    House (UT) 262
Victoria Oaks Inn (CO) . . . 26
Victorian Inn (CO) 90
Voss Inn, The (MT) 182
Walley's Hot Springs
    Resort (NV) 212
Wanek's Lodge at Estes
    (CO) 38
Washington School Inn
    (UT) 248
Waunita Hot Springs
    Ranch (CO) 98
Western Hotel, The (CO). . 118
Wild Basin Lodge (CO) . . . 4

Wingate House (CO). 130
Wingfield House (NV). . . . 216

Winters Creek Inn (NV) . . 204
Woodspur Lodge (CO). . . . 144

Inns with Restaurants or That Serve Dinner by Special Arrangement

Colorado

Alpine Lodge 70
Aspen Lodge at Estes Park,
The 30
Back Narrows Inn. 108
Black Canyon Inn. 32
Briar Rose, The 8
Cambridge Club 22
Crystal Lodge, The 106
Fireside Inn. 82
Fools Fe S2 Gold Inn. 124
General Palmer House,
The 86
Glen-Isle on the Platte 6
Gold Creek Inn. 110
Gold Hill Inn and Bluebird
Lodge, The 10
Golden Rose Hotel, The . . . 16
Grand Imperial Hotel, The . 126
Harbor Hotel 132
Hardy House, The. 42
Helmshire Inn 40
Historic Delaware Hotel . . . 52
Historic Riverside Hotel . . . 100
Home Ranch, The. 84
Hotel Boulderado 12
Hotel Colorado, The 94
Hotel Jerome 72
Hotel Lenado 74
Imperial Hotel, The. 20
Inn of Glen Haven, The. . . 44
Inn of the Black Wolf 66
Millers Inn. 142
New Sheridan Hotel, The. . 136
Oxford, The 24
Peaceful Valley Lodge and
Guest Ranch 56
Pearl Street Inn 14
Peck House, The 28
Ponderosa Lodge. 60
Redstone Inn, The 122
River Song Inn. 34

St. Elmo Hotel 116
Sardy House 80
Silverheels Country Inn . . . 140
Ski Tip Ranch 104
Skyline Guest Ranch. 138
Stagecoach Stop 102
Stanley Hotel, The 36
Strater Hotel, The. 88
Sweet Adeline's 64
Sylvan Dale Ranch 54
Talbott House. 96
Tumbling River Ranch . . . 48
Victoria Oaks Inn 26
Wanek's Lodge at Estes. . . 38
Waunita Hot Springs
Ranch 98
Western Hotel, The. 118
Wild Basin Lodge 4
Wingate House. 130
Woodspur Lodge. 144

Idaho

Cricket on the Hearth 152
Greenbriar Inn 156
Historic Dorsett House. . . . 162
Historic Jameson, The 170
Idaho Rocky Mountain
Ranch 168
Idanha, The. 148

Montana

Averill's Flathead Lake
Lodge and Dude Ranch . 174
Bigfork Inn 176
Chico Hot Springs Lodge . . 192
Crosscut Ranch 180
Foxwood Inn, The. 198
Holland Lake Lodge 184
Izaak Walton Inn 186
Lake McDonald Lodge. . . . 188
Nevada City Hotel. 190
Sundance Lodge Montana . 200

Nevada
Edith Palmer's Country
  Inn 222
Genoa House Inn, The. . . . 206
Mizpah Hotel. 218
Old Pioneer Garden. 220
Orchard House. 208
Walley's Hot Springs
  Resort 212
Wingfield House. 216

Utah
Anselmo Inn 258
Homestead, The 236
Imperial Hotel, The. 20
Mansion House Inn. 240
Manti House Inn 234
Meadeau View Lodge 226

Old Miners' Lodge, The. . . 246
Pullman Inn, The 250
Trappers Inn 228
Under The Eaves Guest
  House 262
Washington School Inn . . . 248

Wyoming
Bill Cody's Ranch Inn 266
Historic Virginian Hotel,
  The 282
Hotel Higgins. 278
Irma, The 268
Jenny Lake Lodge. 284
Lazy L & B Ranch 276
Rimrock Dude Ranch 272
Saratoga Inn 286
Siggins Triangle X Ranch. . 274

City Inns

Colorado
Briar Rose, The   8
Cambridge Club 22
Hearthstone Inn, The 18
Helmshire Inn 40
Hotel Boulderado 12
Oxford, The. 24
Pearl Street Inn 14
Victoria Oaks Inn 26

Idaho
Blackwell House, The 150
Cricket on the Hearth 152
Gables, The 154
Greenbriar Inn 156
Idanha, The. 148

Montana
Voss Inn, The. 182

Nevada
Wingfield House. 216

Utah
Anselmo Inn 258
Birch Trees Bed &
  Breakfast Inn, The. 230
Brigham Street Inn 260
Center Street Bed &
  Breakfast 232
Pullman Inn, The 250

Wyoming
Annie Moore's Guest
  House 280

Guest Ranches and Farms

Colorado
Aspen Lodge at Estes Park,
  The 30
Home Ranch, The. 84

Peaceful Valley Lodge and
  Guest Ranch. 56
Ponderosa Lodge. 60
Skyline Guest Ranch. 138

Sylvan Dale Ranch 54
Tumbling River Ranch . . . 48
Waunita Hot Springs
Ranch 98

Idaho
Idaho Rocky Mountain
Ranch 168
River Birch Farm 164

Montana
Averill's Flathead Lake
Lodge and Dude Ranch . 174

Crosscut Ranch 180
Sundance Lodge Montana . 200

Nevada
Old Pioneer Garden. 220
Winters Creek Inn 204

Wyoming
Bill Cody's Ranch Inn 266
Jenny Lake Lodge. 284
Lazy L & B Ranch 276
Rimrock Dude Ranch 272
Siggins Triangle X Ranch. . 274

Romantic Inns

Colorado
Briar Rose, The 8
Cambridge Club 22
General Palmer House,
The 86
Golden Rose Hotel, The . . . 16
Grand Imperial Hotel, The . 126
Hardy House, The. 42
Hearthstone Inn, The 18
Home Ranch, The. 84
Hotel Boulderado 12
Hotel Jerome 72
Hotel Lenado 74
Inn of Glen Haven, The. . . 44
Oxford, The. 24
Pearl Street Inn 14
Redstone Inn, The 122
River Song Inn. 34
St. Elmo Hotel 116
Sardy House 80
Silverheels Country Inn . . . 140
Ski Tip Ranch 104
Stanley Hotel, The 36
Strater Hotel, The. 88
Tumbling River Ranch . . . 48

Idaho
Blackwell House, The 150
Ellsworth Inn, The 158
Greenbriar Inn 156
Historic Jameson, The 170
Idanha, The 148

Montana
Voss Inn, The. 182

Nevada
Edith Palmer's Country
Inn 222
Genoa House Inn, The. . . . 206
Old Pioneer Garden. 220
Walley's Hot Springs
Resort 212

Utah
Blue Church Lodge,
The 242
Brigham Street Inn 260
Center Street Bed &
Breakfast 232
Greene Gate Village. 252
Imperial Hotel, The. 244
Manti House Inn 234
Pullman Inn, The 250
Seven Wives Inn. 252
Trappers Inn 228
Washington School Inn . . . 248

Wyoming
Annie Moore's Guest
House 280
Historic Virginian Hotel,
The 282
Lockhart Inn, The. 270

Rustic Inns

Colorado

Allenspark Lodge	2
Back Narrows Inn	108
Glen-Isle on the Platte	6
Gold Hill Inn and Bluebird Lodge, The	10
Historic Riverside Hotel	100
Inn of the Black Wolf	66
Little Red Ski Haus	76
Millers Inn	142
Outlook Lodge	50
Ski Tip Ranch	104
Skyline Guest Ranch	138
Stagecoach Stop	102
Western Hotel, The	118
Woodspur Lodge	144

Idaho

Idaho City Hotel	160
Idaho Rocky Mountain Ranch	168

Montana

Crosscut Ranch	180
Fairweather Inn	194
Holland Lake Lodge	184
Lake McDonald Lodge	188
Nevada City Hotel	190
Sundance Lodge Montana	200

Wyoming

Jenny Lake Lodge	284
Lazy L & B Ranch	276
Rimrock Dude Ranch	272

Inns near Downhill Skiing

Colorado

Allenspark Lodge	2
Alpine Lodge	70
Aspen Lodge at Estes Park, The	30
Back Narrows Inn	108
Baker's Manor Guest House	112
Black Canyon Inn	32
Crystal Lodge, The	106
Davidson's Country Inn	120
Fireside Inn	82
Fools Fe S2 Gold Inn	124
General Palmer House, The	86
Gold Creek Inn	110
Grand Imperial Hotel, The	126
Harbor Hotel	132
Hardy House, The	42
Historic Delaware Hotel	52
Historic Riverside Hotel	100
Home Ranch, The	84
Hotel Colorado, The	94
Hotel Jerome	72
Hotel Lenado	74
Inn of Glen Haven, The	44
Inn of the Black Wolf	66
Johnstone Inn	134
Little Red Ski Haus	76
Mar Dei's Mountain Retreat	92
Millers Inn	142
Molly Gibson Lodge	78
New Sheridan Hotel, The	136
Peaceful Valley Lodge and Guest Ranch	56
Peck House, The	28
Ponderosa Lodge	60
Poor Farm Country Inn, The	62
Redstone Inn, The	122
River Song Inn	34
St. Elmo Hotel	116
Sardy House	80
Silverheels Country Inn	140
Ski Tip Ranch	104
Skyline Guest Ranch	138
Smedley's	128
Stagecoach Stop	102
Stanley Hotel, The	36
Strater Hotel, The	88
Sweet Adeline's	64

Talbott House. 96
Victorian Inn 90
Wanek's Lodge at Estes. . . 38
Waunita Hot Springs
Ranch 98
Western Hotel, The. 118
Wild Basin Lodge 4
Wingate House. 130
Woodspur Lodge. 144

Idaho
Ellsworth Inn, The 194
Heritage Inn 166
Historic Dorsett House. . . . 162
Historic Jameson, The. . . . 170
Idanha, The. 148

Montana
Crosscut Ranch 180
Duck Inn. 196
Foxwood Inn, The. 198
Voss Inn, The. 182

Nevada
Edith Palmer's Country
Inn 222
Genoa House Inn, The. . . . 206

Haus Bavaria 214
Orchard House. 208
Taylor House, The 210
Walley's Hot Springs
Resort 212
Wingfield House. 216
Winters Creek Inn 204

Utah
Anselmo Inn 258
Birch Trees Bed &
Breakfast Inn, The. 230
Blue Church Lodge, The . . 242
Brigham Street Inn 260
Center Street Bed &
Breakfast 232
Imperial Hotel, The. 244
Old Miners' Lodge, The. . . 246
Trappers Inn 228
Washington School Inn . . . 248

Wyoming
Annie Moore's Guest
House 280
Historic Virginian Hotel,
The. 282
Hotel Higgins. 278

Inns near Cross-country Skiing

Colorado
Allenspark Lodge 2
Alpine Lodge 70
Aspen Lodge at Estes Park,
The. 30
Back Narrows Inn. 108
Baker's Manor Guest
House 112
Black Canyon Inn. 32
Crystal Lodge, The 106
Davidson's Country Inn . . . 120
Fireside Inn. 82
Fools Fe S2 Gold Inn. 124
General Palmer House,
The. 86
Glen-Isle on the Platte. . . . 6
Gold Creek Inn. 110
Golden Rose Hotel, The. . . 16
Grand Imperial Hotel, The . 126

Harbor Hotel 132
Hardy House, The. 42
Historic Delaware Hotel. . . 52
Historic Riverside Hotel. . . 100
Home Ranch, The. 84
Hotel Colorado, The 94
Hotel Jerome 72
Hotel Lenado 74
Inn of Glen Haven, The. . . 44
Inn of the Black Wolf 66
Johnstone Inn 134
Little Red Ski Haus. 76
Mar Dei's Mountain
Retreat. 92
Millers Inn. 142
Molly Gibson Lodge. 78
New Sheridan Hotel, The. . 136
Peaceful Valley Lodge and
Guest Ranch. 56

Peck House, The 28
Ponderosa Lodge. 60
Poor Farm Country Inn,
The 62
Redstone Inn, The 122
River Song Inn. 164
St. Elmo Hotel 116
Sardy House 80
Silverheels Country Inn . . . 140
Ski Tip Ranch 104
Skyline Guest Ranch. 138
Smedley's 128
Stagecoach Stop 102
Stanley Hotel, The 36
Strater Hotel, The. 88
Sweet Adeline's 64
Talbott House. 96
Victorian Inn 90
Wanek's Lodge at Estes. . . 38
Waunita Hot Springs
Ranch 98
Western Hotel, The. 118
Wild Basin Lodge 4
Wingate House. 130
Woodspur Lodge. 144

Idaho
Blackwell House, The 150
Cricket on the Hearth 152
Ellsworth Inn, The 158
Gables, The 154
Greenbriar Inn 156
Heritage Inn 166
Idaho City Hotel 160
Idanha, The. 148

Montana
Bigfork Inn 176
Chico Hot Springs Lodge . . 192
Crosscut Ranch 180

Duck Inn. 196
Foxwood Inn, The. 198
Holland Lake Lodge 184
Izaak Walton Inn 186
O'Duach'ain Country Inn. . 178
Sundance Lodge Montana . 200
Voss Inn, The. 182

Nevada
Edith Palmer's Country
Inn 222
Genoa House Inn, The. . . . 206
Haus Bavaria 214
Orchard House. 208
Taylor House, The 210
Walley's Hot Springs
Resort 212
Wingfield House. 216
Winters Creek Inn 204

Utah
Anselmo Inn 258
Birch Trees Bed &
Breakfast Inn, The. 230
Blue Church Lodge, The . . 242
Brigham Street Inn 260
Center Street Bed &
Breakfast 232
Imperial Hotel, The. 244
Mansion House Inn. 240
Meadeau View Lodge 226
Old Miners' Lodge, The. . . 246
Trappers Inn 228
Washington School Inn . . . 248

Wyoming
Annie Moore's Guest
House 280
Hotel Higgins. 278
Saratoga Inn 286

Inns with Swimming Pools

Colorado
Aspen Lodge at Estes Park,
The 30
Black Canyon Inn. 32
Crystal Lodge, The 106
Home Ranch, The. 84

Hotel Jerome 72
Molly Gibson Lodge. 78
Peaceful Valley Lodge and
Guest Ranch. 56
Sardy House 80
Sylvan Dale Ranch 54

Tumbling River Ranch . . . 48
Waunita Hot Springs
Ranch 98

Idaho
Idaho Rocky Mountain
Ranch 168

Montana
Averill's Flathead Lake
Lodge and Dude
Ranch 174
Chico Hot Springs
Lodge 192

Nevada
Walley's Hot Springs
Resort 212

Utah
Greene Gate Village. 252
Homestead, The 236
Seven Wives Inn. 254

Wyoming
Irma, The 268
Lazy L & B Ranch 276
Saratoga Inn 286
Siggins Triangle X Ranch. . 274

Inns with Hot Tubs

Colorado
Allenspark Lodge 2
Alpine Lodge 70
Aspen Lodge at Estes Park,
The 30
Black Canyon Inn. 32
Fireside Inn. 82
Gold Hill Inn and Bluebird
Lodge, The. 10
Golden Rose Hotel, The. . . 16
Harbor Hotel 132
Home Ranch, The. 84
Hotel Colorado, The 94
Hotel Lenado. 74
Millers Inn. 142
Molly Gibson Lodge. 78
Peaceful Valley Lodge and
Guest Ranch. 56
Peck House, The 28
Redstone Inn, The 122
Sardy House 80
Silverheels Country Inn . . . 140
Skyline Guest Ranch. 138
Strater Hotel, The. 88
Talbott House. 96
Tumbling River Ranch . . . 48
Victoria Oaks Inn 26
Victorian Inn 90
Woodspur Lodge. 144

Idaho
Greenbriar Inn 156

Montana
Chico Hot Springs Lodge. . 192
Duck Inn. 196
O'Duach'ain Country Inn. . 178
Sundance Lodge Montana . 200

Nevada
Walley's Hot Springs
Resort 212
Winters Creek Inn 204

Utah
Blue Church Lodge,
The 242
Greene Gate Village. 252
Imperial Hotel, The. 244
Manti House Inn 234
Old Miners' Lodge, The . . . 246
Seven Wives Inn. 254
Washington School Inn . . . 248

Wyoming
Bill Cody's Ranch Inn 266
Siggins Triangle X Ranch. . 274

Inns with Working Fireplaces or Wood-burning Stoves in Some Guest Rooms

Colorado
Black Canyon Inn 32
Briar Rose, The 8
Glen-Isle on the Platte 6
Hearthstone Inn, The 18
Home Ranch, The 84
Hotel Jerome 72
Hotel Lenado 74
Mar Dei's Mountain
    Retreat 92
Millers Inn 142
Molly Gibson Lodge 78
Peaceful Valley Lodge and
    Guest Ranch 56
Pearl Street Inn 14
River Song Inn 34
Sardy House 286
Silverheels Country Inn . . . 140
Tumbling River Ranch . . . 48
Victoria Oaks Inn 26

Idaho
Blackwell House, The 150
Ellsworth Inn, The 158
Idaho Rocky Mountain
    Ranch 168

Montana
Duck Inn 196
Holland Lake Lodge 184
Sundance Lodge Montana . 200

Nevada
Edith Palmer's Country
    Inn 222
Old Pioneer Garden 220
Walley's Hot Springs
    Resort 212
Wingfield House 216
Winters Creek Inn 204

Utah
Anselmo Inn 258
Blue Church Lodge, The . . 242
Brigham Street Inn 260
Greene Gate Village 252
Manti House Inn 234
Seven Wives Inn 254
Under The Eaves Guest
    House 262
Washington School Inn . . . 248

Wyoming
Jenny Lake Lodge 284
Rimrock Dude Ranch 272

Inns with Wheelchair Access

Colorado
Aspen Lodge at Estes Park,
    The 30
Black Canyon Inn 32
Briar Rose, The 8
General Palmer House,
    The 86
Harbor Hotel 132
Helmshire Inn 40
Historic Riverside Hotel . . . 100
Hotel Boulderado 12
Hotel Colorado 94
Hotel Jerome 72

Mar Dei's Mountain
    Retreat 92
New Sheridan Hotel, The . . 136
Oxford, The 24
Peaceful Valley Lodge and
    Guest Ranch 56
Peck House, The 28
Ponderosa Lodge 60
Sylvan Dale Ranch 54
Stanley Hotel, The 36
Strater Hotel, The 88

Idaho
Idaho Rocky Mountain
  Ranch 168

Montana
Averill's Flathead Lake
  Lodge and Dude Ranch . 174
Chico Hot Springs Lodge . . 192
Crosscut Ranch 180
Faireweather Inn 194
Foxwood Inn, The. 198
Holland Lake Lodge 184
Nevada City Hotel. 190
Sundance Lodge Montana . 200

Nevada
Taylor House, The 210
Walley's Hot Springs
  Resort 212

Utah
Center Street Bed &
  Breakfast 232
Seven Wives Inn. 254
Washington School Inn . . . 248

Wyoming
Hotel Higgins. 278
Jenny Lake Lodge. 284
Saratoga Inn 286
Siggins Triangle X Ranch. . 274

Inns with Special Features for Children

Colorado
Aspen Lodge at Estes Park,
  The 30
Davidson's Country Inn . . . 120
Home Ranch, The. 84
Peaceful Valley Lodge and
  Guest Ranch. 56
Skyline Guest Ranch. 138
Sylvan Dale Ranch 54
Tumbling River Ranch . . . 48
Waunita Hot Springs
  Ranch 98

Montana
Averill's Flathead Lake
  Lodge & Dude Ranch. . . 174
Chico Hot Springs Lodge. . 192

Utah
Homestead, The 236

Wyoming
Lazy L & B Ranch 276
Rimrock Dude Ranch 272
Siggins Triangle X Ranch. . 274

Inns with Age and Behavior Preferences Pertaining to Children

Colorado
Baker's Manor Guest
  House 112
Briar Rose, The 8
Crystal Lodge, The 106
Glen-Isle on the Platte. . . . 6
Golden Rose Hotel, The. . . 16
Gray's Avenue Hotel . . . . : 58
Hardy House, The. 42
Inn of Glen Haven, The. . . 44
Mar Dei's Mountain
  Retreat. 92

Oxford, The. 24
River Song Inn. 34
Sweet Adeline's 64
Victoria Oaks Inn 26
Wanek's Lodge at Estes. . . 38
Western Hotel, The. 118

Idaho
Blackwell House, The 150
Cricket on the Hearth 152
Ellsworth Inn, The 158
Gables, The 154

Greenbriar Inn 156
River Birch Farm 164

Montana
Duck Inn 196
Sundance Lodge Montana . 200
Voss Inn, The 182

Nevada
Edith Palmer's Country
Inn 222
Genoa House Inn,
The 206
Haus Bavaria 214
Walley's Hot Springs
Resort 212
Winters Creek Inn 204

Utah
Birch Trees Bed &
Breakfast Inn, The 230
Brigham Street Inn 260
Center Street Bed &
Breakfast 232
Imperial Hotel, The 244
Mansion House Inn 240
Manti House Inn 234
Pullman Inn, The 250
Seven Wives Inn 254
Under The Eaves Guest
House 262
Washington School Inn . . . 248

Wyoming
Annie Moore's Guest
House 280
Lockhart Inn, The 270

Inns That Permit Pets

Colorado
Back Narrows Inn 108
Black Canyon Inn 32
Briar Rose, The 8
Cambridge Club 22
Davidson's Country Inn . . . 120
Dove Inn, The 46
Fools Fe S2 Gold Inn 124
Glen-Isle on the Platte 6
Historic Delaware Hotel . . . 52
Historic Riverside Hotel . . . 100
Inn of the Black Wolf 66
Outlook Lodge 50
Pearl Street Inn 14
Ponderosa Lodge 60
Stagecoach Stop 102

Idaho
Ellsworth Inn, The 158
Idaho City Hotel 160

Montana
Chico Hot Springs Lodge . . 192
Fairweather Inn 194
Foxwood Inn, The 198

Holland Lake Lodge 184
Lake McDonald Lodge 188
Nevada City Hotel 190
O'Duach'ain Country Inn . . 178

Nevada
Mizpah Hotel 218
Old Pioneer Garden 220
Orchard House 208
Taylor House, The 210

Utah
Blue Church Lodge, The . . 242
Burr House, The 256
Seven Wives Inn 254
Under The Eaves Guest
House 262

Wyoming
Historic Virginian Hotel,
The 282
Irma, The 268
Lazy L & B Ranch 276
Saratoga Inn 286